The Tragedy of Technology

STEPHEN HILL

The Tragedy of Technology

HUMAN LIBERATION VERSUS DOMINATION
IN THE LATE TWENTIETH CENTURY

PLUTO PRESS

First published 1988 by Pluto Press
11-21 Northdown Street, London N1 9BN

Distributed in the USA by Unwin Hyman Inc.
8 Winchester Place, Winchester
MA 01890, USA

Copyright © Stephen Hill 1988

Typesetting: Ransom Typesetting Services,
Woburn Sands, Bucks

Printed and bound in the United Kingdom by
Billing & Sons Ltd, Worcester

British Library Cataloguing in Publication Data

Hill, Stephen, 1943–
    The tragedy of technology.
    1. Technology. Social aspects
    I. Title
    306' .46

    ISBN 1–85305–009–1
    ISBN 1–85305–069–5 pbk

To Jill, my liberation

Contents

Introduction

The Issue: Technology and Culture

Late in 1987, five events occurred. The American Government dynamited a Trident missile silo, for the weapon interred there in the 1960s was obsolete. The international stock markets crashed, for, with the US living beyond its means, faith in the 'futures' evaporated precipitously worldwide. Then in western France 25,000 people were evacuated from the city of Nantes when a large cloud of toxic ammonium nitrate belched from a blazing chemical fertiliser plant. An upgraded international airport was completed in the tropical and largely traditional paradise of Western Samoa. And Alan Bond, owner of Australia's victorious 1983 America's Cup yacht, announced plans to display movies and advertisements on huge screens attached to the sides of the fleet of airborne blimps that his company, Airships Pacific, was floating across the cities of Australia.

Except for the level of panic that stockmarketers experienced as the storm clouds of Black Tuesday 1929 appeared again over their high rise offices, there was nothing out of the ordinary about these five events. For the horizon of daily life in the late twentieth century is alternately shaded by the darkest of technologically-produced clouds and illuminated by the brightest of technologically-produced sunshine. In the interests of ever-expanding capital accumulation, and with the 'hubris' of Icarus, humankind flies towards this horizon, precariously close to the sun that is both source of power and destruction.

Behind each of the five seemingly unconnected events lies the culture-shaping power of modern technological systems. As a direct catalyst of the stockmarket crash, when the Dow-Jones index started to fall, two New York computers, programmed to buy and sell at pre-set prices, conducted a massive and automated trading spree that foretold panic to those who were watching the market, and who blindly followed the automated lead. The Trident missile silo was only dynamited because technological systems of destruction had progressed over the last 20 years according to a 'baroque' dynamic of increased elaboration and sophistication towards greater technical potency.

1

Meanwhile, as signal to the Soviet Union, the destroyed silo was left open, not for direct inspection but for satellite verification. The international airport in Western Samoa mirrors the technological systems of airports internationally, and draws a remote and largely traditional society immediately into the mainstream of an internationalised 'superculture' that delivers the same standardised high technology consumer products to the sophisticates of New York, the company men of Tokyo and the chieftain-controlled agricultural families of Samoa. Alan Bond's proposed airship video promises to occlude the natural world with the most extraordinary advertising billboard on which a continuous stream of commercialised culture is displayed across the sky. And the release of toxic gas in Nantes warns us, yet again, as did Bhopal, Three Mile Island and Chernobyl, of the precariousness of our productive world – that the most sophisticated of productive technological systems are subject to design faults and minor human error, the human consequences of which can be of megalithic proportions. Yet, as in the case of the stockmarket crash, and the technical system that 1980s 'Star War' technologies imply, decision-making about some of the most critical of economic and human survival concerns has been handed over to technical systems.

The culture of the late twentieth century is deeply penetrated by the command of technological systems, moving along a trajectory that is seemingly commanded by technological opportunity and necessity. However, the technologically commanded trajectory is *accepted* with all its culture-defining power, and its potential for massive error, by society at large.

It follows that to understand the interactions between technology and culture that produce this acceptance is arguably the most central concern that society confronts as we move into the 1990s. For it is only through understanding rather than ignorance that we can have power to assert *human* purpose and render technological systems our servants rather than culture-masters.

Yet the interactions between technology and culture are little understood. The 'myth of the machine' that Lewis Mumford observed in the 1930s persists in a very common view of apparent intrinsic technological inevitability, a view that cannot be sustained when one recognises that technological systems are cultural products, and are therefore products of human agency and choice.

It is the purpose of this book, *The Tragedy of Technology*, to expose the myth, to explore the dynamics of culture–technology interactions, and the role of human agency in the creation and acceptance of technological systems. The book's purpose is *not* to provide a critique of the good versus bad *uses* of industrial technology. Rather, my purpose is to focus on what it is about the link between technology and society that produces the apparent domination of social life by technological change. The title, *Tragedy*, expresses the book's central theme. This theme is to do with the 'remorseless working of things' as in ancient Greek tragedy. Yet, as in a tragedy, the script is a product of human action, and its interpretation is the province of human actors. The script and its interpretation can always be rewritten.

There are a number of highly influential books that have previously approached a similar theme. Numbered amongst them are Jacques Ellul's philosophic work, *The Technological Society*, Lewis Mumford's historic treatise, *Technics and Civilization*, Herbert Marcuse's values analysis of *One Dimensional Man*, Robert Pirsig's journey towards the value of 'quality' in his *Zen and the Art of Motorcycle Maintenance*, David Dickson's critique of contemporary technological values in his *Alternative Technology*, David and Ruth Elliott's analysis of power in their *The Control of Technology*, Langdon Winner's historic and political work, *Autonomous Technology*, and Alvin Toffler's projective accounts, *Future Shock*, and *The Third Wave*. Each of these books presents a valuable context for *The Tragedy of Technology*.

However, the present book is unique. The book makes three distinctive contributions. The first lies in the book's analysis of how the present pattern of interaction between technological systems and culture has been formed historically. The second is to an understanding of how the *cultural* properties of technological systems have power to *penetrate* and shape wider cultural expressions and constructions of meaning, thus drawing these wider values into *alignment* with a technologically inspired social trajectory. The book's third distinctive contribution is in drawing historic and cross-cultural analysis together into an integrated perspective on the relations between technology and society today. Such a project of integration has not been attempted before. Whilst Arnold Pacey's recent book, *The Culture of Technology*, addresses culture-technology interactions directly, its contribution is quite different to the present work. For *The Culture of Technology* is primarily concerned with depiction of the *values* that lie behind contemporary technological use, rather than with the social processes that produce these values and applications, and where these processes originate in history.

The Tragedy of Technology can therefore be of use to scholars, students and educated laypersons who wish to understand the technologically mediated world of the late twentieth century. Equally, the arguments of the book will be of interest to history and sociological analysts of the

newly emergent field, the 'new' sociology of technology, a field that
seeks to identify the social shaping forces and negotiations that create
technological change. The book complements recent works in this area,
such as Thomas Hughes's *Networks of Power*, Donald MacKenzie and
Judy Wajcman's *The Social Shaping of Technology*, and W.E. Bijker, T.P
Hughes and T. J. Pinch's *The Social Construction of Technological
Systems*. The book departs significantly from the existing field,
however, by refusing to separate technological invention from impact,
for *both* are connected within the same cultural frame, and neither can
be understood without the other.

Finally, as a sociological account in which technology is located at
the centre stage of social and cultural action rather than relegated to
the wings of mainstream analysis, the book contributes a new dimension
to sociological theories about contemporary society. *The Tragedy of
Technology* therefore is of use to readers interested in sociology
generally.

Reading the Book

The Tragedy of Technology tells the story of culture–technology
interactions through a variety of accounts, all of which focus on the
manner in which technology when viewed as a *cultural* phenomenon
forges alignments with wider cultural meaning systems. The theory that
makes sense of these accounts *emerges* through the book as new
theoretical tools are needed to explain what went before.

The book can be read in a variety of ways. As a whole, the book takes
the reader through an argument that progresses through the following
stages:

After an introduction to the issues, the argument addresses the
experience of social 'enframement' by technology, and explores the
culture defining power of technology through an analysis of technology
as a 'cultural text' – that is, imbued with cultural meanings that
communicate much more than just the use value of the artefacts
themselves. The book's argument continues by reflecting this analysis
against case studies of what happens along with the introduction of an
alien technology 'text' into traditional societies; and then uses
sociological theory of consciousness and culture to explain what the
journey so far has shown.

From Chapter 6 onwards, the argument then explores how the
technology 'text' was formed in the early industrial revolution; how it
was incompletely communicated to a country at the periphery of
industrial development; and finally, how the 'text' is able to penetrate

to the depths of subjective life and the constitution of culture in contemporary industrial society. The book therefore returns full circle to the experience of cultural 'enframement' where the argument started. The book then concludes by showing that 'enframement', as an intrinsically cultural property, is open to transformation.

To read the book as a whole is to see the overall picture that is composed from the jigsaw pieces of historic and cross-cultural analysis.

At the same time, each chapter, except perhaps for the last, is self-sufficient. Those readers with a specific interest (in, for example, early industrial history, imperialism, developing countries, contemporary society or theory) can, if they wish, view the jigsaw pieces separately. Thus, for example, theoretical arguments about technology as a cultural phenomenon are presented in Chapters 2 and 3 (where the 'technology as text' argument is developed), and in Chapter 5 (where the way in which the cultural 'text' of technology penetrates consciousness and wider culture is presented).

Historical argument about the social and cultural negotiations that produced the early alignment between industrial culture and the cultural frame imposed by its technology text, is presented in Chapters 6 and 7. The historic parallel between core and periphery of early industrial development, and the consequences for culture-technology alignment, is presented in Chapter 8. And analysis of the penetration of contemporary society by the cultural force of technological systems is presented in Chapters 9 and 10.

The concluding Chapter 11 is to some extent an exception to chapter self-sufficiency in that in drawing together the overall story of the book and presenting its implications for sociological analysis, it does assume that the reader is familiar with what went before in the book. However, again, the reader can choose the elements of the conclusions that they wish to pay primary attention to. The first section seeks to demonstrate the potential for more 'open' choice about the future trajectory of technological change that follows directly from the analysis of sources of 'domination' throughout the book. The second section explores the consequences for sociological analysis of industrialisation that follow from the culture–technology alignment perspective that is developed through the book. And the third section presents implications of the argument for those readers who are concerned specifically with analyses of the interactions between technology and society.

The book is therefore intentionally written for several audiences - scholars with varying historic and sociological interests, students, and a general public concerned with understanding contemporary society. According to the reader's particular interest, and as in an 'interrogative text', the book may be followed through in a variety of ways. The purpose of this introduction is therefore to guide the reader in knowing what they can draw from the book. I hope that the style of the text will allow the argument to be accessible to all.

As a way of guiding the reader more specifically, a more detailed outline of the essential features of the book's argument and trajectory follows. Because the book is written so that theory *emerges* throughout the text, a roadmap at the start could be useful as a preview for those who wish to locate each chapter within the overall context of the book. Others however, might like to pass over the summary and return to it after reading the book, as a way of crystallising the connections between the separate features of the argument and evidence.

Structure and Argument of the Book

Chapter 1: A Command Performance

Chapter 1 introduces the argument of the book by pointing to what many people experience as the inevitability and command of their lives by technological change. Yet to attribute this intrusive power to technology *per se* is inherently wrong. Social, political and economic negotiations are involved in bringing particular technological systems into existence. Equally, the impact of technological change varies according to the social and cultural context into which new technologies are implanted. Thus, as the chapter argues, technology is a cultural product, and cannot be reified above the ground of social and cultural forces that create it, or use it, or which fit particular technologies into a meaningful relationship to daily life. The central issue to be explored is how *alignments* are forged between technology – viewed as a *cultural* phenomenon – and the wider culture.

The chapter concludes with three case studies, 'barbed wire', 'trumpets' and the 'electric power plug'. These, at first sight, are seemingly trivial technological developments. But *within* their historic social and cultural context, each had considerable transformative power over class boundaries and social meanings of the time. The case studies therefore introduce the culture power that follows from alignment between technology and culture, a power that can not be attributed to the technologies of themselves.

Chapter 2: The Experience of Technology

Whilst the experience of technology is of artefacts, tools and machines –

of physical objects – the culture defining power of technology lies behind this outward appearance. The power lies in the cultural values and knowledge that is involved in both invention and use of the artefacts. Like all cultural phenomena, the meaning of technologies aligns with the overall world views and cultural mores of the society as a whole. Thus, as the chapter demonstrates, the meaning (and therefore use) of technology in ancient Greece aligned with a pervasive world view that was to do with the harmony of human *engagement* in the cosmos; and the meaning of technology in contemporary industrial society aligns with a world view that identifies harmonious relationship and order as rational, systematic control rather than assertion of human intention that is independent of external technical systems.

Chapter 2 explores the cultural values that reside in modern industrial technologies, and which align with industrialism's enchantment with external rational power.

In particular, the chapter identifies how these cultural values are visited upon everyday experience of technology. It is within subjective experience that cultural meanings are brought into action. Indeed the final resting place of all cultural transmission resides in consciousness. Yet individual consciousness is deeply penetrated by values associated with technological mastery. Experience of relating to and transforming nature is mediated by what technology makes possible. Experience of using a particular artefact is housed in what 'shadow systems' of other technological systems make possible: to use an electrical appliance assumes an electricity distribution system; to use an automobile assumes a road-based transportation system, which in turn implies a wider system of urban design and values. Furthermore, for most people, the technical stock of knowledge that is required to understand fully the technologies of daily life is located elsewhere, within the specialised domains of scientists and technologists. These are all conditions of 'enframement', of acting and perceiving *within* the structures of social life that are allowed by the technological parameters of existence. And these technological parameters are a prism to the overall externalised rational world view that industrial society treats as its commandment.

Here lies the power of contemporary technology to define cultural expression. As with all meaningful symbols, technology is itself a cultural text that people read. Yet what can be read is only that which is allowed by the form of the background 'grammar' of this text. And this is a grammar that implies externalised control and order.

Chapter 2 explores the way in which the assumptions and values of externalised rational order were written into the cultural 'text' of industrial technology in the eighteenth century, and have persisted thereafter. The chapter shows how the base cultural value of system order that is inscribed in industrial technologies injects a process of momentum into the expansion of technological systems into all provinces of social life. However, in keeping with the argument of the book, this expansionary momentum, or the 'authority' of the technology text, *only* exists because of alignment between the internal cultural values of the technology 'text' and the values of the wider society as a whole, an alignment that renders alternatives invisible.

Chapter 3: Uncovering the Technology Text

Chapter 3 continues the argument about the cultural text of technology by exploring its form. Whilst the cultural power of technology is to be found in the implied knowledge, values and assumptions that lie behind the dials, facia-plates and levers, the presented *form* of technology is as a physical object. Seen as a cultural text, technology is therefore metaphorically equivalent to a 'written' text, and like written literary texts, is considerably more autonomous, and intractible to redefinitions, than is an 'oral' text that can be continuously refashioned to make sense of contemporary reality. Chapter 3 develops the analysis of technology as a 'written' text from a comparison of the cultural properties of oral vs. written texts in the discourse of different societies. It is argued that the properties of 'written' literary forms can be translated to apply to the form of the technology text.

As with written literary texts, the text of technology is *presented* to the person within contemporary society, rather than derived or refashioned within the person's experience. As a 'written text', the cultural meanings that are sedimented within the outside covers of the artefact are relatively independent of the subjective intentions of the author, and 'context blind' to the way the technology will be received in contemporary daily life. This autonomy of the text was demonstrated in the opening case studies of the book, 'barbed wire', 'trumpets' and the 'electric power plug'.

The written text of technology that we experience in the present implies all those technology texts that preceded it, even though they may be buried in the library archives of historic obsolescence, out of immediate experience. For each new technological model is built on the incorporation of the most efficient instrumental edge of previous models. Within technological *systems*, the written text of an immediate artefact stands in a direct relationship to an entire library of shadow texts (as, for example, an electric appliance stands in relationship to an electricity generation system). The immediate text only makes sense, and can only be used, in terms of the implied library. To use (or read) the immediate artefact therefore asserts the whole shadow library of interconnected texts (of, for example, energy, transport, communication, productive, and urban 'systems'). Thus the reference point for the technology text in daily life resides in all other technology texts rather than in immediate daily life meanings. And within these interconnected texts lie, in 'written' form, the accumulated values of industrial productive history, the assumed forces and social relations of production.

As in Chapter 2, the autonomy of the text of technology, when viewed as a written text, is a property of 'enframement', a property that limits the values horizons within which social action is enacted and cultural meanings are constructed. The reference point for technology's cultural values (and historic trajectory) even penetrates consciousness, and thus closes the loop between consciousness and cultural objectifications within which culture is formed. For, following Marx, consciousness is formed in praxis – the intentional act of transforming the world through labour, and thereby transforming consciousness. And labour praxis is itself mediated through machine systems.

At this stage the argument of the book moves precariously close to an argument for technological determinism. For the culture defining *power* that is embodied within technological systems stands baldly exposed in the apparent 'autonomy' of the text from daily experience. However, as when one stands at the brink of any precipice, the view is clearer. The power of the technology text is derived from an original alignment between cultural values and technological systems that was forged, not without difficulty, in the late eighteenth century. The form, the 'grammar' and the 'content' of the text are therefore all derived in social history, not as intrinsic properties of technology *per se*. Chapter 6 later carries this story forward. Equally, the power of the technology text depends on its alignment with cultural values and trajectories into which the text is implanted. This was demonstrated in the 'barbed wire', 'trumpets' and 'electric power plug' case studies of the first chapter. Thus, as we stand near the precipice of technological determinism we can see that the platform we stand on is constructed from a cultural rather than an externalised technological fabric.

So far however, the argument of the book has all concerned alignment. To highlight what cultural 'alignment' means, the cultural properties of contemporary technology are now explored when the technologies are implanted into traditional cultures where existing cultural practices and meanings are non-aligned with those implied by introduced industrialised technologies.

Chapter 4: The Extinction of Cultures

Chapter 4 explores what happens to traditional cultures when fully articulated technologies drawn from modern industrial society are introduced. The narrative of this chapter draws on a wide range of experiences and case studies of the introduction of modern technologies into (primarily) Asian, and Pacific island cultures. The story of what follows is remarkably consistent. It is the story of collapse of traditional culture, and its replacement by the internationalised 'superculture' of modernism.

However, a great deal is revealed in what happens during cultural collapse. For, in a way that is hidden in the complexity of modern society, the key entry points for penetration by the written text of technology into culture become visible. Lessons drawn from the penetration of modern technologies into traditional cultures can then be applied back into the greater complexity of contemporary society.

What we see in Chapter 4 is empirical demonstration of the culture-defining 'power' of technological systems that was argued for, theoretically, in Chapters 2 and 3. The introduced technology text is, for these societies, fully 'written', the values and change to social relations that are implied by its use are beyond scrutiny within local cultural meanings. Thus, hidden behind the introduction of the first alien artefact is the entire embodied history of industrialisation, and the entire shadow form of technological systems that make sense of the artefact within the industrialised context from which it is drawn. The tractor may be introduced because it makes labour easier. However the tractor implies the cultural values and power of technical systems, and the connectedness of both the tractor's production and use into wider structures of industrial production. These are cultural values that are fundamentally at variance with those of the traditional society. But their potency is expressed in every act of using the artefact, and at every point along the technology's path of diffusion. The cultural values of the technology text therefore form a 'frame' for the social trajectory that the traditional society embarks upon.

What the case studies reveal is that the cultural 'frame' of introduced technological systems implies an economic and status system that is associated with it in the technology's original host society. The industrialised cultural frame implies stocks of knowledge that are alienated from the traditional stocks of knowledge of the society into which the artefact is introduced. The new artefacts imply and command the development of new productive practices that transform the pre-existing rhythms of life, the patterns of traditional social relations of production, and the traditional sources of collective solidarity and obligation. The new artefacts, arriving from an alien productive world, imply the capital of this world, and require entry into the cash nexus to sustain continued use of artefacts that cannot be produced within the traditional society. And the final power of the artefact lies in its objectification of the symbolism that stands in front of the invading culture, replacing (through, for example, Coca-Cola bottles, tractors, automobiles and videos) past totems and symbols of social cohesion with symbols of technical power. The cultural consequence of the cash nexus that stands behind these new symbols is obscured by the symbols' apparent and immediate power in daily life. Hidden too is the dependency and exploitation that follows close behind.

The power of the technology text to penetrate to the heart of traditional cultures is set in the political-economic pressures and hegemonies that stand behind the cash nexus that use of the artefact implies. However, a political-economic analysis alone is inadequate. For the new technologies have been 'allowed' entry, and their consequences have been 'accepted', both reflections of cultural openness and transformation, rather than economic power and hegemonic coercion.

The key entry points for technology's cultural values into wider culture that are identified in these case studies are those of the social relations of production, stocks of technical knowledge, and superordinate symbols of cultural meaning and cohesion. By penetrating to the heart of traditional culture through these arteries, previously non-aligned cultures are drawn into alignment with the 'superculture' of the societies from which the introduced artefacts are drawn.

Chapter 5: The Culture Factor
Chapter 5 draws what has been learned in the specific domain of traditional societies back into the context of everyday life in the modern world. This chapter penetrates more deeply into the 'secret' of how culture is constituted in everyday life as a basis for demonstrating the influence of the technology text over everyday life through social relations of production, stocks of technical knowledge and superordinate symbols.

Culture is a 'secret' because daily life is so deeply embedded in the background cultural 'grammar' of the society, that culture itself is rarely visible. One has to move outside one's own culture – like a 'fish out of the water' experiencing what water is – to understand what culture is. Chapter 5 uses cross-cultural and historic analysis therefore to demonstrate the basic social properties of culture, the *way* that culture penetrates and is carried in consciousness, and the way that the grammar of culture frames daily life experience. This analysis is necessary at this stage in the book's argument, for it provides the other side of the two-way relationship between the cultural properties of technological systems and the wider culture within which these systems are housed, and within which the technology text is 'read'. As with Chapters 2 and 3, the intention of Chapter 5 is that of theoretical analysis. It provides the theoretical platform for the remainder of the book.

Chapter 5 penetrates theories of consciousness (drawn particularly from phenomenological analysis) and culture (drawn particularly from anthropological analysis) to demonstrate how different forms of cultural alignment with technologies are likely to arise. In particular, the analysis demonstrates that along with the historic transformation of the industrial and urbanised context for daily life, there is a self-reinforcing cycle of enframement by the culture-defining properties of the technology text. For culture is formed and carried in inter-subjective engagement, yet the structures of daily experience that have been produced by technological systems are ones that de-emphasise inter-subjectivity and enhance anonymity. This is a condition that is handled in daily life by erecting objectifications to subjective meanings – in the commodities that stand *for* personal worth and social status – an open invitation for further entry of the cultural values of the technology text, a stance of passive acceptance. The symbolic content of technological commodities implies an order that is beyond active constitution in daily life, an order of inevitability.

A similar alignment between the technology text and power is demonstrated. For power to *do* only exists in a context of power to *define*. Legitimacy persists only as long as daily experience aligns with perceptions of meaning (and horizons of accepted privilege), and the trajectory of the order as a whole. Authority of a ruling class's power is predicated on *alignment* between the legitimating ideology that the people accept and the continuous constitution of the order and its meaning *within daily life*. Thus power, legitimacy and ideological hegemony all depend on the constitution of culture in everyday life. And this process of culture constitution depends on its alignment with the cultural text of technological systems that circumscribe it. In this sense, power, culture and the society's technological form will all tend towards mutual alignment, but the technology text performs as a 'frame' for cultural negotiations rather than merely as one actor amongst culture-forming equals.

It is these theoretical conclusions that are carried through into the historic analyses of Chapters 6, 7 and 8. These later chapters explore the social negotiations that went on as the industrial technology text was originally formed. The significance of these negotiations depends on the key entry points for cultural transformation identified out of Chapter 4, that is to do with social relations of production, stocks of technical knowledge and superordinate symbols. The following chapters therefore use the theory developed up to Chapter 6 as a context for understanding early industrial history, a history that reveals the manner in which an alignment between the technology text and wider culture was forged in the first place.

Chapter 6: Industrial Capitalism on Cue

Chapter 6 presents this history, particularly as it relates to the use of coercion to drag society out of its feudal heritage, and as the history reveals the mechanisms that produced the industrial discipline that had to be established before technological systems could take off as a dominant productive mode.

Chapter 6 commences with a case study that bridges earlier discussions of traditional cultures and the culture of eighteenth-century English society that experienced, for the first time, the onslaught of industrialisation. Whilst industrial technology was introduced to both kinds of society for the first time, the cultural negotiations and consequences were very different indeed.

The case study is of a Cook Island society that buried the one pick-up truck they had acquired in a formal funeral ceremony, thus symbolically rejecting modernism. In the case of the Cook Islanders, traditional culture was (temporarily) reasserted, for it could retain its resilience against the onslaught of the modern technological text – though this was only a transitory resilience.

The link to the culture of the people of eighteenth-century England who confronted industrialisation for the first time also concerns resistance and adjustment. The difference is that by the time the first industrial factories appeared on the eighteenth-century social landscape, the culture had already been deeply penetrated by world views, philosophies, and social practices that prepared the way. Rejection was quashed. And adjustment was inevitable, for the wider cultural order was already set in place.

The technology text of systems was introduced into industrialising society with difficulty. Its formulation and acceptance was a product of cultural negotiations, not only between the vested power interests (for whom the text implied economic advantage) and the powerless (for whom the text implied fundamental cultural adjustment). These were also negotiations in which classes that stood between these two groups were involved. All were seeking order within daily life, though with different interests. This was an order that had to be established in an environment of decaying social order and a transforming physical reality for which new meanings had to be found.

The promise of a new order already existed within the ideology of Baconian science – both within the method of disciplined (moral) observation and within the ontology of a cosmos (and therefore, as in 'political economy', a social order) that was guided by natural external laws. However, whilst the principles were accepted by the ideologues and the capitalists alike, the level of transformation of culture that was implied, was not.

Thus, the late eighteenth and early nineteenth centuries were characterised by debates, protests, and resistance concerning the new 'machinery question'. Early industrialisation depended as much on direct and naked coercion and repression, as it did on technological efficiency *per se*. Within this period, technological systems still stood as an equal within a wider game of actors. But once admitted to the stage through acceptance of the underlying grammar of the cultural text of technological systems, the power of technological systems within cultural negotiations increasingly assumed the role of stage director. For, because of the enframing quality of the text's written form, because of the intrinsic potential for spreading that was written into system's cultural grammar, and because of the content of the text that implied penetration to the very roots of culture constitution – the technology text expanded in its dominance. By the 1840s, a previously divided and resisting culture had therefore been drawn into alignment with the 'calculated life' that the machine system implied.

Once the culture–technology alignment was set in place, the cultural values of the written technology text took command. Even ruling class interests and ideologies that were in conflict with the cultural frame imposed by industrial technology thereafter were swept aside by the culture defining properties of the technology text. But this did not happen *before* culture alignment was achieved. The values and dynamics of the technology text were sedimented into wider cultural values at this point, and have persisted since, within continuation of the (constantly readjusting) culture–technology alignment, an alignment that increasingly rendered the technology text into a 'frame' for the constitution of culture itself.

Chapter 7: Ideological Choruses

Chapter 7 also deals with the early Industrial Revolution. The focus of this chapter, however, is on the transformations that occurred in background ideologies, belief systems and knowledge.

The chapter demonstrates the ideological import of the emerging middle classes both before and during the Industrial Revolution. For the middle classes stood in an interstitial location within the superordinate and subordinate social order, and had greatest need of legitimation of the order as a whole. The middle classes played an essential role in balancing the interests of the exploiters against those of the exploited. They sculpted the shape of ideological legitimation whilst tenuously seeking to maintain this balance. The chapter shows how the 'interstitial classes' did this, through first preparing the way for industrial discipline in schooling, and then in proselytisation for an acceptance of the ideologies of political economy amongst the 'lower' classes. Legitimation was based on the order of 'science', but the techniques of the Industrial Revolution were not. Science only came to connect with industrialisation directly after the culture–technology alignment was set in place, and when corporate organisations had incorporated the central values that provided the connecting tissue of this alignment into organisational practice. Prior to that, the import of science for industrialisation was primarily ideological and legitimating.

As the chapter goes on to show, legitimations and power can only persist as long as they align with the 'reality' that the society *as a whole* experiences and ascribes meaning to. Thus, where ideological legitimations moved out of alignment with the experienced order of daily life, these legitimations were demolished. Such was the case with the fall of British-inspired political economy as the US took over the leading edge of progress in the culture–technology alignment. Similarly, power interests transformed or fell as they moved out of alignment with the culture–technology nexus. And the meanings of boundaries of social and class solidarity were entrapped in a shifting field of negotiations as the culture–technology alignment outflanked past sources of collective solidarity and interest.

Chapter 8: Waiting in the Colonial Wings

Chapter 8 explores what was happening at the furthest corner of the world from Britain whilst Britain was pursuing the path of industrialisation. The chapter analyses the history of Australia, a colony of Britain, that economically and socially fed Britain's industrial might, but at the same time, was excluded from industrialisation. The historic case study of Australia provides empirical middle ground for a comparison of the development of deeply embedded cultural alignment (as in Chapters 6 and 7), the articulation of deeply embedded cultural alignment in contemporary international society (as in the subsequent Chapters 9 and 10), and the impact of industrialisation on non-aligned cultures (as in Chapter 4). The case study of Australia follows Chapter 7, however, for it focuses particularly on the themes developed in Chapter 7 concerning ideological and knowledge interactions with the technology text of industrialisation.

Australia stood throughout its modern history as an outpost to Britain's evolving industrialisation, and formation of a culture–technology alignment. The colonial economy of Australia was used by Britain to feed the centre's industrialisation strategies. In so doing, the colony became wealthy. But as with Nauru today – a nation that became suddenly wealthy through compensation for past exploitation – wealth did not guarantee either productive alignment, or continued health. In Australia, because of wealth, the people continued to accept the fruits of colonialism rather than resist the centre's control. They imported the ideologies, the lifestyle, and the technologies of industrialisation, that – at a distance – made the emerging nation wealthy. But the central element of cultural alignment with industrialisation, that is, development of an aligned technical stock of knowledge, did not occur. The imported ideologies were institutionalised, in education, political and scientific systems. But each was alienated from, rather than integrated with, an aligned technical stock of knowledge. Whilst the society remained wealthy from reflected industrial might, the ideologies persisted. But once the *reality* of non-alignment confronted the Australian people when isolation from the centres of international industry was enforced during World War II, the culture *had* to escape illusion, and enter into the construction of the missing technical knowledge component of alignment. Inability to do so, because of the nation's historically weakened position, has meant that wealth derived from a culture–technology alignment has atrophied further, and national culture is left in a severely dependent posture in relation to the international fashion houses of industrial development that are in command of the contemporary culture–technology alignment.

Chapter 9: Winning the Audience

Chapter 9 continues the exploration of the features of culture–technology alignment by progressing from history to the culture of modernism, specifically to explore the cultural dynamics that produced 'consumer society'. The chapter demonstrates the prior culture–technology alignment that had to be set in place for such a society to arise. The chapter explores the mechanisms that came into being to capitalise on an emerging cultural demand for consumer products of the technological system – principally, consumer credit, obsolescence and marginal differentiation of products.

These social mechanisms worked *because* of prior expansion of the technology text into everyday life. By the time that consumer culture came into being in the early twentieth century, technical systems, and their implied cultural values, had already spread across the social landscape, transforming the social and urban order into territory that was only socially intelligible in terms of its technical systematisation rather than its neighbourhood or community meaning. This was experiential territory that reinforced cultural values of privatisation and anonymisation, both values that, in keeping with the argument of Chapter 5, underlie the need for object props for personal identity – the cultural base of consumerism. However, in parallel with the need for coercion in early industrialisation, the conversion of industrial society's inhabitants into consumers also required ideological manipulation. The mechanisms employed to convert the middle classes therefore played on guilt and the absence of servants from the labour force, both products of the prior adjustment of industrialised culture to the burgeoning demands of the nineteenth century technology text's progress. Thus, as was shown in Chapters 6 and 7, cultural adjustment to the technology text is not necessarily automatic, but is mediated by interests that have the products of adjustment within their capitalist hearts.

Chapter 9 therefore demonstrates the construction of a critical cultural bridge between the technology text and subjective life, a bridge that industrialism had to cross in order that the values of the technology text could be mirrored in subjective life, the last domain yet to be ordered by the cultural values of technological systems.

Chapter 10: A Hall of Mirrors

Chapter 10 completes the story. It presents the final (to date) stage of the culture–technology alignment that was forged in the fires of industrial history, that is, the mirroring within subjective life of the cultural values of the technology text itself, the final act in the conversion of the technology text into a 'frame' for culture.

The narrative commences with a demonstration of the metaphorical salience to the modern world of the ancient Greek and Roman legend of Echo and Narcissus. The narrative thus returns to the Greek cultural roots from which the depiction of 'tragedy' originated in Chapter 1. The dominant mode of the culture of modern industrial society is *dependent*, passively constituted within the culture–technology alignment that has been erected historically. It is the culture of mirrors to an evolving 'tragedy of technology'. As in the Echo/Narcissus legend, the culture–technology alignment projects cultural atrophy in the face of self-absorption within a cultural world view that is seemingly commanded by the values of technological systems, rather than by participation and engagement within everyday life. For the 'oral text' of participation is commanded by the 'written text' of technological systems. It is this culture of command that is exported, in its finally articulated form, to the traditional cultures of developing countries.

The chapter concludes with an analysis of the forms of social adjustment and reaction that are housed within the contemporary moment of culture–technology alignment. It is demonstrated that protest is itself generally enframed or co-opted. Political reaction and social movements tend to function more as a 'governor' (as in a steam engine) to limit excess, rather than as a 'cybernetic control device' (as in electronically balanced systems) that fosters continuous balancing and adjustment of technological advance, and its penetration into cultural values. Thus, the dynamic that produces political enframement is the same as that which produced the trajectory of industrial history, the marginalisation of Australian society, and the collapse of traditional societies – namely, the culture-defining power of the technology text.

Chapter 11: Culture, Technology and Liberation

The appearance is similar, but the consequence is different. The *power* of the text of technology in forging cultural alignment has been demonstrated. But, whilst this *appears* to be a consequence of intrinsic qualities of technological systems *per se*, what the book has revealed is that the power lies in a cultural process, not in technology. The power of the technology text is therefore exposed as lying in its cultural form and mechanisms of cultural co-optation. 'Technological determinism' as an explanation, dissolves in the face of an argument for a theory of cultural alignment. The basis for such an 'alignment' argument is strong, for it evolves in the book from a full exercise of 'sociological imagination', the exploration of culture and technology interactions across history and across widely differing cultures. As a way of concluding, Chapter 11 explores the consequences.

Chapter 11 therefore demonstrates what there is to be learnt from viewing technology as a *cultural text* for analyses of the history of industrialisation, and for analyses of contemporary culture and options that exist within it. The chapter shows how such an analysis is informed by sociological theory, and at the same time reforms this theory by placing technology as a cultural phenomenon at the centre rather than at the margins of theoretical insight.

This chapter also demonstrates how a culture–technology alignment perspective contributes a theoretical perspective to the 'new sociology of technology' debate, the scholarly pursuit of explanation of the *social* shaping of technological invention and innovation. Within a culture–technology alignment perspective, a contribution can be made to an understanding of the shaping of social negotiations that produce innovation, and of the general trajectory of innovative change.

Chapter 11 returns to the question of liberation or domination, the subtitle of this book. What has been demonstrated through the book is the depth of penetration of the technology text into everyday life, and the consequent co-optation of the perception of alternatives that follows. Thus, we have come to accept the dynamiting of Trident missile silos, the role of technology in economic collapse, the release of toxic gas at Nantes, the international airport in Western Samoa, and advertising airship blimps – as inevitable and normal.

A 'technological determinist' position offers little alternative, for it reduces cultural constitution of meaning and action to automatic adjustment to technological command. However, when the enframing power of the technology text is revealed as a cultural power, the possibility for the questioning and transformation of this power lies at the point where culture is ultimately constituted – in choices within the everyday lives and actions of the people, and within the institutions that represent their interests. Based in the analysis of the book, and as a way of demonstrating that the argument of *The Tragedy of Technology* leads to optimistic 'possibility' rather than pessimistic 'determinacy', the final chapter therefore offers examples of social action that show that such choice is possible, and that the apparent 'determinacy' of the technology trajectory *can* be dissolved.

Part I
The Culture-Technology
Connection

1

A Command Performance

Technological versus Social Command

> The essence of dramatic tragedy is not unhappiness. It resides in the solemnity of the remorseless working of things.[1]

The experience of modern technology is, in these terms, a dramatic tragedy. The plot is written around the abrogation of personal choice as actors recite the recurrent chorus, '*You can't stop progress!*' The script frequently refers to a shadowy deity whose commandments are to be obeyed. These are the four commandments of the modern age – etched on silicon chips rather than inscribed on blocks of stone: 'Thou shalt bow down to efficiency!'; 'Thou shalt adjust!'; 'Because it *can* be done, it *must* be done!'; and, 'Thou art not responsible! What else canst thou do?'

Even behind the spotlight of technological liberation there lies a shadow of new forms of social domination. Information technologies promised freedom, ease and knowledge in the 1960s; but in the 1980s, freedom has been transmuted into military repression, ease has been transmuted into unemployment, and knowledge has been transmuted into infinite but mindless information. Meanwhile, the unseen god of the technology drama appears to reward, not the meek, but those who are wealthy in capital and strong in efficiency.

The *experience* of technology is the experience of apparent inevitability. It is the experience of being 'framed' by an immutable and 'tragic' power, even though this is a power that at the same time offers continually new and enchanting means of mastering the problems humanity confronts.

The most influential critics who have sought to understand the experienced 'command' of technological change over twentieth-century life have turned to the machines for explanation, and asserted the 'autonomy' of technology. This 'technological determinist' argument is a prevailing theme in a considerable body of both academic and popularist literature, in, for example, Lewis Mumford's *Technics and Civilization*, and Jacques Ellul's *The Technological Society*. Technological determinism is a recurrent theme in general social and political thought, as Langdon Winner's *Autonomous Technology* demonstrates.[2] Each of the technological determinist positions tends to see the technological 'frame' as autonomous, with social and cultural transformations being the consequence of a technologically-inspired trajectory, not the creators of this path. Thus, as Ellul suggests, daily life is controlled by an 'imperative' that allows no scope except for adjustment, for abrogating responsibility to an immutable system. In daily social, economic and political life, technologically-determined 'progress' is so strongly legitimated that resistance is therefore seen to be 'immoral'.[3]

Yet 'technology', as it is commonly understood, simply consists of collections of technical tools and artefacts – 'things' that offer humanity opportunities to transform the world to human advantage; 'things' that lie dormant and benign until they are picked up and used according to the wilful action of living, breathing, sensuous human beings. New technologies are the product of human action and intention, not of some inhuman process. New technologies that persist do so because their 'time is right': they *fit* into contemporary expectations and structures. New technologies diffuse through a society, and transform it, more because the technologies align with people's desires, than because of the singular power of repressive interests to enforce ownership and participation.

We are confronted therefore in our experience of technology with a paradox that is not resolved within a technological determinist perspective. Technological systems and patterns of change are experienced as a frame of inevitability within which we paint our life-picture. Yet the frame is a product of human action. The frame aligns with human needs and only assumes power when humans actively engage with it. As a mirror of human agency, the technological frame *ought* thus to be infinitely plastic, mouldable into any shape of our collective will. The frame *ought* to be plastic, but the remorseless tragedy of technology continues to unfold, continually displacing the technological frame of social experience with a progression of more encompassing frames, a progression in scale and international connectedness between technological systems of production, consumption, transportation, communication, urbanised living, and military destructiveness.

Consequently, whilst the technological determinist stance aligns with many people's everyday experience, to assume that technological systems are independent from the culture that creates them is untenable as an explanation. Such a stance removes human agency from a role both in shaping the particular technologies to which invention gives birth, and in shaping the impact on the human family of the maturing technological child.

The new sociology of technology that has arisen over the last decade in response to this paradox is grasping for an alternative.[4] This perspective has reoriented the attention of history scholars towards social forces that were previously not noticed in many accounts of the invention and application of technology. In supporting the new sociology's position, Thomas Hughes points out, for example, that the prior technological determinist view of the evolution of technology was bad history for it was largely informed by 'non-contextual, internalist histories of technology'.[5]

The new sociology focuses largely on the social forces that shape the *invention* and initial use of technologies. And clear evidence is emerging that particular social, political and cultural forces do shape the birth of technologies. The evidence also shows that social, political and cultural forces shape the maturation of the technologies and their impact.

For example, Bruland observes that one of the main stimuli for development of technologies of the early Industrial Revolution was the *need to control discipline and industrial conflict* rather than a natural progression of technical efficiency *per se*.[6] Thomas Hughes, observing the national shaping of electricity distribution systems at the turn of the twentieth century, shows that *social and geographic* factors shaped the particular form of technological systems.[7] *Political* hegemonies can command the particular shape of regional or national technological systems. Charles Cheape's comparative study of New York, Boston and Philadelphia at the turn of the twentieth century observed the effects of *local politics*, political traditions which (along with urban size and timing) 'forced modifications in the organization of trolley operations and restrained strategies and structures in technologically oriented firms'.[8] Chicago's 'tumultuous politics' endorsed the value of personal mobility and therefore encouraged innovations in highway and traffic systems to accommodate motorists at the same time as discouraging public transport innovation.[9] Bailes observes shaping at a *national political* level, where Stalin's promotion of a Soviet aircraft industry prior to World War II was oriented towards international prestige rather than defence, even though 'defence' was a prime design parameter elsewhere.[10]

Mary Kaldor shows that the *institutional context* of the US' state/military client relationship produces a distinctive style of technological innovation in weapons systems, which progressively become more complex, more elaborate, more sophisticated and grotesquely more expensive. She describes this trajectory of 'over-elaboration' as 'baroque'.[11] In a similar vein, *institutional structures* that form around particular technological systems will, for a variety of social and economic reasons, be resistant to radical advance to more efficient systems. This is demonstrated to be the case with Edison's DC electricity generation system.[12]

Meanwhile, wider social forces offer resistance to an established technological trajectory. Success of political protest can redirect the trajectory of technological systems, as is shown to be the case with the success of the anti-nuclear power movement. As Melvin Kranzberg observes, as a result, 'we have spent billions of dollars on nuclear power plants that we have had to abandon before they were completed.'[13]

Equally, social and ideological alignments with what is offered by a technological trajectory must be set in place before further development of the trajectory can continue. Donald Schon demonstrates the necessity for a new form of corporate structure, the 'learning organisation', before science-led consumerist innovation could proceed after World War II.[14] Jean Baudrillard shows that the progression of 'fashion-based' innovation in automobile manufacture depended on prior *social acceptance* of the idea of 'obsolescence'.[15] Ruth Cowan shows that progress of consumerism (and therefore for the invention of future 'appliances') depended on *psychological acceptance* of the advertisers' appeal to housewife 'guilt'.[16]

Finally, it is clear that the technological context for daily life, once created, limits and focuses the future social developments that are likely to follow, and thus creates a particular *shape of demand* for subsequent technologies. Mark Rose shows the consequences for industrial location and urban design that followed from particular technological choices about DC versus AC electricity distribution systems in Denver and Kansas City. Whilst Rose does not deal with the social consequences directly, they are implied. For the emergent urban design, he observes, is one that displaces neighbourhood cohesion in favour of individualistic isolation, and hence fosters demand for consumer products that align with privatised urban living.[17]

This is a strong and expanding field of evidence. What it shows is that social forces and action are intimately intertwined with technological advance. So the technological determinist position dissolves to the extent that it does not admit social shaping forces. However, the picture of social shaping has been painted close to the social canvas of particular inventions where particular social negotiations are very clear. The wider social and technological context, and the influence of its historic trajectory in shaping *interactions* between inventions and the wider society remains less clear. The possibility persists that when one stands back to see the social shaping picture as a whole, the immediate social shaping brush strokes may all be contained within a wider frame, the frame that everyday experience communicates to us is a consistent and apparently immutable technological 'trajectory'.

Thomas Hughes does, for example, demonstrate that whilst social and geographic factors shaped the particular forms of electricity generation systems at the turn of the twentieth century, the limits of national 'shape' were set within the technical possibilities that were available within the international community.[18] Similarly, whilst local politics in Chicago encouraged highway systems over public transport, the resulting automobile-based city is now mirrored in virtually every metropolis of the world, as the emergent Chicago system aligned with an international trajectory of technologically inspired individualisation and commodity-based urban living. The over-elaboration of the international baroque nuclear weapons arsenal aligns with a consistent trend of technological systems towards greater system complexity and control generally. Resistance to nuclear energy production played a secondary role to absolute spiralling cost for 'fail-safe' systems, thus redirecting energy decisions to other centralised and large-scale systems of production, rather than fundamentally altering the trajectory towards large-scale energy production and use. And the dynamic in technological systems design of controlling discipline and industrial conflict that Bruland observes is located at a particular point in industrial history, where the use of technological systems of production *required* the disciplining of a labour force that had yet to learn to *fit* into the systems.

Thus, the paradox between 'experience' of technological determinism, and evidence for the social shaping of technological advance, is not yet resolved. The theoretical programme that follows must seek to resolve this paradox, that is, between the apparent 'autonomous' command of technological enframement, and the social 'autonomy' that creates this frame.

The starting point for a theoretical programme that resolves the autonomy paradox lies in treating technology for what it is, a cultural phenomenon. As the previous 'social shaping' evidence showed, the particular forms of technology that develop and bed into society are shaped by cultural meanings and social negotiations. Equally, the experience of technology and its impact on everyday life are shaped according to cultural meanings that reside within the wider society. Thus, by exploring the *cultural* properties of technology (as distinct from technology's instrumental power or use value *per se*), we can look behind the evidence to identify how technology as a *cultural* force *generally* interacts with, forms, and is formed by the wider culture of industrialising society. Technology presents us with a cultural 'text' to be read in everyday life. If we 'read' this text as communicating a message of inevitability this is because our wider cultural values allow us to read the text in no other way.

As this book goes on to show, the apparent social *power* of a technological trajectory lies in the embodiment (or 'objectification') of cultural meanings *within* technology, and within the *alignments* that come into being between present cultural meanings and the objectifications of the past that we confront in contemporary technological artefacts. Thus the social negotiations that go on in the development of particular technologies are themselves shaped according to a broader culture–technology frame. The immediate social negotiations are therefore not infinitely plastic in the technological products that could be produced, but severely constrained. Equally, the depth of impact of particular technological changes will depend on the alignment between the changes and the social and cultural context into which the innovations are implanted, a context that has already been formed according to technological and social changes that went before.

Three deceptively simply cases serve to introduce the analysis of the book. These cases observe what might seem trivial technological changes – the introduction of barbed wire to Britain, the cultural salience of improved brass trumpets in England's northern towns, and the diffusion of the electric power plug in the United States. Arguably, it can be claimed that 'barbed wire' brought down the English aristocracy; that 'improved trumpets' raised the British working class; and that the 'electric plug' proletarianised middle-class American housewives. Together, the three cases reveal the overall picture of the revolutionary social power that follows from cultural alignment of simple introduced artefacts. It was not the artefacts themselves that transformed social class relations. Nor was it class relations that brought the technological innovations into being. Instead, it was the *alignment* between cultural change and technique that reveals the dynamic of the 'tragedy of technology' – the seemingly remorseless march of technique through the centre of life-experience.

Introductory Cases: 'Barbed Wire', 'Trumpets' and 'An Electric Power Plug'

The fox, 100 years ago in England, probably did more for the preservation of rural aristocratic privilege than any economic, political or cultural hegemony the lords could still lay claim to.[19] The social function of fox-hunting was much deeper than mere privileged and destructive amusement might suggest. The brotherhood of the fox-hunt reached well beyond the loyalties bred by estates and regally connected lineage. In what could be viewed as a nineteenth-century arcane precursor to Rotary Clubs, included within the hunt were men from many positions within rural society: the fox would find itself pursued by not only lords and squires, but also by a collection of farmers, the local village parson, doctor and solicitor, and even the village sweep. Except perhaps as subservient 'beaters' who flushed the fox out of hiding to ease the burden of the gentry's 'search-and-destroy' mission, the only social group missing were the labourers. Thus, as Schneewind observes, 'the fox did more for the unity and strength of the landed interests than rent rolls'.[20]

By the late Victorian era, 100 years of industrialisation had torn the foundations of traditional legitimacy out from under the aristocracy. The emergent capitalist bourgeoisie was firmly entrenched in control of both political and economic forces of change. Death duties, perhaps the most potent contradiction to inherited privilege, had been approved by Parliament. The working classes had started to discover the power of their own collective action – as in the successful dockers' strike of the 1880s – and were no longer merely breaking machines as protest. The industrial landscape was an inescapable fact, and as source of Britain's imperialistic might, industrialism had transformed the geography and perceptions of England: the new machine age not only raised smoke-stacks to economic wealth in the cities, far removed from manorial sylvan bliss, but rushed right past the aristocrats' doors, in smoke-belching steam trains that left in their wake a landscape etched with the steel tracks of the industrial system. And education was, for the first time, finally shaking itself out from the classics and tradition, and teaching the populace to look forward to 'progress' rather than backwards to the power of religion and the structures of power and privilege that were associated with it. The aristocracy was under siege. But, they could still hunt foxes.

As with all atrophying ruling classes in history, the gentry sought to protect the penultimate bastion of privilege that was represented in the fox-hunt. But in their action, they virtually shot themselves in the foot.

Concerned about the continuing encroachment of the outside industrialising world and its people on their cherished fox 'coverts', the aristocracy imported barbed wire from the US in order to fence in the fox coverts and the foxes' own territory. The production of barbed wire had been made possible by the early ninteenth-century invention of galvanising processes; barbed wire had been conceived of in the US, because through the 'American System' of automated production, it offered a relatively cheap way of fencing the vast open spaces of the American frontier. As an innovation within England, barbed wire was initially effective in protecting the aristocrats' hunting territories. However, the success was short-lived. Because of its relative cheapness and the ease of fencing it offered, others followed the aristocracy's example, and fenced their own boundaries, areas that the aristocrats had formerly crossed with divine privilege in the course of their fox-hunting. It was not long before the intimate, manicured landscape of England was criss-crossed by unjumpable barbed wire fences that not only protected the fox and his vixen, but also meandered along the edges of non-aristocratic territory and across the path between the lord's front vestibule and where the foxes had decided to live. Thus the fox-hunt became severely restricted, and in many locations, impossible. The foxes survived, and had their revenge, for the aristocracy atrophied: the source of aristocratic solidarity that the fox-hunt provided was fast disappearing, assisted in its demise by the barbed wire fences that blocked the path of the traditional hunting grounds. It could be said that the British aristocracy disappeared as a traditional ruling class because of barbed wire.

In the same vein, it could also be said that the working classes became strong because of the brass trumpet. Whilst the aristocracy were at leisure on the backs of thoroughbred horses, galloping around a shrinking countryside, the labouring classes were at leisure marching on foot down the thoroughfares of expanding industrial towns and cities, playing in brass bands. Admittedly, the working class had distinctly less time for leisure than the aristocracy, and could afford considerably less money for their enjoyment. But by the mid-to-late nineteenth century, the working class had become a class-conscious social force of gathering momentum, and had already won some freedom from the outright, numbing exploitation of early capitalist repression. Beginning about the middle of the nineteenth century, around the same time as the advent of mass spectator sports, brass bands had marched into the industrial towns as a burgeoning form of recreation for the emerging urban working classes. This was particularly so in the industrialising north of England, where by the late nineteenth century, Yorkshire and Lancashire alone were reported to have 4,000 to 5,000 such bands.[21] The bands formed the basis for social cohesion of the labouring classes, in much the same way that the fox-hunt did for the aristocracy. Workmen in mills, collieries and factories formed their own bands, thus extending their class interests within the industrial employment domain out into the wider culture of the town community. Again, cheapness was a critical factor in the impact of technology on the boundaries of class cohesion. Workmen could not afford expensive instruments; nor could they afford the luxury of time involved in learning difficult musical apparatuses. However, several industrial innovations came together in the first part of the nineteenth century that helped to solve both problems. An improved method of making brass tubing was patented in 1838; a method of compounding copper and zinc into large brass sheets of much improved workability was developed in 1837; and valves were developed that simplified the performance of any melody on the cheaper brass instruments that the other technologies made possible. So, whilst new technology could be said to have brought down the traditional aristocratic ruling class, new technology could also be said to have given birth to the wider social cohesion of the emerging proletarian class, a class that was itself a direct and repressed social product of the very technological system that now provided the means of their liberation and cohesion in leisure.

Whilst the technical artefacts of barbed wire and trumpets played a role in the social transformations that these two stories reveal, these actors only assumed power because of the particular social stage on which they performed. Both of the events depicted are framed in a wide and diffuse social context. Whilst it might be claimed quite validly that these two particular technologies played *a* role in the transformation of class boundaries as industrialisation marched across the landscape of society's life-world, causality can be attributed to neither. The aristocracy were besieged not only by the barbed wire devil of their own making, but by the whole march of industrialisation. As a result of a *wide* range of forces, the proletariat were emerging as a socially-cohesive cultural group, rather than as a minority that recognised their collectivity only within the bounds of factory-based repression. Trumpets may have helped to bring down the walls that separated workers from each other within their life-worlds both within and outside the factories, but the tune the trumpets played was in harmony with a symphony of forces that were all leading towards the formation and strength of the proletariat.

In the case of the aristocracy, their power as a ruling class commenced its downward plunge as soon as the authority of a hierarchical church (and its intimate link with the State) was undermined by Protestantism. For, along with this social force came de-legitimation of the nobles' inherited privilege to act on behalf of God in controlling rural estates and the peasant's employment and life-space. The demise of the aristocratic ruling class was fostered by the authority of individualism and rationality that followed the Enlightenment, for this questioned the legitimacy of all tradition. The fall of the aristocratic ruling class was finally actualised by the new source of economic power, the capitalists, who, legitimated by political-economy philosophy, ruled the spread of change across the physical and perceptual landscape of the nineteenth century. By the time that fox-hunting started to disappear, the nobles were besieged by a complex array of forces that the changing times had yielded: Trollope, in a contemporary report, talked of the 'perils' confronted by fox-hunting, as the perils of outsiders, new-fangled prejudices, more modern sports, over-cultivation, extended populations, increasing railroads, indifferent magnates, decrease of funds, and increase of expenditures.[22] All of these were the perils for aristocratic privilege that were directly produced by the transformation of structures of power, hegemony and culture that were associated with industrialisation.

In the case of the working classes, their very formation as an objective class was a direct product of industrialisation as well. Formed originally from the margins of eighteenth-century society's displaced and marginal peasants, women and children, by capitalists who had an economic interest in collecting a machine-disciplined workforce under one roof, the class had not realised its cohesion for some time. There had been some success, such as within the northern town of Oldham, within the early days of industrialisation, in forming a self-conscious social class from the mill-workers.[23] But in general the early proletarian-based revolts that were potentially a source of class cohesion, simply involved the breaking of machines that were identified with the source of worker unemployment and repression.[24] These movements invariably failed. They did not provide a sense of power in cohesion, a necessary base for the development of class consciousness and identity. By the later part of Victoria's reign however, the proletariat was both numerous and concentrated in working-class neighbourhoods within the towns and cities. And, along with development of increased education and literacy of the lower classes, along with the victories that the proletariat as a force had won over some of the capitalist restrictions on free time and cultural separation of the people from each other, the class was becoming conscious of itself as both a social and political force. Trumpets may have provided a means for collective action in leisure, but this collective action was built on a trajectory that was directly associated with the whole process of emergent industrialisation.

The two stories may not be simple. But both convey important messages about the relationship between technology and society. The technologies of barbed wire and trumpets did play a part in both the dissolution and affirmation of class boundaries and solidarity. However, the particular technological artefacts only did so because of the particular, historically determined, social context into which they were introduced. The respective impacts of both technologies were therefore *framed* in a wider social context that was intimately bound into the force of transformation that industrialisation and its prior technological changes had unleashed. Both technologies impacted on boundaries of social cohesion and identity. But barbed wire and trumpets only did so because these objects had a particular salience to the social practices that produced social cohesion within the everyday life-worlds of the participants.

Both technologies were produced from production systems that in no way had these social transformations as objectives. Technical efficiency, social control of the labour force, and profitability for those who controlled the means of production, and market, were the guiding principles for implementation of the innovations. Yet the unintended consequences of production were to assist the demise of a ruling class that resisted industrialisation on the one hand, and to *foster* the emergence of a proletarian class that combated the new bourgeois rulers, on the other.

In both cases, the technological artefacts presented a message, a text to be read, to both the producers and the users. But neither group could read the message for it was opaque in its subsequent social connotations. The text was opaque because neither group could see anything but the meaning of the technologies for their immediate life-world. Neither group could see beyond this life-world to the wider 'system' of technology-social relations that produced both the technologies themselves and the life-world consequences that the system implied.

These are the fundamental principles of the technology-society relationship. Technology is produced by particular social forces. Technology produces both intended and unintended social change. Technological systems *enframe* the meanings and consequences of particular technological artefacts. But the meanings and social consequences of technological change come to rest at the level of the life-world experience of the people. Technological change therefore is not, by itself, productive of social change. Instead, the direction of change is a product of the particular alignment between the technological possibilities and the society and culture that exists. Meanwhile, technologies are themselves shaped by the society, and the meanings that enjoy power within it. The technology-society relationship is interactive, and at the same time enframing of possibilities. The key to what is produced in technology-society interactions is *alignment*.

One has not to look too far to find an infinite variety of cases that reinforce these assertions. To take one further, seemingly trivial, example, it could be claimed, in line with the flavour of the two cases presented, that the electric power plug caused the proletarianisation of the suburban housewife, through plugging middle-class women into an emerging consumerist system that gained only through the household becoming its servant.

When Thomas Alva Edison introduced the electric (or 'incandescent') lighting system for urban populations in 1881, the power plug was the one thing he forgot. Under an extraordinary five pages of inventions that Edison presented under the 1881 patent No. 251,551, everything else that could be envisaged within a 'system of electric lighting for houses' was included[25] – but not the obvious device of a power plug that could use this system *flexibly* within the home for a *variety* of other appliances. The *system* of electric lighting that Edison introduced was immediately successful as its time was right, and the world was quickly beating a path to his door to participate in the modern electricity generation. Just two years after Edison patented his invention, a central power station was generating electricity for 8,000 light bulbs within New York's Wall Street area.[26] By 1890, central electricity generating stations powered urban areas throughout the world. But meanwhile, whilst the first electric appliances (fans and sewing machines) were demonstrated in the same year as Edison's patents (at the Paris Exhibition of 1881),[27] electric phonographs were exhibited at the Chicago Columbian Exposition of 1893[28] and 'electric appliance' appeared for the first time in a US patent in 1887,[29] the use of these electricity-powered appliances had to depend on an expensive fixed circuit wiring of the home. Thus the commodity revolution did not hit the home until about the time of World War I, when a standardised system of convenience outlets and interchangeable appliances was introduced.[30] From then on, the industry engaged in active promotion of domestic appliances, a marketing initiative that underlay the subsequent consumer revolution and the final capture of society as a whole in the interest of continued industrial expansion.[31]

Edison had his head turned towards building an industrial system, and could not see the domestic lifestyle consequences that could follow from a flexible way of using the centralised system he designed. But the domestic household was ready. George Walsh, writing in the *Independent* in 1901 projected the edge of a revolution in housekeeping: 'It only needs the cheapening of electrical power to introduce them (electrical appliances) in nine-tenths of the houses in this broad land.'[32] Servants were becoming expensive (with the rising wages associated with industrialisation) and hard to come by.[33] Middle-class women were being made to feel guilty by marketers if they did not adopt the latest in consumer products and gadgetry.[34]

And the result was that middle-class female spouses, instead of being primarily involved in the *management* of domestic labour, became involved in doing it themselves – with the apparently labour-saving devices that the marketers not only made available, but morally necessary.[35] Instead of being managers, middle-class housewives became workers, labouring on tasks that had no end, but which were required in service of both their husbands patriarchal interests, and the morality of modernism.

Thus, it could be said that the electric plug caused the proletarianisation of the middle-class housewife.

As with the examples of barbed wire and trumpets, such a 'technology determinist' explanation is not adequate. Certainly this simple invention of a flexible power outlet 'opened the door of opportunity' as Lynn White claimed for technology generally.[36] But this invention was set in both a technological and social context, and could not have worked, or even been relevant, without it.

The invention and distribution of electricity unleashed a massive technological system across the whole urban landscape. This 'system' 'determined' the subsequent structure of urban settlement and industrial location, an assertion I will develop later in this book. But most importantly, the emergent electrical system *enframed* the life-world of the housewife. A range of choices existed for the particular consumer products that followed – both for inventors and the housewife. But all of these choices were set in a trajectory of response to individualist needs rather than communal sharing. Communal designs for the provision of household services thus existed, but were never brought into operation.[37]

The wider 'system' was invisible to the housewife plugging in the fan or sewing machine, but it was still there, enframing the choices and possibilities she could capitalise upon. The wider industrial system had produced the social conditions that led to the demise of employment for domestic labour, thus enframing the choices that 'managers' of the domestic household confronted in deciding on the household's management. The wider industrial and emerging marketing systems *aligned* with the social needs that the values of the systems themselves had created. It was the result of these *wider* social-technological alignments that led to the proletarianisation of the middle-class housewife and the commodification of domestic culture. These transformations did not follow from the artefacts themselves.

It follows from these examples that technological determinism as an argument is an entirely inadequate explanation of the way that technology and society interact, even though life-world choices were enframed. It also follows from the examples that the application of particular inventions as well as the impacts of technological change are directly connected to the wider social and technological context in which they are housed. Finally, it follows from the examples that the last resting place of this intersection between 'enframing' technological systems and social change, lies deeply within the life-world, and the meanings that are constructed within it by the people who are living their daily lives. Thus the shape of technological application and its impact is produced in *cultural* interactions. However, sources of the culture-defining power of technology are yet to be revealed.

The Experience of Technology

Harmonies and Disharmonies of Technology

Following a concert given by Fritz Kreisler, a woman came up to him and said, 'Maestro, your violin makes such beautiful music.' Kreisler held his violin up to his ear and responded, 'I don't hear any music coming out of it.' Melvin Kranzberg, in presenting this story, then observes, 'when men and machine work together, they can make some beautiful music.'[1] In this context, Kranzberg is viewing machines, tools, technical artefacts and technique as one, a conflation that I will show later is misleading. Each of these manifestations is however a member of the general species, 'technology'.

The story and Kranzberg's observation directly align with the original Greek conception of what technique and knowledge were, the two Greek epistemic roots from which the modern-day meaning of 'technology' was derived. The ancient Greeks had a world view that asserted human engagement with the natural world. This world view is quite different to the contemporary world view of industrialised society which places science on a pedestal as an independent arbiter of what is valid in human experience and constructions of meaning. Science, for the Greek philosopher Pythagorus, involved 'the study of the comely and harmonious order of the world.'[2] Greek science was more to do with the human engagement in the aesthetic of the 'Kosmos' (or 'comely order' of things), as in Pythagorean geometry, than it was to do with the separation fostered within post-Baconian science between an external reality and its human observation. Similarly, the Greek root for 'technology', *techne*, is to do with not only the activities and skills of the craftsman, but also comprises the arts of the mind, and the fine arts. *Techne*, like science, involves an aesthetic, or as Heidegger describes it, a 'bringing forth to poiesis', or the human *construction of* poetic meaning within technique.[3] For the ancient Greeks,

Beauty lay in the potential for meaning which realized the object, an object simultaneously useful, integrated and integral, or rather, both the product and production of nature prescribed by a unifying vision of the world, gathering about it and in it the milieu from which it took root.[4]

The 'ology' part of the word 'techne-ology' refers to knowledge about techne, literally, 'words of knowledge'.[5] Thus, the cultural roots from which the word 'technology' has been derived are deeply planted in *human* engagement in a world that the people are crafting, transforming and gaining knowledge about, as a harmonious and poetic synthesis constituted within the relationship between humans and nature. This perfectly expresses the relationship between Fritz Kreisler and his violin.

However, by the time 'technology' came to be defined by the American Webster's Dictionary, its meaning had fundamentally shifted to 'the application of science to industrial use'. Within this definition, 'technology' still concerns a mode of *revealing* to human consciousness, as Heidegger would claim.[6] However, what is 'revealed' is only that which can appear through the filter of rationality and the application of rationality within industrialism. As opposed to the holistic view of the ancient Greeks, contemporary 'technology' is seen more as associated with a means to an end than it is with human activity and construction of meanings. Within the modern experience of technology, the person is a component in a collective enterprise that connects technical means with productive ends. Thus, the end that Kreisler could accomplish as a virtuoso violinist may express human harmony. But the experience that people have of technology generally is very different indeed.

Factory workers (and, increasingly, office workers) experience technology as a powerful, external force that enforces a rigid and subservient discipline on the employees' experience of work, and their relationships with others in collectively producing and transforming the natural world. Employees generally see technology in the 1980s as an alienated force that stands somewhere behind their left shoulder, and which, with one new breath of change, may extinguish their means of livelihood. The aesthetic is one of externally imposed order rather than human harmony; the words of knowledge are opaque, controlled by those who are masters of the technological system and the variety of specialists who inform them. The technological aesthetic is unreadable to the layman, but is embodied in words of knowledge that say 'you shall adjust'. As Philip Slater observes, 'We talk of technology as the servant of man, but it is a servant who now dominates the household, too powerful to fire, upon whom everyone is helplessly dependent.'[7]

Fritz Kreisler's experience of technology is therefore an exception to everyday experience of the technologically penetrated world that people of the late twentieth century inhabit. Through today's technologies we stand apart from the world, whilst our relationship to this world is *mediated* through an opaque 'black box' of technique. The relationship of people to this world is thus enframed by what technology *does*, its *use value* in transforming the world for human advantage, and an aesthetic that views harmonious relationship and order as rational control.

As Marcuse proposes, 'The industrial society which makes technology and science its own is organised for the ever more effective domination of man and nature, for the ever more effective utilization of its resources.'[8] And the world itself is seen as a *standing reserve (Bestand)*, as Heidegger suggests,[9] a field of energy or power that can be captured and stored: earth is no longer 'mother', but a coal-mining district or a mineral deposit. Human activity is taken into the process of rationally ordering this world, and seeing this world through the foggy mediating lens that technology provides. Thus, even the act of labour *praxis* that Marx identified with joining consciousness and action in transforming the world[10] is itself mediated by technological filters; and world transformation (as well as consciousness) is enframed in the ordering principles that lie behind the technologies that join consciousness and the world transformed. In contrast to Fritz Kreisler's experience, the world and our experience of it is *enframed* by technology, and revealed only within the on-going dynamic of order that this frame implies, and not within the aesthetic that is humanly constituted in everyday action and individual control.

Consequently, whilst the definition of 'technology' has been derived from ancient Greek cultural roots, the aesthetic order that houses human experience, and the *meaning* of 'technology', is now fundamentally different. As far as the Greeks were concerned, the aesthetic was one of harmony derived within human engagement. As far as modern society is concerned, the aesthetic is one of harmony between smoothly integrated technical systems, a harmony that mirrors the assertion of 'instrumental' over 'communicative' action.[11] The modern technological aesthetic has as its fundamental dimension externally-mediated power and control over both the use of nature and humanity's definition of it. Thus, whilst 'men and machines working together can make some beautiful music' in any culture, for the Greeks the harmony is the music of human engagement, and for the modern world, the harmony is the music of smoothly meshed, quietly humming technical systems.

Experiencing the Technological Drama

The order, the harmony, of a modern technologically-integrated society is largely invisible. The order is maintained in the networks of power transmission that weave the whole urbanised landscape together into an energy system; though the wider system *inclines* people's choices (to use Don Ihde's term),[12] few people contemplate the system when connecting the kitchen blender into a power outlet. The technologically-based order is maintained in the networks of roads, railways, airlines, telephones and media transmission that together provide transport and communication access; but experience of the system is not so much of the system itself, and the organisational order that lies behind its operation, as it is of traffic jams, the quality of airline steward service, mother calling at an inconvenient time of night from overseas, and of seeing the world paraded in two-dimensional vibrant images within our lounge room. We contemplate taps when we need water, not dams and reticulation systems; plasticised cartons of milk on a supermarket shelf, not cows, dairies and trucks; digitalised numbers that represent time, rather than the turn of the earth on its axis or even the silicon chip logic that mediates this relationship between being at work on time and where the sun is in the sky.

In other words, most of the harmonious order of the technological world is *background*, or 'technological texture'.[13] This background is at the same time mediating our experience of nature and others, as well as providing an assumption or grammar for direct experience of particular technological artefacts that stand in front of the wider systems and embody them. We therefore participate within a technological code that remains a perpetual and unexamined context for lived experience, until crisis, such as system breakdown or strike, slams the significance of this background directly into our awareness.

The physical objects of technology that we confront in our life-world objectify this code. According to how centrally the physical objects represent the entirety of the code, they therefore draw superordinate symbols of the whole technological culture into lived experience, in much the same way that Emile Durkheim observed,[14] how religious totems symbolise and draw into experience the whole social order and solidarity of traditional societies. God is sitting in the driving seat of the automobile now rather than on the church altar. The code enters into our daily experience in a number of quite different ways, ways that vary according to the different sorts of relationship we have with technological artefacts.

Our *focal* experience of technology can embody our relationship to the natural or social world *through* technology: in using a simple tool such as a pencil or a knife for example, the tool provides a means of extending or accentuating our physical capability to achieve an end that dirty or sharp finger nails (respectively) would be incapable of accomplishing. Meanwhile we *see* the world through the tool as astronomers see the cosmos through, and within the limitations of, a radio-telescope. We experience the world's natural texture and usefulness (or, for that matter, the cosmos) through what the tool makes possible; and at the same time, we close off sensuous experience (of, for example, coolness or sensual stimulation) by what the capability and design of the tool excludes. All technology *mediates* our life-world experience according to technological design parameters.

In using a more complex machine, the artefact also allows us to extend human capability and to experience the world through the machine. However, along with an increase in the complexity of the inner workings of the machine, the experience is increasingly mediated by the machine itself. All but what the focused purpose of the machine allows us to perceive is locked away in shadow. With a front-end loader rather than a shovel, our efficiency in digging larger tracts of earth out of the backgarden is massively enhanced, but direct sensuous experience is unlikely to be of the earth's texture, coolness and wetness, or of the onion-grass and orchid bulbs that are embedded within the soil, or of the worms and arachnids that populate it. Our experience of the earth is as one tonne bucket loads of undifferentiated rubble. More importantly however, this experience of the earth is secondary to the more immediate experience of the machine itself. In operating the front-end loader we must devote considerable attention to the actions of pressing pedals, changing gears and operating pneumatic drive mechanisms. Unless we as actors pay attention to the machine, unless we abide by the technological logic embodied *in* the machine, then not only will we be unable to achieve the end of digging out a large sodden hole, but in trying, we could well bring down the power-lines, take out the side wall of the house or run over the neighbour's dog. The *focus* of our experience is of the technology itself more than it is of the world that we are relating to or transforming via the mediating device of the machine. When the focus of our experience is on the technology and *its* capabilities, the world remains a distantly perceived 'standing reserve' as I observed earlier from Heidegger: the world's meanings derive from what the machines can do to it.

Thus, the distinction I have observed here between tool and machine allows us to see that from the most simple to the most complex technological artefact, there is a continuum of mediation of our direct experience of the world that tools allow us to transform. The entire spectrum of technological artefacts stands however as foreground to the entire harmony and interconnectedness of the background technological systems that produce, maintain, transform, repair and give meaning to the artefact in our hand, under our feet, or at the end of our button-pressing finger tip.

Action, Knowledge and the Cultural Text

The machines are brought to life, and thus illuminate this background, *only* through human activity. Unless we know what the machines are for, and how to use them, they remain as rusting and inconvenient pieces of matter that we must negotiate our way around in everyday life - in the same way that we avoid junkyards and derelict buildings. The tool or the machine in this sense embodies a *cultural text*[15] that is set within the grammar of the background system, but remains unreadable in everyday life unless we know the action-and-meaning cypher.

The artefact text is *totally opaque* to those who are ignorant of the particular activities that are required to bring the machine to life. That is to say, it is totally opaque except to the extent that the machine is a familiar symbol within life-world experience of the passively received background cultural code. 'Everyone' knows what an automobile means in terms of transportation potential and status salience, but still the *reading* of the artefact text that brings these meanings to life requires knowing how to use the machine: the same automobile that was acquired to show off to the neighbours only serves to kill the grass it occludes from sunlight unless we know how to drive.

The text is *relatively opaque* to the extent that we know only how to *use* the machine, and are unable to scrutinise or comprehend the machine's inner workings or logic. The relative opacity of the machine text is one of the most fundamental problems encountered in the transfer of Western technical artefacts into developing countries, when the technique but not the whole knowledge context is all that is transferred. For example, workers at an externally introduced tin-plating factory we observed in Thailand knew how to operate the machines but had no comprehension of the total system concept, or of how to tune the integration of the separate machines into optimal production: a retired American foreman who could read the system text therefore saved the factory owners some $250,000 per year when he was brought in to help, simply because he turned a few dials, adjusted a few levers and harmonised the system into an optimal technological flow process.[16]

The artefact text is *transparent* to the extent that we have the knowledge not only to use the machine and understand its inner workings, but also to *intervene actively* in designing, fabricating and modifying the machine and its use. Transparency comes with a level of active engagement that involves not only reading, but also *writing* the text. The post-World War II technological power of Japan originated primarily from precisely this transition, between 'reading' the text of machines the Japanese copied, and 'writing' the text of machines they modelled and improved on, having learnt to read.

Consequently, what determines the level of opacity or transparency of the artefact text is the level of alignment between the stock of knowledge that we have access to within our life-world experience, and the stock of knowledge that is hidden within the artefact. Thus, returning to the original derivation of the word, 'technology', the 'species' is defined in terms of knowledge rather than mere physical object, but within the species, the distinction between the separate identities of tool and machine – as far as life-world experience and mediation of relationships is concerned – is a distinction between the *level* of knowledge embodied, and the accessibility of this knowledge to life-world experience and construction.

Cultural Influences on the Technology Text

The stock of knowledge 'appears' as technical knowledge. But this technical knowledge stands in front of the cultural meanings and assumptions that make sense of it. Thus, standing immediately behind knowledge of the inner workings of machines is knowledge of the implied interconnections of the machine with other systems, as well as knowledge of the whole system grammar of technique within which the immediate artefact stands. Standing further back in the shade of this immediate background is knowledge of valued social goals (to which the machine systems contribute); the background stock of knowledge is also to do with intelligibility and ontology of the world (that the logic of machine systems mediates); and the knowledge implies a morality that aligns individual and social norms with the wider frame of meanings that the technological system implies. The physical artefact that stands before us is therefore a cultural symbol that is imbued with acquired meanings that are salient within the *overall* cultural grammar of our society.

Furthermore, the text of the artefact stands in a wider *con*-text, against which the textual meaning makes sense. A machine-system only makes sense as a machine when it is located in a physical and cultural context that indicates its machine-usefulness. This is the same as the way that a Bible – as cultural symbol – assumes a different meaning when found in an antique shop or as a door stop, rather than on a church altar.

Technologies born in the womb of Western industrial culture are therefore likely to assume quite different meanings when introduced into non-Western traditional cultures. Aeroplanes and consumer goods were introduced into the experience of Papua New Guinean natives during US occupation throughout World War II. The physical artefacts entered a culture that had no way of incorporating them within traditional stocks of knowledge, nor within existing productive or cultural practices. The life-world stock of knowledge of the tribespeople permitted efficient agricultural production, ritually managed inter-tribe warfare, and the hunting of cassowaries for status-exchange gifts. But the Papua New Guineans had no way of understanding either the American technologies that now stood in front of them, or the implied industrial system that stood behind the 'cargo' that arrived miraculously out of the skies. The meanings of technology were transmuted into the culture that existed and made sense of the people's lives. The people incorporated the meaning of the 'powerful' new artefacts into their existing stock of knowledge, and into what they *could* do, and therefore built ritual airstrips to attract aeroplanes after the Americans went home, as if building animal traps. The 'cargo' never arrived.[17] This same cultural transmutation of technological meaning was evident in remote areas over 20 years later when Neil Armstrong walked on the moon, a feat that symbolised within the West the most extraordinary level of technological mastery. A friend of mine who was present in the Upper Sepik district at the time, told of a native who returned to his tribe, having heard of the moonwalk on the radio in Port Moresby. In the tradition of the people, he presented a masterful oratory on rockets and space capsules, and on men journeying through the skies to land on the moon that the people could see above the skyline of their jungle habitat. The people were transfixed. The orator was heard in complete silence, unusual as normally there is a considerable amount of cross-talk whilst an orator presents his speech. At the end, the people asked him two questions. The first was 'Why did they go? – was it for pigs or women?' The second question was 'Who were they? – Roman Catholics or Seventh Day Adventists?'

The physical artefacts of technology embody cultural meanings, and in the Papua New Guinean case, these meanings were alien to the indigenous culture, so the cultural clash and transmutation can be seen in high relief. Within our own industrialised society the meanings of technology equally exist, but they are harder to see, because the meanings are taken for granted and are deeply embedded within the cultural assumptions of the wider social-technical system that provides the context for our lived experience. The contemporary cultural meaning of technology has, however, not suddenly sprung into life as in a flash of inspiration, or in a charge of new knowledge outputted to us by computers. Artefact meanings, like all cultural properties, have evolved historically, and contain within them their historic residues. Meanings and experience are in constant negotiation within culture, as is demonstrated also within the Papua New Guinean examples. In a traditional culture, where the context of meanings is locked into a seamless web of tradition rather than change, and into an unvarying ecological niche, there is little disharmony between cultural context and the meaning of immediate experience. There, the evolution of transformed meanings is very slow. That is, the transformation of meanings is very slow until the culture is suddenly confronted by alien cultural objects and practices such as has been the case in Papua New Guinea where remote tribal people confront Western technologies and urbanisation and progress 'Ten Thousand Years in a Lifetime'.[18] Within Western society, however, the seeds of cultural change were planted deep in the soil of an emergent assumption of 'progress' well before industrialisation cast the shadow of its smoke-stacks across the ecological niche in which the societies were housed. And the dislocation between the changing cultural context and immediate experience was continuous. Thus the acquired meanings of technology today have been derived within a historic negotiation process, where originally people negotiated the meaning of their life-world space within existing technical and cultural contexts, and gave birth in their *active* constitution of the world, to new techniques, new meanings, new frameworks of cultural values – in a continuous dialectic process wherein new meanings emerge out of what went before.

Thus, tools, and even machines and factories have accompanied Western civilisation's progressive development since antiquity. But the cultural frameworks into which these technologies were cast and their meanings were quite different to those which emerged from post eighteenth-century society. Neolithic society had potters' wheels; the ancient Egyptians employed powerful leverage machines to raise the pyramids to the eternal well-being of their rulers; the ancient Romans employed both freedmen, craftspeople and slaves in factory systems to manufacture (respectively) the craft lines of clay lamps, metal wares, jewellery and water pipes, and the mass produced lines of bricks and red-glazed pottery.[19] Furthermore, the *systematisation* of labour in alignment with productive techniques can be traced at least back to the early Middle Ages. Lynn White describes the emergence of a social system of agriculture in Europe between the sixth and ninth centuries

AD, and the dependence of the emergent system on technological innovation. The heavy alluvial soil of the northern European plains required a heavier plough than the two-ox scratch plough commonly used previously on the Roman peninsula. In order to move the heavier plough that developed, farmers had to harness six oxen to it. Very few farmers were rich enough to have six oxen, so the technology required that they pool their resources, that they combine strips of land into open fields, and that they develop a regime of shared, scheduled work. Consequently, decisions that the farmers made about when to put the crops into the ground, and when to harvest, had to be binding on the collective. As White observes, the communal pattern of manorial life across northern Europe developed out of these new technologically-induced social alignments.[20]

Finally, the mechanical logic that was basic to later self-regulating and automated industrial production predated the take-off of industrialisation by centuries. The mechanical clock, invented within the confines of thirteenth-century Benedictine monasteries, was, as Lewis Mumford observed, the model for all later automata. The clock embodied standardisation, the intricate connection of technical parts, a means of ensuring an even flow of energy through a complex technical system, strict regularity of movement, and a means of governing the overall pace of this movement.[21] The printing press of the sixteenth century was a paragon of mass production, using standardised, interchangeable components to produce a uniform product in large quantities. Even the 'automaton' that seeks to model life itself, as does the present-day robot, has existed since antiquity: Mark Anthony employed a wax model moved by means of a special mechanism hidden behind the bed to create a realistic automaton of Caesar's body, a secretly constructed automaton that he used with dramatic affect to create a popular riot at Caesar's funeral: 'From the bier Caesar arose and began to turn around slowly, exposing to their terrified gaze his dreadfully livid face and his twenty-three wounds still bleeding.'[22]

All of the elements of modern technology and technological systems therefore existed well before industrialisation. However, housed as they were in a different productive and cultural context, the artefacts and systems had a quite different cultural salience to the life-worlds of the people to that which has emerged with industrialisation. Thus, *the meanings of modern technological artefacts cannot be found in the objects themselves, but in relating the symbolism of the object to the cultural context and world-views within which the meanings of the immediate objects are located*. In Chapters 6 and 7 I will show *how* the modern meanings of technology emerged out of the cultural negotiations –

between life-world and cultural context – that underscored the take-off of industrialisation. Here, it is sufficient to observe just the fundamental shift in the alignment of technique with the social relations of production that characterised the industrialisation threshold. For this movement, a transformation of world view injected a totally new condition into the modes of interaction between people, and thus a new *code* into the social process within which culture is constituted. Modern meanings of technology have emerged in the continuing dialectic negotiations between immediate life-world and its cultural context that have followed on from this premise. By scrutinising their origins, we can see that which is hidden in the taken-for-granted cultural assumptions of the present.

The Basic Code of the Technology Text

Standing precariously at the edge of industrial transformation of the meaning of technology was Jacques de Vaucanson's mechanical duck. In 1740, de Vaucanson presented his mechanical duck to admiring audiences within the French Academy of Science, along with two other automata, a drummer and a flautist. The duck was the last of the great, useless, automata. It could waddle and swim; its wings imitated nature in detail and beat the air; the duck could wag its head, quack, pick up grain, swallow it, pass it through a miniature internal chemical laboratory to decompose it, and ... defecate. The automata, such as de Vaucanson's ingenious duck, was *the* machine of seventeenth- and eighteenth-century European society. As self-regulating, self-running mechanisms, they portrayed the image of the autonomous individual. Like the machinery of the heavens, the automatic man (or duck) was a self-enclosed system, and could maintain its regular and orderly motions whilst free from external interference.[23] The physical object of the automaton was a vehicle for the positive values that in preindustrial society were associated with the self-determining subject.

What is significant about de Vaucanson's duck is that it waddled, quacking and defecating, into the history book just at the moment when the *usefulness* of such mechanical ingenuity was recognised. Cardinal Fleury, Prime Minister of France at the time, immediately set de Vaucanson to work as Inspector of Silks, with the express purpose of automating spinning and weaving machines: de Vaucanson's inventions directly underlay the development of key elements of the cotton-spinning factories, which from the late eighteenth century revolutionised productive relations and the culture of industrialising society. Along with de Vaucanson's march out of the curiosity-inspired halls of the French Academy into the utility-inspired walls of factories, the toy, an *adjunct* to human purpose, was transmuted into the machine system, a *substitute* for human labour.

Jacques de Vaucanson did not *create* this cultural shift. But his 'time was right' within the emerging life-world/cultural context negotiations that were going on within European culture. The movement in meaning was not only fostered by a new and exploitative class, the capitalists. At a deeper level of the cultural order, the recognition of machine power salved a fear of bondage to the uncertain, capricious, dangerous but nurturing power of *nature's* rhythms. In its assertion of human *power* to regulate nature's uncertainty through technique, the move in world view provided a legitimacy frame for the capitalist class to take charge of the mechanised means of production, and fit people into their designs. As I will show in Chapter 7, carriage of the the emerging bourgeoisie's legitimacy was pursued through assertion of ruling-class hegemony (in, for example, new educational practices, and political-economy ideology) rather than through popular assertion; enforcement of the new machine system discipline also involved naked self-interest; and the 'machine question' was a source of considerable conflict, not only between ruling and labouring classes, but within the ruling class itself. But these conflicts and hegemonic powers were all components in the life-world/context negotiations that produced the shape of the industrial order within a quite new world view that valued human power and skill to order the natural universe to suit humanity's needs.

Inscribed in the mechanistic assumptions of industrial technology then, is the fundamental cultural principle of *ordering human arrangements to align with the actualising of technical power*. This cultural principle is an inheritance from history and the social forces of production that were drawn into the development of machine systems.

Three other fundamental cultural principles have also been embodied in machine systems. The first concerns the philosophic logic that was an emergent property of proto-industrial society. The second concerns the particular forms of an accumulating stock of knowledge that were drawn into machines from the total social forces of production. And the third cultural principle concerns the 'objectification' of this focused stock of knowledge into object forms that increasingly mediate the relationship between humans, and between humans and the order of the natural world to which the machine systems relate. Together, these sediments of history align with the superordinate world view of human control, the *code* that underscores industrialisation. Together, these sediments of history are embodied within the process of change in industrial technology; they are embodied within the meaning of technological artefacts we confront in everyday life; and the sediments are embodied within the technical and social context of values that circumscribe life-world experience. For the dynamic momentum and properties of systems , along with the social alignment and enframing command of technological systems, are derived from these cultural roots.

Fundamental Grammar of the Industrial Technology Text

Systems Philosophy and Logic

In direct alignment with the world view liberation of humans from the capricious control of nature into the new bondage of humans in technologically-ordered arrangements was the emergence of a liberating philosophy. This was a philosophy that liberated thought from the tradition-constrained interpretation of what God's will said about nature and human arrangements. Liberation was embodied in a philosophy which sought, through the power of autonomous thought, to reach behind the appearance of nature to comprehend nature's underlying structure – whether the scriptures, or priestly interpretation of them, had anything to say about this underlying order or not. The new mode owed its birth to the Renaissance and assumed a body in the Baconian science that arose out of Bacon's abstraction of an epistemology from observation of Renaissance craft activities. The new mode of thought specifically connected transformation of nature with progress of knowledge,[24] and thus emphasised systematic and controlled observation of the natural world. The new mode of thought employed rational logic to connect cause and effect, and led to the application of derived theory to the instrumental control of empirical phenomena.

As with all cultural ontologies and epistemologies, the emergent philosophy was moral as well as demonstrably workable. Whereas in Greek science the harmonious order of the world is *in the world* whether we see it or not, the inherited Baconian view was that reality is what we *see* in front of us. Yet, according to Bacon, 'human understanding resembles not a dry light, but admits a tincture of the will and passions, which generate their own system accordingly.'[25] Thus, human cognitive capabilities were seen as instruments that required maintenance, supervision and correction – to understand nature was a matter of disciplined observation. The attainment of disciplined observation was therefore a never-ending contest with human weakness.[26] This was a morality that aligned congenially with the evolving liberation of religion from the traditional authority of the Church into the Protestant affirmation of salvation through disciplined, ascetic, individual labour.[27]

Intrinsic to the new mode of thought is the recognition of regularities and interacting systems beneath the world of appearances, regularities and interactions that can ultimately be represented in their purest form through mathematical logic, rather than through cultural interpretation. The complexity of nature's systems can be grasped and manipulated through specialised and disciplined knowledge. Whilst the earliest industrial machines cannot be attributed to the *direct* application of science to production, their invention *was* a product of disciplined observation and was set within the frame of logic that Baconian science offered.[28]

The earliest machines, even of the modern age, were designed to perform a single set of functions – such as crushing grain or spinning cotton. But the logic that informed their design offered far more. For the logic of science offered a way of comprehending and creating *systems* of technical action. The aesthetic implication of this logic followed, that is, that the systems should smoothly interconnect, and inefficient or dislocating components within the systems should be eliminated. This observation leads directly to a fundamental difference between the machines of the industrial age and those that went before. For the inefficient component of a technological system lies not so much in the technical arrangements as in the human labour skill that connects them. Consequently, whereas preindustrial machines primarily were concerned with the embodiment of human labour *power*, the design of industrial machines sought to embody not only power, but also human labour *skill*, for this more than power was the weak and poorly controlled link in efficient technological systems, and therefore was the source of unprofitability in a competitive environment. With an external source of mechanical power that could be integrated into the system, such as was provided by Boulton and Watt's steam engine for a factory at Papplewick, Nottinghamshire in 1785,[29] the machine system was freed from 'inefficient' (system) dependency on either nature or collective labour to provide power. Thus, designers were free to capitalise on eliminating internal 'inefficient' connections within the production systems. The logic was still the logic of the superordinance of technique over social arrangements. The aesthetic was one of system-harmony. And the attention that now needed to be paid to the internal system aligns directly with Thomas Hughes' concept of 'reverse salience', where a retarded component in the smooth development of integrated systems is the focal point of greatest design effort.[30]

Informed by the political-economic ideology of Adam Smith (which also aligned directly with the systems logic of science), the clear design problematic was to develop specialised, repetitive mechanical components that could be interrelated into smoothly operating systems that required minimum dependence on a labour force that was resistant to systems-based machine discipline.[31] Power can thus be converted into a level of accuracy and speed of repetition that is well beyond the capacity of a skilled tradesperson, and with increased embodiment of tradesperson technical skills into repetitive and uniform operations, a level of flexibility could be achieved that emulated the advantage that the tradesperson had over a machine. Independence of the machine-system from operator skills permits automation, the next 'reverse salient' under system logic; and eventually, with increasingly sophisticated application of specialised technical knowledge to the system process, application of machine intelligence replaces even the role of human thought in holding the system's productive activity together. Indeed, with increasing complexity not only within individual systems, but also within their wider interconnection, the application of machine intelligence provides the key 'reverse salient' for further system momentum.[32] All of the presently experienced de-skilling consequences of industrialisation, along with the progressive displacement of prior craft skills,[33] follow from this basic system-design principle. The principle was born within the alignment of philosophy with economic advantage, and more fundamentally was in keeping with the world view transitions that were occurring within the wider proto-industrial culture.

Stocks of Knowledge and 'Objectification'

In our experience of contemporary machine systems we therefore confront our own history. Behind the appearance of external facia plates, knobs and dials lies the accumulation of stocks of knowledge from which the industrial fabric has been woven, and also the sedimentation of cultural meanings that paved the way for the system's momentum. Or, as Thomas Hughes observes, 'Durable physical artefacts project into the future the socially-constructed characteristics acquired in the past when they were designed. This is analogous to the persistence of acquired characteristics in a changing environment.'[34]

Karl Marx saw this embodiment of history in machines of the present as a capture of the 'social forces of production' into machine technique, that is, a capture of all the forces that allow a society to produce – past thinking, prior social relations of production, productive knowledge and meaning systems that make sense of what the machines are for, and whose interests they serve.[35] Thus the whole collection of technologies that characterise a society at any point in its history represents the general productive power that the society's *collective intelligence* has produced over time. The technologies are 'dead', however, lying dormant until brought to life in the present through 'living labour', that sensuous activity of humans involved both intellectually and physically in transforming the world. What living labour *can* bring to life is not the whole of the social forces of production. Human craft skills of prior generations are resting there in between the computerised wiring, robotic arms and pneumatic drive mechanisms. But the whole of these skills are not in residence – only that instrumental component of human labour that is amenable to systematisation, repetitive and mechanical movement, or which can be manipulated through repetitive and rational machine intelligence. In other words, what the alignment of systems-thinking with capitalist private property allows, is the siphoning off of just the instrumental edge of past labour, and the 'objectification' of living labour's instrumental capabilities into the machines that confront contemporary labour's everyday experience. 'Living labour is appropriated by objectified labour.'[36] And the richness of the whole spectrum of the social forces of production is filtered through the prism of capitalist ability to purchase and control history, into machines that inevitably get bigger, more complex, more commanding ... more enframing of living labour's freedom to engage in liberating praxis. As Marx concludes,

> Labour ... [is] ... subsumed under the total process of the machinery itself, as itself only a link of the system, whose unity exists not in the living workforce, but rather in the living (active) machinery, which confronts his individual, insignificant doings as a mighty organism.[37]

Dynamic Principles of the Technology Grammar

This dynamic, whereby capital interests 'objectified' human productive history to elite economic advantage, has injected a series of interrelated momenta into the *shaping* of industrial technologies of today. The shape is first one that is commanded by a momentum of increasing *complexity*,[38] where technical stocks of knowledge and craft skills of the past are embodied ingeniously into new capital. Secondly, the shape of industrial technologies is commanded by a momentum in *scale*, as increasing levels of capital acquired from past exploitation of labour allow surplus value to be turned back into larger, more competitively efficient, machine systems. Thirdly, technological shape follows the momentum of increasing *power*, as increasingly efficient sources of energy production – steam, electricity, petrochemicals and nuclear – can be brought into alignment with production systems, and as more specialised technical and scientific competences are brought into direct service of production efficiency.

Finally, the shape of the technological system is directed by a momentum of increasing *ubiquity and interconnectedness*. The two principles mirror each other in the increased pervasiveness of industrial technological systems throughout the whole world. Operating together, the ubiquity and interconnectedness momenta drove the machine-systems out of the industrial towns of northern England and along a path defined by economic primacy to the most remote corners of Bhutan.

'Ubiquity' is a natural property of the momentum of systems. A system involves an ordered relationship between specialised parts, control over the smooth integration of this order, and closure from an unordered environment from which necessary system inputs are drawn in a strictly uniform or ordered form that can be incorporated into the internal order of the system.[39] Thus, the most efficient systems are those that can draw from an 'environment' that is itself in ordered alignment with the standardised requirements of the system itself. Thus, radical change in the mode of production in any one sphere of industry must spread – like ripples from a stone dropped into the pool of the social process of production, for the change, guided by the momenta of complexity, scale and power, offers opportunities (or system requirements) for expanded alignment in environments. As Marx observed in 1867,

Thus spinning by machinery made weaving by machinery a necessity, and both together made the mechanical and chemical revolution that took place in bleaching, printing and dyeing, imperative ... So too, on the other hand, the revolution in cotton spinning called forth the invention of the gin, for separating the seeds from the cotton fibre; it was only by means of this invention, that the production of cotton became possible on the enormous scale at present required. But more especially, the revolution in the general conditions of the social process of production, i.e. in the means of communication and of transport.[40]

Ubiquity and interconnectedness are thus intimately related momenta behind the shape of technological systems. The systems dynamic intrinsically eats into system environments, drawing out from them those elements that allow conversion of the environment into a connected system. As criterion example, in the worldwide standardisation of McDonald's hamburgers, the corporate system has stretched back to the production system's agricultural environment to standardise both potatoes and beef that are supplied. Meanwhile, the observation by

Marx in the 1860s of the intrinsic spread of interconnection between production systems and communication and transport has continued to enframe virtually all patterns of subjective life into interconnected, ubiquitous systems.

A multiplier effect is added to these momentum principles behind technological shape, and this directly derives from the interconnected-ness principle. Higher scale, more complex and powerful technological systems will tend to displace less sophisticated technologies, and also dig out the foundations on which less sophisticated technologies could later be constructed. In Uttar Pradesh, India, the introduction of semi-automated weaving looms eliminated the market for peasant cotton spinning that the looms were intended to service. The reason was that peasant spinning technology could not produce thread of adequate standardisation and strength for the mechanical looms. The result was that owners of the weaving factories had to import synthetic thread from the cities (thus accelerating the higher technology) and the peasants had no market for their spun cotton (thus accelerating the demise of the lower technology). Not only that, the peasants could only purchase woven synthetic cloth, a situation of double jeopardy, for the increased market expanded the power of the higher order systems at direct expense of the peasants' ability to generate wealth. In the same Indian state, the introduction of tractors meant that farmers sold off their power-providing buffalo herds. When attempts were made subsequently to introduce methane-gas production into villages, the percentage of families who still had enough buffalo to provide the dung to make the system work was so small that the lower-order technology was brought into production in a very small number of cases.[41]

The momentum that derives from the interactions between the dimensions of the technological dynamic is powerful. It is also self re-enforcing. Within each of the dimensions of technological momentum – complexity, scale, power, ubiquity and interconnectedness – the same process of objectification of labour is operating. Within each dimension the same cultural symbolism persists as that which established the alignment between industrial technique and society in the first place - that is, symbolism of a world view that asserts the dominance of technique in the design of social organisation, symbolism of a philosophy that applauds the superordinacy of disciplined rational thought over engagement and cultural interpretation in relating to reality, and a symbolism of praxis that separates thought from action and aligns thought with control.

Authority of the Technology Text

The cultural symbolism of the original industrial technology-culture alignment persists. It is there to be confronted in every technological artefact that we experience in daily life (and in the technological systems that lie behind direct experience and provide *con*-text for what can be 'read'). All that is different (compared with the cultural pattern that was asserted by technique in the transition towards industrialism), is the seemingly immutable power of these cultural meanings, and the ubiquity of their framing of active engagement in the world. This is a power that ascended as the 'system' increasingly spread its network of relationships across all physical, productive, social, cultural and subjective life.

There is no general popular 'Machinery Question' now as characterised early nineteenth-century debates about whether industrialisation should proceed or not,[42] or be exported to the colonies where it could have little impact on the quality of life in England.[43] In general, contemporary popular scepticism of the technological system emerged out of reactions against the (American) State in the late 1960s, and were against the State's use of technological control for social violence, in particular in Vietnam.[44] The almost 'tribal' protest that emerged was directed more at abuse of technological power rather than at technology itself. 'Reactions' have primarily fragmented into reactions against particular technological system excesses – of, for example, nuclear power, armaments, wood-chipping, expressways and high technology whaling, or against the impact of particular technological change on employment levels. But reaction is against the State (or particular corporations) that stands in front, rather than against the background technological system itself. *All* reactions, including that of the more general 'Green' movement and politics are set within the wider world view, philosophy and praxis of the system's momentum. From the far left to the far right of politics, the technological system is inviolate though the politics of its management, and the role of a social 'governor' on its programmes, is not. As the head of a revolutionary women's organisation in the Philippines said recently, what women want from the revolution is 'peace and a washing machine'.[45] It is virtually impossible to live outside the contemporary technological system, even for those who deeply deny its potency or necessity. Thus, within the technological artefacts that stand before us in everyday life, we experience an inevitability, and an assertion of the priority of technique over life itself, within the grammar or code of the objects' cultural meaning.

This is not to say however that the overall momentum of the *system* itself – as a series of interlocking subsystems – follows a singular expansionary path where all dimensions operate equally. The simplistic 'technological determinist' argument of inevitable system structure and impact is demonstrably wrong. This is so, because even with its extraordinary power to advance, the technological system is still shaped and transformed because of social and cultural alignments with the trajectory the 'system' is following. I will deal in some detail with the nature of these alignments within the next few chapters. Suffice at this stage to observe, as I did in Chapter 1, that a whole range of social forces have already been shown to shape both the invention and diffusion of particular technological forms within the ongoing trajectory of system progress.

The particular path of technological progress will depend on the *whole* infrastructure of knowledge-generation, education and cultural expectations into which the technological system is embedded, a lesson that is shown in high relief in the discussion of 'technological imperialism' in Chapter 8. As in ancient Greek society, where the epistemic roots of 'technology' originated, as in *all* societies, *all* of the components of a total social and cultural system interact[46] with the shape of the technological base for societal production. What is different in contemporary society is only the enframing *power* of the technological system within the technology/society balance.

The primary source of this enframing power lies in the second-order form and cultural grammar that resides within and behind the first-order text of technology that we are confronted by in everyday life. The technological momentum that is written into this text creates a sense of inevitability about the shape and possibilities of this experience, for the context frame itself is continuously moving – enframing even the frame that existed before. Such an 'outflanking' momentum co-opts challenge to the authority of the technological text as well as cultural alternatives along the way. The moving frame thus picks up and sediments cultural meanings into its trajectory but filters these meanings according to the grammar of its systems-logic. And objectified *within* the technological artefacts that represent the moving frame we confront a powerful interpretation of all that civilisation has already achieved through its labour; we confront a powerful definition of what we are now humanly capable of achieving; and we find our own definitions of who and what we are to be dependent upon mirrors that the technological system presents to us.

Contemporary technology is therefore not merely a set of tools or artefacts that assume meaning according to a wider cultural frame of values and assumptions. Instead, contemporary technology symbolises the frame itself, within which our cultural possibilities are cast and played out – a frame that industrial society willingly embraced when instrumental logic was welcomed as master rather than servant to social arrangements.

Interestingly, at the time when the application of instrumental logic was born and just about to move through the labour ward, Jonathan Swift predicted in satire what was to come, with the objectification of human skills into machines. In 1726, when Swift published *Gulliver's Travels*, the Royal Scientific Society was just becoming an object of public attention in England, and thus a target for public humour. In lampooning the Society as the 'Academy of Lagardo', Swift presented a satire of the 'mechanical calculator' that had been recently invented by one of the Royal Society's members – Liebniz. The caricature is uncannily close to what the mechanical calculator became 250 years later. In Swift's satire the calculator was represented as a 'word making machine', a project of the Academy of Lagardo that Gulliver came across in his travels. The 'word making machine' was a square box with a great number of elements and many handles to be turned manually so that, by using it, 'the most ignorant person, at a reasonable charge, and with little bodily labour may write books in philosophy, poetry, politics, law mathematics and theology without the least assistance from genius or study.'[47]

3

Uncovering the Technology Text

Artefact Meaning as Written Text

Technological artefacts are solid. The cultural meanings that have been historically sedimented into them are objectified, and whilst remaining closed to scrutiny – as in Swift's 'word making machine' – they are at the same time removed from immediate negotiation and reinterpretation. In this sense, the cultural text which stands in front of us is a closed book. Because of the sheer sedimented weight of its covers the book is difficult to open. But because of its physical property of being (metaphorically) a 'book' that contains fixed words of print, it retains the same message as last time, when we can finally prise open these hide-bound covers to peer inside.

The 'words' that symbolise remain the same. And in the case of industrial technology, the words were those that were written at 'creation' ... of the industrial age. Reinterpretations will emerge – as with the refashioning of religious ideologies from Catholic to Protestant to fundamentalist to Appalachian snake-handling Christian interpretations of the Bible. Reinterpretations will emerge as the *con*-text surrounding the text is transformed, thus signifying a different cultural salience of the text itself. But the original text stays there. Whilst context for the text directs attention to the text itself rather than to the symbolic quality of an unread text (a Bible as antique commodity or door-stop), reinterpretations will be limited by the basic assumptions of what is written. Interpretations of the Bible are set within the fundamental assumption that the text presents God's last (and original) word. Equally, the original text of the industrial machine stays there, and presents the last (and original) word of artefact meaning that is based on the fundamental cultural assumptions of industrialism.

As with reinterpretations of the Bible, the new meanings derive from new alignments between social experience and the text's message. Protestantism focused attention on personal responsibility, an orientation that aligned with the person being set adrift in a world of transforming structures of authority. Prior catholicism focused attention on the priestly hermeneuts who, in religion-centred social structures, mediated the relationship between the individual and God. The shift in interpretation was associated with experience of crisis in the alignment between experience and the prevailing ideology. Similarly, the technology artefact text of the industrial machine has shifted in meaning throughout industrial history. For example, the 1960s presented a crisis in confidence to the young concerning the State's use of technological power for violent political control (particularly with the US' use of technology in Vietnam). Through both conscripted involvement in the war, and through continuous prime-time television coverage, the young were confronted with the visibility of naked and repressive power within the war technology's artefact text. The consciousness that resulted led, amongst other things, to the rise and acceptance of 'alternative technology movements'. Similarly, the confrontation with a general faith in technological infallibility by the breakdown of nuclear power systems at Three Mile Island and Chernobyl, have fundamentally shaken the foundations of popular acceptance of the benign power of high technology systems.

However, as with the Bible, so too with the artefact text: the meanings may change with new experience/text alignments, but the text itself remains the same, its meaning being fundamentally predicated on an assumption (of God or industrialism respectively) that is stable. The stability of textual meaning remains because the machines can only be brought to life and used for social purpose within a cultural context that focuses attention on the text and the knowledge and power it implies.

Even the apparent contradiction to text stability – that is, of continuously new technology – is incorporated into reassertion of the artefact text's original formulation. With a continuous series of new physical objects, we experience what appear to be new versions of the original text. But the text is rewritten the same in each new case, even though the covers change. This is so, because written into the original text is the inviolability of continuous change, as well as the increasingly pervasive enframing of experience by the new text versions that emerge. The process of enframing follows the trajectory that the original text had written into it. Protest and reinterpretations are thus co-opted rather than constitutive of new texts, in the same way that 1960s counter-cultural values have been co-opted into the manufacture and marketing of industrially produced, processed 'organic' foods.

Technological artefacts of the industrial system therefore embody a resilient cultural 'text'. The text is 'written' rather than constituted afresh with each new interaction between person and artefact, a process that directly parallels the relative interpretive intransigence versus flexibility of written versus oral modes of communication. A number of significant characteristics of the artefact text can be identified by exploring this parallel further.

The Contrast Between Oral and Written Texts

Oral Texts

At the turn of the twentieth century the British annexed northern Ghana and the colonial administrators recorded the number of divisional chiefdoms that existed within the resident Gonja tribe. Seven divisions were noted, and the legitimacy of the divisions was attributed by the Gonja to territory distribution amongst the seven sons of an invader, Jakpa, in what was for the Gonja an ancient past. Shortly after the British took this record, two of the seven divisions disappeared, one being deliberately incorporated into a neighbouring division because its rulers had supported a Mandingo invader, the other because of some boundary changes introduced by the British administration. Sixty years later, when the myths of State were again recorded, the original king, Jakpa, was credited with only five sons, and the Gonja made no mention of either the founder's other two sons, or of the two divisions that had since disappeared from the political map.[1]

The Gonja had an oral culture, and the reformulation of history to meet the experience of the present that is revealed in this example is a basic property of such orality. In non-literate societies cultural traditions are brought to life continuously within the present by the performer,[2] whilst the conditions of transmission – speaker/hearer interaction – tend to draw cultural traditions into alignment with present experience, into consistency between past and present. Such continuous realignment is possible because the word-as-record is not separate from immediate human memory or experience (as written records permit), but instead depends for its meaning on the continuous re-currence of the word-as-*event within* immediate life-world experience.[3] Immediate lived experience therefore embodies all history, interpreted and refashioned to make sense of present events, social practices and relationships. As Evans-Pritchard observed of the Nuer tribe of northern Nigeria for example, distance of kinship relationships and obligations was related to the original location of joint heritage within one of six possible age sets that extended back in time (and therefore in social distance) to a horizon where time (and relationships) dropped into mythology and prehistory some 60 years before. Thus mythology was constructed within lived experience from all events that stood outside present direct tribal memory; and the categorisation of time that was encompassed in living memory was played out in every kinship interaction.[4]

Within an oral culture the symbol (the word) and referent (experience) are immediately experienced together, and the symbol is fully coloured in within this experience – by vocal and physical gestures that combine to particularise what the word means, what it can refer to, and what it implies of tradition, immediate social relationships and the events or objects that the word refers to. Operating within a domain of immediate time, or at least a continuously moving but experienceable time range, oral cultures therefore connect the participant directly to the world around them. This is particularly demonstrated in Benjamin Lee Whorf's observation of the American Hopi Indians. The Hopi language compels the speaker to consider their own concrete observations as fundamental, to see for themselves what the speaker is referring to. For example, for two Hopis in the same observational field, the word 'wari' can mean 'he is running' or 'he ran': the hearer distinguishes only by observing for themselves whether the runner is in the field or not.[5] As in all oral cultures then, words cannot accumulate successive layers of historically validated meanings, but are ratified in a succession of concrete situations.[6]

Some resistance is built into oral cultures against the continual refashioning of meanings. As in all cultures, both oral and literate, the culture must 'work' in terms of relating social practices and cultural meanings to the 'reality' the people must deal with in order to survive. So whilst meanings accumulate or transmute, they also have a persistent reference point in the culture's relationships to definitions of a workable reality – as long as the boundaries of this reality or of the society's ecological niche do not change. Historic consistency is also built into oral cultures however through specific social practices. Mnemonic devices exist in formalised story-telling and revivification of myths, in formalised patterns of speech, recital under ritual conditions, the use of drums and other musical instruments to texture the rhythm of the present in terms of the past, and in the employment of professional remembrancers. Together, these mnemonics shield at least part of the content of memory from the transmuting influences that flow from the immediate pressures of the present.[7] In revivifying tradition, the devices also act as hegemonic controls over the maintenance of traditional authority, traditional expertise, and the social relations of production that both of these hegemonies imply. To take but one example, in a situation under considerable influence from modernism, and literacy (in a language that was only in the last century written down by Christian missionaries), the king of feudal Tonga in the South

Pacific still maintains ritual language for gift-giving ceremonies. A small number of 'kingly-language' speakers are the only people who can speak in this ritual language that has been passed on from generation to generation within the nobility. When a formal gift is presented to the king, two of these elite 'kingly-language' speakers are employed, one to represent the king, the other to represent the gift-givers. As a Tongan resident recently observed of the experience of presenting a formal gift to the king, only the interpreters speak. With little alternative opportunity to display their competence, the exchange of formal pleasantries can continue for hours – following a protocol of demeaning the gift by the interpreter who represents it, or praising it by the interpreter who represents its acceptance. The gift-givers chat amongst themselves, and the king often falls asleep. But the ritual, the formalised speech patterns, and the employment of professional remembrancers reasserts the traditional power and hegemony of the king and the feudal system that he heads.[8]

Given that Tonga has entered the international culture of television, national airlines and high technology aid, the king's gift-giving ceremony is arcane. But its significance persists – as revivification of the seamless web of meanings and authority that once existed in an oral culture. The mnemonic of ritual brings the past to life in the present, preserves traditional social structures, and provides boundaries for the transformation of meanings. The oral text – here, of the 'kingly-language' speakers – only exists and comes alive however in direct face-to-face interaction, where meaning is constituted in terms of the personal life-worlds of the speakers.

To highlight the fundamentally human constitutive property of oral texts, a momentary aside to Marshall McLuhan is called for. McLuhan claimed that with the ubiquity and efficiency of electronic broadcasting media the world would see a new 'secondary' or 'literate' orality period arise. Electronic media, he claimed, would shape the whole world into a 'global village' where mentalities would be shaped in much the same way as the oral media of communication shaped the mentalities of pre-literate societies.[9] In terms of the way that an oral culture is shaped, however, this position is fundamentally wrong. Within an oral culture the world and its meanings are continuously and actively shaped within the people's own life-world experience. History and events outside this direct subjective experience is rewritten to connect with and make sense of this immediate life-world. This is not so when the medium is technological. Experience of the rest of the whole world is brought into reach, but is already mediated by interests that have no connection, or for that matter interest, in the immediate life-world of the receivers. The experience that can be presented is only that which is accentuated by the mode of its presentation, i.e. anonymous reporters, received television images and two-dimensional aural or visual symbols. The experience is preselected according to (commercial or ideological) interests of capital-rich media controllers. The experience of others who reside outside the immediate life-world is therefore passive, its immediate construction of meaning not actively engaged with either the full human circumstances of the event or the actors who are presented to consciousness. Thus, instead of breaking down the individualistic barriers that McLuhan claims a print-based culture fostered, what the electronic media offer is an extension of the basic enframing forces that 'written' texts offered in the first place.

Written Texts

A culture that is based on written rather than oral texts is quite different to a culture that is based on texts that are actively and orally generated within each moment of life-world experience. Writing *records* a past in a form that, as long as the texts remain accessible, can be returned to as in a time-jump out of the present into the past. History does not disappear over the horizon of the past beyond which direct memory of those who are now alive cannot penetrate. The written text captures only that which can be represented within the grammar and extensiveness of representation that the language allows. So the subjective *experience* of history is not brought into the present in its experiential totality, just those elements that are deemed to be worthy of written record in a past and different age and culture.

In written languages, history stands as a partial representation of past experience in an autonomous relationship to interpretation and presentation in the present. As with the objectification of sedimented cultural values that I observed before in machines, written language stands there, offering a text that is waiting to be read, the independence of which we must accommodate or negotiate our way around. As Socrates observed to Phaedrus, when the text is independent of direct and reflexive interrogation,

> Written words seem to talk to you as though they were intelligent, but if you ask them anything about what they say, from a desire to be instructed, they go on telling you just the same thing for ever.[10]

Written texts draw historic record into the present. Indeed with the richness and length of literary traditions, and with contemporary ability to read geological 'texts' scientifically, the factual text of history can be extended through millions of years. But the texts remain autonomous, are not related *in our experience* or in the experiential events they refer to, with the life-world we directly inhabit and make sense of in continuously constituting our culture. The written text is 'context blind' whilst the oral culture presenter could not be. The autonomous text does not therefore connect, except as 'reminder' (rather than self-referent 'memory') with the person and their meaning world. The autonomy of written language separates the author from the receiver – even across millennia and radically different cultures. The autonomy of written language allows an enormous proliferation of cultural utterances, as the whole is not limited by just that which can be passed on in direct oral interactions. Within a writing-based culture, life experience is therefore set in and informed by the autonomous culture that surrounds it, but can never encompass either the fullness of meanings that the written form 'accentuates' and obscures, or the breadth of information and events that the written form can refer to. A writing-based culture is therefore *enframed* by a trajectory of the past that accentuates what both the medium and grammar of written language allows, and what the recorders paid attention to; and a writing-based culture, by virtue of the inaccessibility of *all* texts, *enframes* immediate life experience within a sea of what cannot be known or directly experienced. Within the vast array of written texts available to us today (including, in particular, the 'information' data bases of computer systems),

> we moderns [as Nietzsche asserted back in 1909] are 'wandering encyclopaedias', unable to live and act in the present and obsessed by a 'historical sense' that injures and finally destroys the living thing, be it a man or a people or a system of culture.[11]

Whilst intrinsically having the effect of pauperising the individual's ability to grasp the whole in life-world experience, the autonomy of written texts at the same time allows the injection of choice and scepticism that would not be possible within the continuous present of oral cultures. The choice is, however, conditioned according to what elements of past experience the written texts *accentuate*, and how these accentuations align with contemporary events and experiences. Thus, histories are continuously rewritten in tune with the ideologically-conditioned attention of the time of writing. But the prior histories and events they refer to remain as accessible sources not only of knowledge about the events themselves, but also (by comparison) of the ideological grammars that housed their presentation and interpretation in the first place. Written language, by virtue of its autonomous domain, therefore allows a perception of change (even at the level of cultural and belief change), of 'progress', of cause and effect, and of a 'truth' that stands in an independent relationship to one's direct experience of the world in the present, and of myths, superstitions and fictions.

Furthermore, particular cultural properties follow from the nature of the language, in particular, from the distinction between written languages based on phonetic versus non-phonetic symbols. Phonetic scripts imitate human discourse, so that, rather than symbolising the objects of the social and natural order as such, the scripts are capable of expressing thought, personal meanings, and reactions as well as items of major social importance. Non-phonetic writing records only those cultural items that are deemed by the literate elite to be significant for cultural expression or action. Non-phonetic writing therefore is the text of central and literate authority, rather than the text of speech, consciousness and participation. Thus, amongst the Sumerians and Akkadians, non-phonetic writing was the province of scribes, and was preserved as a 'secret treasure' that even the royalty had only secondary access to.[12]

Literacy in non-phonetic writing requires the learning of a large number of separate specialised symbols, rather than of a central speech code from which the rest of the symbolic universe can be derived. Literacy in Chinese, for example, requires the learning of a minimum of 3,000 separate characters, but full literate proficiency involves knowing a repertoire of some 50,000 characters, a task that usually takes about 20 years to accomplish.[13] Thus, in non-phonetic writing, not only is the cultural code asserted and fashioned by literate authorities rather than being an organic product of social participation, but also the very nature of the code reinforces the hegemony and power of an elite specially trained professional group.

Inheritances from the Written Text of Technology

With the 'objectification' of cultural symbols into written text there is a major transformation of the manner in which 'text' both enframes and commands the construction of cultural meaning within a society. Each of the observations that follow can be applied directly to the character of cultural 'text' that is written into the technological artefacts that we confront in daily life.

The text that is presented to us in machines is 'written' in the sense that it is embodied, autonomous, not derived from immediate life-world cultural participation, but from sedimented meanings and stocks of knowledge that are 'objectified' in the machine. As 'autonomous' text, the machine text is severed from any relationship to the intentions or subjective world of its author. The text is 'context blind' (as far as the subjective world of participants is concerned) and is *presented* to contemporary observers in much the same way that a new book is, to be made sense of in terms of the observer's own subjective world.

As autonomous text, the machine text potentially conveys the power of historic consciousness and scepticism that the written text allows. Here, the machine text is different however. Historic contextuality is in continuous process of removal, as old machines give way to the new, so what is confronted in the contemporary world is rewritten history, the older versions of which are removed from consciousness in 'useless' piles of scrap or occasional 'quaint' museums. Thus, the experience of newness itself is one that implies the deeper cultural code of 'efficiency' and system-expansion that the text's grammar implies. The experience of newness does not therefore allow for scepticism concerning the trajectory that newness is following, for the old 'books' containing similar messages at a more primitive level have been burnt in the fires of industrial history. Experience of the code of newness is therefore experience of the trajectory's inevitability. Those who are instructed to intervene in the code – in science and engineering – are usually educated within this same frame: the curricula for science and engineering principally concern current knowledge and the most advanced means of accomplishing instrumental efficiency; if ever these curricula consider historic and cultural contexts for the accumulation of this contemporary knowledge, the courses are usually regarded as unconnected 'soft' course options that have a token purpose of 'humanising' the technocrat.

The presented text implies varying levels of literacy on the part of the observer: the text is opaque to the 'illiterate' who have no subjective stock of knowledge that allows them to *use* the machine for the purposes the author intended; the text is relatively opaque to those who can use, but not comprehend, peer inside and modify the machine and its functions; the text is transparent to those who have access to a stock of knowledge that allows them full control over design. All, however, are only able to bring the machine (and its design) to life through abiding by its background grammar – of technical-systems logic, and inter-connectedness to associated systems. This is a *con*-text that, by aligning directly with the meaning of the immediate artefact, focuses attention inescapably onto the written text that stands before us. At a deep (or second-order) level, the contextual grammar accentuates properties and purposes to which machines are to be put – particularly those that align with the technical superordinacy world view of industrialisation. At the same time, both the form of the text and its grammar obscure and mediate all that the machine cannot do – particularly those human purposes that cannot be accomplished through technique. At the level of 'literacy' *within* this grammar frame, the text accentuates and obscures human purposes according to what can be achieved through machine logic. As in non-phonetic texts, *command* is not in the hands of even the moderately literate participant, but lies outside, and frames what is indicated and can be acted upon. The logic grammar of machine texts is at root mathematical, and implies highly specialised stocks of knowledge both to comprehend and to manipulate these mathematical symbols in the design of machine systems. This is a non-phonetic text, so that in parallel with the power of Sumerian, Akkadian and Egyptian scribes, the power of command lies with highly specialised modern-day scientific 'scribes'. As opposed to even the extensiveness of Chinese non-phonetic script however, the written text of machine systems is almost infinite. No one specialist can ever encompass anything but an infinitesimally small component of the whole. The specialist world is therefore collectively literate, but not individually literate, yielding power not to the specialist as such but to the corporate or state interests that control the collective literati. Not even the most technically literate can grasp or participate in the whole, so no subjective human agency has the power to fashion or refashion the whole, only to participate within it. This situation is fundamentally different to the power of the performer in a culture predicated on oral text. The character of the 'written' machine text is therefore one of alienation from life-world accessibility and participation, and the power of the 'written' machine text lies in its enframement even of the scribes that write it.

To the extent however that the written text implies collective participation by human actors, the written text indicates an oral text as well. The characteristics of oral texts are therefore to be found in the social relations of production that follow from the written text's direction. 'Performance' (in 'living labour') brings the written text (and its objectification of past labour) to life, as the performance of an orator in an oral culture draws history into the present life-worlds of the people. The machine 'word', and the subjectively experienced 'event' of acting in relation to the 'word', are synthesised. However, the 'written' word enframes what can be constituted and reflected upon within 'oral' participation. Following through the metaphor of oral cultures, mnemonics are inscribed onto the 'oral' text that limit the degree of contemporary reformulation that is possible. Formalised patterns of speech are paralleled in the superordinacy of rational–technical dialogue that connects human action with machine system texts. Recital under ritual conditions and the use of drums is paralleled in the ritualistic regimes of employment activity connected with collectively participating within machine systems – going to work at 7.30 am and returning at 4.00 pm, ritually performing specified tasks that are indicated by the machine-word, and so on. The drum is the mechanical clock and the rhythm of the machine. Professional remembrancers are the technical specialists who recite in their practice the inevitability of the written code's consequences for social relations of production and the limits to human flexibility that can be encompassed whilst serving the written code. Meanwhile, in parallel with 'public' readings or story-telling, the oral (or participative) code is asserted over the written code when conflict between the system-masters and servants draws industrial relations into the collective arena for debate and resolution; and the oral code is asserted when conflict between system-masters and the community draws technology 'issues' (such as those concerning the use of nuclear technologies) into the political arena. The 'myths', for example, of the inevitability of progress, of the democratic power of the American way, and of the enlightenment that follows access to the 'scientific' text, are laid out by the 'old men' (or 'establishment'). And the myths serve the same function as in oral cultures of making sense of the present and the moral action that should follow (for example, pursuing the American SDI programme), in terms of the past that is written into the whole configuration of machine systems. The myths and political rituals that surround them serve the same function as in oral cultures, of reinforcing the hegemony and legitimacy of those who present and fashion the myths.

However, all participation in this 'oral' dimension of machine text culture is enframed by the 'written' word within the technique artefact itself. Thus, severe restrictions are placed on the capacity to reformulate meanings within the oral discourse. The horizon of oral discourse lies at the point where the inevitability of the machine script comes into question (thus, enframing what *can* be achieved, for example, in labour disputes concerning factory conditions before the factory itself goes out of business). With no human agent in charge of the whole, the horizon is itself relatively intractable to transformation, except along the trajectory that the 'inevitability grammar' of the machine system dictates, that is, towards increased enframement of human participation.

Influence of the Technology Text over Cultural Life

To return to the example of Chapter 2, where the discussion of the 'technology text' commenced, Fritz Kreisler could not hear any music coming out of his violin. As was demonstrated by the brilliant concert he had just performed, the music only came into being because as performer he could use considerable skill to bring it to life out of an otherwise 'dead' and useless tool. Thus, Kreisler could comprehend and master the written scripts of previous composers, and he could draw them into the present according to the instrumental 'text' of the tool. He brought past music to life in much the same way as an orator could draw the whole history of an oral culture into the people's immediate life-world experience.

Melvin Kranzberg's observation of Kreisler's performance, 'when men and machines work together, they can make some beautiful music' is entirely appropriate to Kreisler's relationship to violin technology. This was a relationship that could be seen as parallel to active engagement with an oral text. However, as this chapter has demonstrated, the observation is severely misleading when generalised to a description of the relationships between industrial technologies, the cultural texts they imply, and contemporary society. For the contemporary relationship between people and machines is far more guided by the dynamics of relationship to the 'written' text of technology.

The single most dominant feature of the contemporary technology/human relationships is the *enframement* of humanity by the superordinance of the 'written' text of technique. Thus, the 'harmonious order' that we experience is not within the direct relationship between person and technology – as with Fritz Kreisler. Instead, the order is background, lodged deeply in machine-system co-ordination, a harmony that lies outside immediate life-world experience. The 'aesthetic' order therefore is fundamentally at variance with the humanly constituted order of the Greeks, from whom the epistemic roots of the word 'technology' have been derived. The harmony is, to follow the Fritz Kreisler example through, being broadcast throughout the concert hall from an overbearing Muzak system. Kreisler can only play out of tune with the dominant system at extreme peril to his performance.

Whilst enframing, and beyond immediate life-world constitution, this larger aesthetic order is brought to life within *direct* experience by performances we enact with physical technological artefacts that are both produced by, and connect with, the wider harmonic order. We stand within an order that is based on cultural values that intrinsically mediate our experience of anything but this order, and therefore assert the order above immediate life-world experience itself. The aesthetic order is like an advertising billboard on which is depicted a representation of the natural world the billboard itself obscures, a billboard that remains on its concrete foundations even though the picture can be repasted and modified every fortnight. With increasing machine complexity, the world itself is made distant, a 'standing reserve' that can only be experienced *through* the technology that mediates our relationship with this world.

The message of the billboard is obscure. Within daily experience we only perceive its meaning indirectly, through the textual prisms that immediately experienced technological artefacts provide. To use the example presented earlier, the electrical distribution system that stands behind the power plug remains invisible until the power outlet does not work anymore, and we need to determine whether a tree has fallen on the electricity wires, or whether we need to employ an electrician to reconnect the household circuitry.

The picture pasted on the billboard is obscure because its meanings are not immediately apparent. The picture – or the wider contextual harmonic order – embodies deeply sedimented meanings that have been derived from historic capture of human experience and skill. But what has been captured from the whole of human productive activity, or from the 'social forces of production', is just that instrumental component of human skill that can be 'objectified' in the machine system to ease the burden of inefficiency that wider human productive participation in the machine-system perpetrates. Therefore, both the billboard that the wider system presents, and the artefact prism through which we see it, align with the geometry of instrumental skill rather than with the archaeology of the accumulated human meanings of the skills within the historic periods from which they have been drawn. As both frame (billboard that obscures the natural world), and artefact content (prism) of experience, the technological system allows us to experience the world only in terms of the instrumental logic that the system objectifies, and with which the system encompasses our immediate life experience. Cultural meanings are enframed rather than in control. Enframement of cultural possibilities therefore implies a trajectory that joins past and future – in terms of the progress of instrumental logic. As a consequence, enframement also implies an inevitability in the continuing expansion of technical logic over life-world experience.

The dynamic of this trajectory is deeply woven into the cutural meanings that the machine-system implies. Drawn from the culture/technology alignment that precipitated the industrialisation order, these original meanings have provided the second-order grammar for the technology text ever since. At root is a cultural world view that asserts the importance of human power to control technique over the importance of direct human engagement in the natural world. Equally, at the base of sedimented cultural values within the machine-system, is a philosophy that asserts the power of rational logic, and a praxis that alienates thought from action. Inscribed within this grammar are subordinate momenta of increasing technological complexity, scale, power, ubiquity and interconnectedness. These are system-control properties that actualise the underlying grammar in present-day innovation, but at the same time accentuate the framing process that the grammar implies – for each immediate system-artefact implies the other elements in the system. As a result, the artefact and its context mutually imply each other, and rigidify the meaning that *can* be read from the artefact text.

Within this second-order text-context grammar, what we can read of technology's meaning resides in the cultural text that is presented to us in the artefacts that we experience directly, and can draw directly into the reach of consciousness. As metaphor, this is a 'written' text, and encompasses all the properties of written versus oral texts in language's cultural symbolism. Not only that, but the text of machines is a written non-phonetic text. As such, the text represents social and cultural codifications that the specialised literati design, whilst themselves enframed within the grammar and trajectory of instrumental inevitability.

As 'written' text, the text is autonomous from immediate social reconstitution. As an autonomous text, the machine-text presents all history. However, the *machine-text* version of 'written' text at the same time paradoxically denies its antecedents in the continuous revisions of technological process and products that the inevitability of 'progress' allows. Thus, whilst the original texts lie outside contemporary consciousness, the original grammar is reasserted in each new technological version, for each new version lies further along the same continuum. Just the ability to scrutinise and be sceptical of 'progress' (a capacity that is retained with the maintenance of written records) is removed because previous texts disappear into the junkheap of obsolescence.

As 'written' or 'objectified' 'non-phonetic' text, the machine-text is infinite. Consequently, no one member of the technically specialist literati can envisage or design the whole. Power to define resides in the corporate or state interests that can employ the collectivity of literati, not in the literati itself. External control and vested interest hegemony is therefore inscribed into the machine-system text itself, and thus into the harmonic order, the aesthetic of the total enframing system. This power is itself shored up – as long as the power centres retain alignment with the technological system's grammar – for the experienced frames of everyday life that could be questioned are continuously moving to wider, more encompassing frames that paralyse or co-opt prior popular protest. Neither left nor right ends of the political spectrum have power to persist unless they retain alignment with the technological trajectory.

The technological text embraces participation. Although the heart of this text is one of cold technical logic, the text implies the full range of human meaning, as with all cultural symbolism. In addition to technological logic, the stock of knowledge that the text encompasses also implies or asserts valued social goals (that the machine-system contributes to), intelligibility and ontology of the world (that the machine-system mediates), and morality of what one should do (according to what one can and *should* do within the machine-system's grammar and logic). The 'written' text is therefore not *experienced* as alienated or partial. Instead, the text deeply penetrates and circumscribes *all* cultural experience. 'Participation' and active constitution of meaning is cast *within* this cultural frame. Participation is constituted as in an oral text, but within a written inscription of the oral text's limits. Thus the 'orality' of daily life is guided by oral culture mnemonics of the order that visit past stabilities on present performances – through ritual, rhythm, recital, formalised patterns of 'dialogue', mythology and 'public readings' or 'orations'. However, because of the written frame, participative mnemonics abide by the patterning that the written text sanctions. The oral mnemonics therefore reinforce and sustain the written text itself – in terms of, for example, continuance of a trajectory of social relations of production, and continuance of a trajectory of co-optation of protest into the ongoing march of the technological sytem.

Thus, the technological text is one of enframement in the logic of its own trajectory. Every act of reading and writing the text in daily experience of technological artefacts reasserts the text, as well as the 'inevitable' character of the grammar that underlies it, and the *con*-text that makes sense of it. This enframement is not a product of technology as such, but instead is a product of the culture-technology alignment that precipitated industrial society in the first place.

This chapter and the last, which set themselves the task of defining what technology means within contemporary experience, has concluded with the assertion of an enormous technological power to enframe this experience, as well as to enframe the culture that makes sense of it. Yet the trajectory is continuously creating new social and cultural alignments, and whilst dragging them into new alignments with technique, is by no means socially autonomous. As a product of collective *human* enterprise, the trajectory *could not be* wholly autonomous. The trajectory is just very powerful, according to its alignment with vested power centres that retain hegemony over the trajectory's direction whilst alignment persists with the power centres' interests.

The next step in exploring the alignment between the cultural force of technology is therefore to penetrate the dynamics of culture itself, and the manner in which power and hegemony are built on the foundation of power to *define* culture for its participants. This is the task of Chapters 4 and 5, chapters that will demonstrate the richness of the cultural world that interacts with, and alternately commands, and is commanded by, the trajectory of industrial technology.

'When men and machine work together, they can make some beautiful music.' However, the cultural meanings that bring the music to life must harmonise with the melodies that the machine system allows. And the music is an electronically synthesised version of what is presented on the billboard that advertises the concert, a billboard that stands between the performer and his or her audience.

4

The Extinction of Cultures

New Technology and Traditional Cultures

The introduction of steel axes by Christian missionaries into Australian aboriginal society played a critical role in the transformation of aboriginal culture. Within traditional aboriginal culture in Australia, stone axes were a valued possession. Stone axes were possessed by tribal elders; the axes were used as key exchange objects between tribes, so that stone axes migrated across tribal boundaries for thousands of miles throughout the continent of Australia. When Christian missionaries arrived in the nineteenth century, their overt purpose of Christianising the 'primitives' was supported by social practices intended to bring the natives into the modern world. Missions were established to educate and clothe the indigenes, to save them from the sin that the missionaries aligned with traditional tribal ways, and most importantly, to draw the aboriginal people into the modern world through work discipline, and introduction to modern work practices. In line with more modern work practices, the missionaries gave the tribes steel axes. But the axes were given to the young men who were strongest and most likely to use them, or so the missionaries thought. The result was profound, for the steel axes, as well as being more powerful than stone axes in their function, were artefacts that could not be produced by tribal technology. The steel axes therefore embodied a special symbolism of the power that aboriginals had come to associate with the invading white culture that marched irrevocably across their land, building fences across traditional hunting grounds, and conquering with guns and mission schools. The new power symbol was now in the hands of the young rather than the elders, so the effect was to interfere directly with the traditional symbols of cultural authority, and thus seriously erode the control of the tribes by the elders.[1]

This story is repeated again and again wherever modern industrial society encroaches on a traditional culture. In a mirror of what happened with Australian aboriginals, young Papua New Guineans were employed straight out of their timeless tribal society in the copper mines of Bougainville, and with their entry into a money economy, purchased Western consumer products that they took back to their villages. The wealth of powerful artefacts they could present as 'bride prices' was far in excess of that of the traditional exchange gifts of pigs, cassowaries and tribal artefacts. As with stone axes for Australian aboriginals, the symbolism of tribal goods used in exchange was deeply woven into the cultural fabric of the society, and directly associated with acquired status and exchange-induced obligations. The effect therefore of the young men entering the money economy through the Bougainville Copper Company was deeply to penetrate and erode the traditional structures of authority, obligation, status and cultural meaning of tribal society.[2]

Similarly, the older people of the Skolt Lapplanders of Finland were displaced from their former position of authority and usefulness by the introduction of snowmobiles. The machines were given to the people to replace traditional reindeer sleds as means of transportation. Introduced in the 1960s, the snowmobile was intended to enhance the efficiency for the Skolt Lapp people in gaining easier access to trading posts, better health care and more varied diet and recreation. Old men did not have the muscular dexterity to run the machines. Reindeer, previously a source of meat as well as transport, were reduced in cultural significance for the society, and along with this loss of salience the significance of the knowledge and wisdom of the old men concerning the care and use of reindeer were lost. The reindeer herds themselves declined as 'de-domestication' caused by the noise of snowmobiles caused a significant decline in the number of calves born. And, most importantly of all, the society had entered a path of modernisation that was virtually impossible to reverse, because of a new dependency on imported petroleum and spare parts to maintain the usefulness of the new technology that had been imported.[3]

Together, these three case studies demonstrate that technologies introduced from a more instrumentally powerful culture into traditional society 'burn like a cigarette on a silken fabric' into the wholeness of the cultural patterns that existed before. The artefact itself is an invading alien. It does not *have* to be backed by the repressive might of the alien political and cultural system that stands behind the object – although, as with the conquering of American Indians and Australian aboriginals by white society, repression and warfare were close behind. The invasionary power of the alien technological artefact lies instead in its cultural salience, and its resilience as a physical object in which the external culture is objectified, to being defined *into* the existing traditional cultural system. Invading technological artefacts are capable of eroding traditional culture at every level at which the culture is constituted and asserted in daily practice.

As the three case studies demonstrate, the alien artefact symbolises a powerful new productive force. The traditional society has no access to this productive force except through joining in with the encroachment of modernism from outside. The artefact enters as a virus into the body of existing social practices, but the culture of the body has no immune system, primarily because the productive roots of the old culture are torn out from beneath the meaning system of the whole society. Apart from the direct changes to productive practices demonstrated in the examples presented above, this transformation can also be indirect and unintended – as the *wider* technological systems that affect traditional life are changed. In Western Samoa for example, a small scale hydroelectric system that was introduced into mountain country dammed and rerouted the river system from which the people of the village used to obtain their staple fish diet. The villagers had to find another source of protein, a requirement that placed increased dependence of village life on the external cash economy. More importantly though, the mythology, the meanings, the symbols that were previously central to the culture were all based on fishing – the productive activity that stood at the centre of village life. With no fish, the mythologies, the fabric of meanings of communal village life, were torn apart for they no longer bore any relationship to the reality into which the children were socialised. The new electricity-generation system therefore was timely, for it then provided the power for consumer products that subsequently started to invade the village as the people sought new meanings in the cash economy they were forced into. But the need to enter the cash economy was a direct product of the introduction of the electricity system in the first place.[4]

Thus, because of the depth of connection between the society's whole culture and its productive practices, the infection caused by invasion of new technological artefacts or by change to the society's technological frame spreads to command the *whole* social productive system. For the wholeness of the culture that held previous practices together into a meaningful system is shattered, leaving the path to complete invasion wide open. The traditional culture can do nothing but adjust or disappear under the onslaught of the assumptions and social practices that stand behind the modernist artefacts and techniques.

The virulence of infection is demonstrated in a case study of the introduction of new fishing technologies into Sri Lankan villages. From 1960 to the mid-1970s, 2,000 inboard motor craft were brought into the fishing villages of Sri Lanka to improve fishing yields, a programme that was devised on the advice of foreign 'experts' whose fisheries experience was mainly of large industrial enterprise. At a cost of some

30,000 rupees (or 10 to 15 years' worth of income for village families), the boats were very expensive. Thus, to ensure maximum diffusion, the boats were introduced under a hire purchase scheme. Prior traditional production systems however generated only marginal savings that could be used for entry of the village fishermen into this cash economy. As a consequence, the cost of boat repayments together with wage and maintenance expenses, resulted in the majority of the 'new' fishermen going bankrupt. Repairs to the boats were the critical cost, as traditional practices embodied no way of comprehending or maintaining Norwegian boats with Japanese motors. So, when the boats broke down the fishermen could not fix them, and lost their source of fishing income from which they could continue repayments on the original boat purchase. The richer, more successful boat owners, who could afford to keep the boats running by *paying* for repairs, managed thus to purchase the second-hand boats, and built up fleets that increased their elite advantage over the distribution of the village fishing trawl. The previous 'inefficient' canoe-based fishing system was almost entirely displaced.

Paul Alexander observed the effects on one fishing village of 1,200 to 1,300 people.[5] Fishing output rose by a factor of 7 or 8, from 30 tons in 1960 to about 200 to 250 tons in 1975. The increase was directly attributable to the introduction of mechanised boats. However, the total number of people employed in fishing decreased by about 50 per cent, and the total number of unemployed rose to the point where, in 1974, 35 per cent of males under 25 years had no job at all. Formerly, there had been a very small elite of one or two families and a large class of free peasants; now there was a large elite of ten to fifteen families, but at the same time, about 200 families were living close to or below subsistence level, and were being kept alive by government rations or rice and other foodstuffs. The more wealthy and successful boat owners increasingly moved to a financial management position, owning several boats and employing other villagers merely as labour. Social boundaries within the village had therefore been converted into a mirror of the industrialised capitalism that surrounded it, with the proletarianisation of the majority and the embourgoisement of an emergent elite. Prior obligations of village life had disappeared along with the erosion of traditional social relations of production.

Not only that, but the process of change also led inevitably to closer dependence on the external urban-based economic structure. The size of financial transactions meant that the loan economy could no longer be located within the village. So villagers became increasingly dependent on external financial sources. With the larger catches it became worthwhile to transport yields to the capital city, Colombo, a linkage into the wider technological and economic system that increased the imbalance between urban and rural equality. Whereas most of the catch used to be eaten locally, most of the increased catch now went to the capital city – some 120 to 130 miles away.

In some villages where the geography was unsuitable to mechanised boats, a similar effect unfolded with the introduction of nylon fishing nets, again a technological artefact that fundamentally assumed and connected with the wider technological system. The nylon nets were expensive in that they were worth approximately six months of family income. But they were not so expensive as to be out of reach of the majority of families, nor did they require expensive repairs, as did the mechanised fishing boats. The nets were however a major technical advantage over the traditional rope nets. The new nets – drifting a mile in the current across the incoming fish shoal – were extremely efficient. Formerly, when a fleet of 25 to 30 boats went fishing, one or two might catch more than the others, but the catch was spread quite evenly throughout the fleet. After the introduction of the nylon nets, the first boat to spread the nets across the incoming shoal took 75 per cent to 80 per cent of the catch, the second net might take a very small yield, and the other 28 boats took nothing at all. Owners of the fastest boats became significantly richer, whilst the others were not harvesting enough food to eat. The size of the fishing fleet diminished rapidly. And the traditional production of woven rope nets disappeared entirely.

Originally within the Sri Lankan villages there was willing acceptance of the new technologies of mechanised boats and synthetic fishing nets. Both technologies appeared to provide greater ease of labour, greater wealth and greater power. But neither technology could be *integrated* into existing productive practices or stocks of knowledge. So, behind the immediate artefacts stood the modern industrial production system that villagers had to depend upon for the new production practices to survive. This same observation applies to the use of snowmobiles by the Skolt Lapps. Those within the Sri Lankan villages who had first-level access to the modern industrial and economic system – through previously acquired wealth or power – generated a multiplier effect in their advantage. The traditional ways, meanings and obligations of production were destroyed; the villagers as a whole became increasingly dependent upon the urban technological *system*; yet the majority were pauperised and proletarianised in the process. And they couldn't turn back because the past pattern of social relations had been demolished.

For anyone with experience of the introduction of Western

technologies into developing countries the Sri Lankan story is so common as to be virtually universal. To finalise the picture, one has only to look at the failure of probably the most concerted attempt to employ modern practices to alleviate poverty and starvation that has been attempted – the so-called 'Green Revolution'. As a largely (American) aid-inspired venture, the 'Green Revolution' sought to introduce high yield, genetically modified crops into the farms of the developing world, and to support the increased growth potential through modern farming technology and chemicals. Apart from unintended and gross impact on ecology caused by the run-off of chemicals into the water table, the programme failed in its social and economic goals because of precisely the same dynamic identified in the Sri Lankan case study. As a key player in this aid initiative, the Ford Foundation, in establishing its 'Intensive Agricultural Assistance Program' 25 years ago, explicitly identified its target group as the rural middle classes. This definition followed from the assumption that only middle-class farmers could take the risk involved and would show the creativity to respond to new technology. It was also assumed that the innovation of middle-class farmers would have a demonstration effect that would allow spin-off of new techniques throughout the entire rural economy. Both of these assumptions specifically were targeted at using technological change to break the relationship between traditional agricultural practice and existing patterns of social, economic and cultural relations.

The tractor was central to the strategy. The tractor replaces muscle or animal power, and therefore provides a mechanised quantum jump in efficiency in agricultural exploitation. Along with inputs that were required by the new seed varieties, of irrigation, pesticides and fertilisers, the programme was successful in increasing the absolute quantity of food available – much as was the effect of mechanised boats on fish harvesting in Sri Lanka. However, chiefly because of the replacement effect of tractors on labour power inputs, the effects on employment prospects for landless labour were considerable. In Pakistan, for example, 9.5 to 11.8 full-time jobs were lost for each tractor purchased. After purchase of a tractor the average farm size increased by 20 per cent within three years, mostly through the eviction of tenants, and employment per cultivated acre dropped by 40 per cent.[6] Michael Howes shows how this happened in a case study of a village in Thailand.[7] A trader in the village (already joined into the external capitalist market economy) acquired the first tractor and through hiring it out to the larger landholders acquired 60,000 baht (or $3,000) in the first year. Over the next seven years, the larger landholders followed the trader's example and also purchased tractors. Because of the size of their landholdings, the purchase and use of tractors were, for them, an economic proposition. Smaller landholders followed the larger landholders' example and also sought to use tractors – entirely in keeping with the Green Revolution's philosophy. However the smaller landholders could not afford to spend the large amount of capital required to purchase tractors, so they hired them from the large landholders. For the smaller landholders, the use of hired tractors was an uneconomic proposition: the size of their land did not justify the cost of hiring, especially when surplus labour was available from their (generally large) families; and the smaller landholders were only able to hire the tractors once the richer farmers had finished using them – thus delaying the smaller landholders' ploughing and harvesting and reducing crop yields. Meanwhile, richer farmers had no use for the agricultural labour of those who were landless peasants. Richer farmers got richer and poorer farmers had to sell their land. It was the same story across the whole Asian region. In Indonesia, only 25 per cent of peasant farmers benefited in any way. As Perelman observes, increased urbanisation progressed across the whole region as the poor were driven from their fields and forced into cities, to buy expensive cereals grown in the fields where they once harvested inexpensive legumes.[8] And the culture and economics of the modern industrial system marched further into the whole life-experience of the traditional societies, its assumptions written in the face of the tractor that got there before.

The impact observed in these cases of alien technologies on the existing social relations of production is not only the impact that follows from artefacts that by their power 'open a door of opportunity' as Lyn White would suggest.[9] The power of the artefact to transform instead is a product of its *association* with economic power and new social statuses that are derived from participation in the invading economy and culture.

Basic to this power is the alienation of existing traditional stocks of knowledge from the stocks of knowledge that stand behind the use of the invading artefacts. Within the Sri Lankan fishing villages there were expert fishermen, but no one who could repair a carburettor or even who knew how an engine system worked. There were expert craftspeople who could weave rope nets, but there was absolutely no productive capacity to produce nylon. Thus the old social practices and obligations that were associated with traditional social relations of production gave way to dependency on stocks of knowledge that cost *money*, and had to be imported from outside. In one case of my own experience, a farmer in India told me he could not use his almost new tractor because the carburettor was blocked: no one in the village could repair it, and the cost of bringing in a mechanic from the nearest large town just to look at it was 200 rupees – or 25 times the average daily wage of the villagers.

The stock of technical knowledge in a traditional society can be very rich. The average adult of the Philippine Hanunoo tribe could identify 1,600 different botanical species – 400 more than had previously been identified by a systematic botanical survey. The Hanunoo had four different terms for describing the firmness of soil; nine colour categories to reflect soil properties; ten basic and thirty sub-types of rocks; five different topographical types; three different ways of categorising slopes; and, six major and ten minor types of vegetation grouping. The average !KO bushman of Botswana was able to identify and name 206 out of the 211 varieties of botanical specimens collected by a professional taxonomist, and could make finer distinctions than could the taxonomist between different types of plants. The !KO could quickly locate individual plants of a particular species through their intimate understanding of the principles governing the co-location of different plants according to soil conditions.[10] In the Kingdom of Tonga, traditional medical knowledge encompassed surgical practices that mirrored those used in modern medicine today. For example, in the early nineteenth century a marooned English sailor observed the surgical procedures that were used in treating a warrior with a spear wound. The barb was cut off and removed, and the wound was then inserted with a trachoma tube made from furled banana leaf in order to drain the wound. The banana leaf had been heated over a fire thus making it sterile. Although using more sophisticated instruments and sterilisation procedures, the same principles are applied today in modern medicine.[11]

This common stock is the knowledge that weaves social practices into the ecological niche that the society inhabits. But, as with the knowledge of reindeer for the Skolt Lapps, the common stock of technical knowledge is useless as far as the acquisition or production of modern technologies is concerned. With the power of alien technological artefacts, the indigenous knowledge – as common amongst the traditional people as is the knowledge of automobile makes and train timetables within modern society – becomes 'common', useless, and associated with a past order the people are escaping.

The traditional stock of knowledge tends to be learnt according to a process that Lévi Strauss calls 'bricoleur',[12] or by imitating the ways of technically proficient older people of the tribe – 'learning by doing'.[13] The knowledge is learnt as an 'oral text'. The acquisition of knowledge therefore directly supports traditional structures of status legitimacy and authority. As an oral text, traditional technical knowledge is deeply interwoven with cultural meanings, life-world experience and rhythms of daily life and productive activity. Thus the introduction of tractors – and the associated introduction of fertilisers and pesticides – not only challenges prior traditional knowledge of agriculture and the process by which agricultural practices are learnt. The introduction of tractors also transforms the rhythms of labour. It changes the regime of planting and harvesting time and practices, and the solidarities and obligations of collective labour. Moreover, the introduction of tractors challenges the wisdom of the old whose authority depended on integrating technical knowledge with all life and its meaning – as was shown to be the case with the challenge caused by the introduction of snowmobiles to old peoples' wisdom and authority amongst the Skolt Lapps.

Technical knowledge is therefore surgically excised out of the cultural framework into which it was originally set. In the hole that remains, the cultural pulse of prior technical knowledge dies, and the whole surrounding culture implodes. The culture stays stitched together, but only with dissolving thread. For the central heart of technique starts to beat to the cultural rhythm of the social and economic assumptions of the invading industrialised culture.

Along with this process of transformation the salience of old cultural symbols is rendered impotent. In an order that is reeling, physical artefacts of the powerful alien culture provide a new superordinate symbolism of an order yet to be achieved, an aesthetic yet to be grasped. The physical artefacts represent the invading culture, and the power of order that is associated with it. This is a power that can be held by an emergent elite who are first to move into the strong grasp of modernism. It is a power that offers to make sense of a world that is falling apart within people's lives and life-expectancies. As Arthur Koestler observed of what he described as the 'Coca-Colonisation of the world', the most widely known symbol throughout the world today is not the cross or other representations of deities; it is 'Coca-Cola'.[14] In my own experience, Coca-Cola and Pepsi can be found in the most remote villages of northern Thailand, Nepal and Papua New Guinea. The symbol is closely followed by modernised fast-food systems and their trade symbols. A friend who hiked for three days into the hinterland of American Samoa found an American hamburger stand in the midst of a coconut and fish based society. Marion Christie observed the increasing prevalence of fast-food shops in the Highlands of Papua New Guinea.[15] Indeed, the symbolism of fast-food even broke up a major riot in Papua New Guinea. A teacher who lived at Mount Hargan during the 'Mount Hargan Dispute' of the late 1960s told me of a very tense moment in the dispute when the tribesmen, dressed in warpaint and armed with spears, were confronted by a line of police nervously fingering their crowd-control batons. At that moment, when the violence seemed to be imminent, the sound of 'Greensleeves' suddenly broke from the surrounding jungle, followed shortly thereafter by an enterprising 'Mr Whippy' truck. Both tribesmen and police broke ranks to purchase ice-cream and the confrontation dissolved.

The new cultural symbols imply new saliences of foods that are associated with industrial culture. They draw the Westernised culture *directly* into the life-world of the people. Processed foods – like white flour and white rice, and drinks – like beer and Coca-Cola therefore replace preference for traditional food supplies. The health effect of nutrition changes can be profound, and directly reinforces the encroachment of Western technically-rational institutions. This effect is shown in caricature within Paul Zimmet's study of the Island of Nauru in the Pacific.[16] For generations the British Phosphate Company had been removing guano deposits (bird droppings) from the centre of the island, transforming all but the outside edge of the island into a moonscape. On final settlement of recompense for this ecological damage in the courts of London, the island was given a perpetual income of $25,000 per person. The people basically went on a spending spree. The entire adult population bought automobiles – to drive around the one circular road of the island. Work practices changed – towards the market and bureaucratic centre of the towns, rather than village life. Virtually all food was subsequently imported and sold in supermarkets. Backed by Madison Avenue-style advertising hype, the food purchased tended to be Westernised – that is, processed white flour, white sugar, white rice, tinned fish and meats, tinned fruit and vegetables, soft drinks and beer – food that was mostly high in carbohydrates and calories but low in nutritional value. Traditional agriculture and fishing disappeared – except for occasional pleasure jaunts to fish from twin-engined launches.

As Zimmet observed, a direct consequence of these changes in lifestyle was that the island was hit by an epidemic of the diseases of modernism – hypertension, heart disease, ulcers, obesity, and in particular, diabetes. Diabetes rocketed from zero incidence to a point where it was suffered by 40 per cent of the population. The people loved sugar and would add three tablespoons to an already sweet glass of processed cordial. Obesity aligned with the traditional symbols of status of chiefs, that is, enormous physical bulk: average calorific intake was now approximately 6,000 per day, two to three times higher than the average nutritional requirement; and *average* weight was 18 stone. Whilst under the prior traditional system of food type and patterns of consumption, the storing of sugar in the body had been a survival advantage, it was now a direct threat to mortality. Diabetes had been nascent in the society for centuries. But with a limited gene pool that concentrated the inheritance of diabetes, and along with new food acquisition and consumption practices and the cultural meanings that supported these practices, the introduction of processed sweet foods unlocked the disease from the cultural shell that had suppressed it. Nutritional and lifestyle changes thus injected a secondary multiplier into the dynamic encroachment of modernism, for the diseases of modernism required new hospital based approaches to medical intervention.

Though seen in caricature in Nauru, the story is common across the Pacific. In societies that have experienced the precipitous invasion of wealth such as occurred in Nauru, the seductive attraction of Westernised foods to societies being shaken out of traditional ways has had similar, but less dramatic effects. In the Kingdom of Tonga, for example, during the 1970s, a bakery commenced the baking of bread for the first time in the capital city, Nuku'Alofa. The demand was initially very small for a people whose staple diet was taro, coconuts and fish, and only one sack of imported flour was used a day. Today, the demand is hundreds of times higher. With improved roads – a product of aid-assistance – access to the capital is considerably easier, and people flock to the town to purchase bread. Children from schools buy bread for lunch rather than eat traditional foods. The need to *purchase* a staple commodity that cannot be produced from local resources has required villagers to enter the cash economy, so many young people (particularly) congregate in the town looking for work that the modernist elements of the economy can not yet provide adequately – and the traditional relations and obligations of village life are being demolished with each new loaf of bread that is baked. Because of the low level of wealth of the nation, the flour that is imported is the lowest quality that can be obtained, and whilst rich in starch, is very poor in nutritional ingredients. Diet-related health problems are accelerating along the same trajectory that Nauru has followed – all because, as the senior Tongan official who told the story said, 'the people had got used to buttered bread.'[17]

The impact of *high* technology intrusion on lifestyle in the Pacific is even more dramatic. Satellite-based television is, during 1987, being introduced into Fiji and Papua New Guinea, with programming that will promote the cheaper US and Australian soap dramas, police shows, and so on – all to do with the most dramatic and violent images of Western individualised lifestyle. But the ground is already prepared.

Video has made enormous inroads already. The main Tongan island of Tongelavu for example boasts the sale of 2,000 video systems, which people in a marginal cash economy are at times paying off on hire purchase at the expense of money needed to give their children lunch at school. There are virtually no controls over video films that are imported throughout the region, with the singular exception of the Cook Islands. Video marketing outlets are generally not licensed. So, what the people are voraciously consuming is the worst X-rated movies, replete with sex and violence, that cannot be sold in many developed country outlets. As with cigarettes, banned drugs and chemicals, and polluting industries, the developing countries are a burgeoning market for the international capitalist interests that can find profit from products that can no longer be marketed in the West. Thus, what the people, often still living in traditional village communities, are seeing, and modelling, is the worst of the excrescences of advanced industrial life. The contrast, the shock of change from traditional communal mores and ways, is enormous.

The people and the cultures of the Pacific are adjusting – at times with precipitous speed. The economies however are not, remaining dependent for one-third of foreign income on aid, and one-third on expatriated earnings of nationals who have moved through the locally presented images of the advantages of modernisation to New Zealand, Australia and the US, where they join the advanced nation culture and are submerged within it. The drive to move through local modernisation into the modern societies of advanced nations is very strong indeed, and is further exacerbated by high technological intervention. In the Cook Islands for example, under an aid-sponsored initiative, an international airport was built at Raratonga in 1972, intentionally to improve the wealth of the islands through tourism. But the people had 'tasted buttered bread', and saw the airlink as a way *out* of traditional society's restrictions on access to modernism. Thus, over ten years there was a net *outmigration* of over a quarter of the population – principally to New Zealand. The situation is even worse for the tiny nation of Niue, where following the construction of an international airport, today's population stands at *less than half* (46 per cent) of the population that inhabited the islands before.[18] Needless to say, those who leave are also those who are likely to have the greatest skills either to redress the imbalances of modernism, or to build up some level of national, technical or decision-making autonomy.

When introduced into traditional societies, the transformative power of industrialised technologies is profound. A single technological artefact has the power to penetrate to the heart of traditional cultural stability and meanings. The power does not lie however in mere technical usefulness, as a non-cultural analysis might suggest. Nor does it lie only in the abuse of economic hegemony, as a political–economic analysis might propose. Rather, the most basic source of transformative power lies in the cultural context from which the technology is derived, a context that is implied at every point along the technology's path of diffusion. The cultural context of technological systems implies an economic and status system that is associated with it. The Western cultural context of values implies stocks of knowledge that are alienated from the traditional stocks of knowledge into which the artefact is introduced. The introduced or implied stocks of knowledge are therefore capable of tearing the heart out of the cultural salience and authority of traditional knowledge and its meaning within the life-world of the society.

The introduced artefacts imply and command the development of new productive practices that transform the pre-existing rhythms of life, the patterns of traditional social relations of production, and the traditional sources of collective solidarity and obligation. And the final power of the artefact lies in its objectification of the symbolism of the invading culture. This is a symbolism that stands in front of the invading culture's social implication, and obscures the dependency and exploitation that follows close behind. The new superordinate symbols maintain their ascendent trajectory because they replace the symbols of cohesion that went before by symbols of power. The meaning and seductive property of this power however resides in *participation* in the invading system, and acceptance of the new cultural assumptions – the final nail in the coffin of past ways. The culture is smashed into obeisance, leaving only remembered colourful dances to be performed in Hilton Hotel lobbies for curious tourists, dances that by the location of performance, and the cash nexus that brings them to life, are robbed of their integrative communal significance.

From Jungle to Mantle Shelf: Lessons for Contemporary Society

The discoveries that we have made in the jungles of traditional culture can now be brought back for display on the mantleshelf of everyday life in industrial society.

What can be seen in the impact of introduced technologies on traditional societies is the enormous power to transform that resided *in* technologies that came from an alien cultural context. Rather, the power lies not in the technologies *per se*, but in the cultural symbolism they embodied, and in the *non-alignment* of the introduced cultural 'text' with every force that constituted cultural meanings within the traditional societies. Even modern technological means that may be used to try to *consolidate* traditional relations rather than break them, are therefore likely to come to grief – primarily because the technologies imply economic and cultural assumptions that are at variance with traditional ways. This was demonstrated with the introduction of direct international dialling into Western Samoa. The system was introduced to the people as a means of retaining contact with members of their families and villages who had emigrated to New Zealand, as a means of retaining kinship ties. The effect was the reverse. The people did indeed call their relatives, but soon realised that the cost of telephoning for long periods of time was impossible to bear given their low levels of cash income. Consequently, they started to reverse the charges for the calls. As a result, the family members in New Zealand, who also could not afford the cost, started to refuse calls from their relatives in Western Samoa, an action that antagonised their kin and caused *greater* social distance between them, rather than bringing them closer together.

As in all the case studies presented in this chapter, the meanings of the alien technologies were at variance with the traditional social relations of production – relations that, in joining meaning and action with physical survival, most fundamentally constitute the premises of social discourse. Through the social relations of production, the boundaries and content of social solidarity are maintained. So too are the sources of legitimacy maintained, as well as the hegemony of the society's ruling class – in these cases, the elders of the tribes.

The alien technological artefacts implied stocks of knowledge, and through these, the socialisation practices and power structures that are predicated on control over stocks of knowledge. The implied stocks of knowledge of alien artefacts therefore disenfranchised the authority of the prior ruling class. This was so, except where, as in the cases of tractors and fishing boats introduced to middle-class farmers and fishermen, the elite retained hegemony over what was introduced, and therefore accentuated their power. The new (implied) stocks of knowledge were alienated from the wider cultural meanings into which traditional knowledge was embedded. They therefore distanced the new elite from the traditional patterns of obligation and meaning that previously held the societies together, fostered the identification of the emergent elite with the outside capitalist culture, and split the society in two.

And the alien artefacts implied a new superordinate symbolism, where symbols of technical power replaced totems of group solidarity. The whole nest of cultural symbols and meanings that rested beneath the umbrella of master symbols was therefore demolished by replacing the overall symbols that made sense of everything else. The effect was to enforce on the societies a desperate and disoriented search for new meanings. This is a search that ultimately leads the people into the bright lights of the cities, or leads the culture of the metropolises down through the electric power cables and television sets into the villages.

Traditional cultural practices may sometimes hinder the encroachment of modernised technological practice, even unintentionally. For example, as John Standingford reports, a United Nations Food and Agricultural Organisation (FAO)-based scheme was introduced into Western Samoa to supply village fishermen with small catamaran launches powered with outboard motors so that the fishermen could make day-long fishing trips outside the reef. The aid agency also paid attention to transferring the technical knowledge that was necessary to keep the boats operating, and provided both tool kits and training in the care and maintenance of outboard motors when the boats were delivered. But,

> community and family obligations in Western Samoa are such that the owner of an outboard motor frequently comes under irresistible pressure to lend it for many purposes, economic and otherwise. Indeed, he may come to his boat prepared for a fishing trip only to find he has lent his motor to a person or persons unknown during the night. Toolkits suffer the same fate and, like books in our own society, seldom find their way back to their original owners.[19]

Indeed, from personal observation of this same case, resistance to the introduction of the boats was also becoming overt (rather than unintentional) some years later. The people had realised that in order to maintain payments for the boats under the suspensory loan scheme by which they had been purchased, the men had to go fishing for at least two to three days each week. Previously, they had fished only for immediately needed food. The people resisted the change to their lifestyle that was required by such a regime, and were far less attracted by the apparent advantages of the boats. However, the same people are now purchasing videos, and wishing to participate in the modern consumer society that has continued to encroach on Samoan life over the past few years. They are therefore being *forced* to find means of participating in the cash economy. And, as with what appears to be a universal lesson of what happens when a modern technology frame encroaches on traditional society, resistance is being swept away, along with traditional fishing practices, as the people rush to participate in the new society that is surrounding them.

Standing restlessly behind the scenes of each of the cases presented in this chapter was the cash nexus that ultimately joined the traditional societies into the world economy and into the interests of capital that this economy serves. Standing more intrusively at the edge of each culture drama were the political-economic interests that were incessantly searching for new markets to invade. However, both the cash nexus and external economic interests were allowed entry, at least in the first instance. Their transforming and coercive power was not immediately apparent, but was invisible behind the symbolism of power and status that resided in the introduced technological artefacts. A political-economic analysis thus sets a context for understanding the level of cultural change that the case studies present. However a political-economic analysis is not of itself an adequate explanation. For it was the culture power of the artefacts that led the way and which implied participation in the cash nexus, not external imposition of economic hegemony.

The picture of culture-technology interactions is printed in vibrant colours in these Third World examples. But the interactions between culture and technique that the picture displays are universal. What makes the clarity of the picture obscure in contemporary industrial society is simply that our own culture has had time to embody much of the interaction process into the basic grammar of social interaction, and therefore into taken-for-granted assumptions. Even so, the culture-technology interactions follow the same general line of trajectory as in the Third World case studies. To erect the products of analysis of the 'jungle' on the mantle shelf of everyday life, it is therefore worth pointing to what is universal about all culture (including industrial), and to what is universal about the linkage between culture and consciousness in everyday life. From this, we can then identify the specific 'cultural inclinations' of industrial society that shape the universal culture-technology interaction into a particular trajectory. This is the subject of Chapter 5.

5

The Culture Factor

Culture and Consciousness in Everyday Life

The average tribesperson of the Papua New Guinean or Philippine Hanunoo societies did not *choose* to change their culture. Or at least they did not choose a vision of an industrialising future at the time when the process started. Neither did the peasant fishermen of Sri Lanka. Indeed, if they could have foreseen the consequences that the introduced technologies carried with them the people may well have done everything in their power to reject the social trajectory that lay in front of them. The people did not choose. Rather, they took advantage of what lay in a seemingly unproblematic way in front of them, and then *lived* the experience, and sought to make sense of the changed meanings with which they were confronted. By accepting the alien technological meanings into everyday life, the people were therefore irrevocably enmeshed in a social trajectory, the shape of which they could not even imagine, but which incremental adjustments of experience actualised.

Culture is not constituted somewhere else and given to us. It is constituted in daily life – in the negotiations and incremental adjustments to experience of day-to-day existence. Culture is rarely seen, except where a sudden trauma throws daily life into an 'existential wobble', or where contact with an alien culture throws one's own cultural patterns into sharp relief. We cannot see culture as an object of scrutiny because daily life is so totally enmeshed within it. As Ralph Linton suggests, it is about as difficult for us to reflect on culture as it is for a super-intelligent fish living within the depths of the ocean to understand what water is. It is only when the fish, by some accident, is brought to the surface and introduced to air that it experiences something different.[1] Anthropology came to grips with culture by a somewhat analogous process, that is, through confronting and needing to explain totally different kinds of society. What anthropologists thus came to realise was that all societies hold together because they have come to a shared view of what social reality is, and how the people should act together in order to maintain this reality, and survive within it. Culture therefore concerns the *meaning system* of society - conveyed through expectations, norms, taboos, rules, symbols and structures of discourse. Culture embodies 'shared ways of thinking and believing that grow out of group experience and are passed from one generation to the next'.[2] But, most fundamentally, culture lives not in some external etiquette text, but in the interactions and constructions of meaning of daily life, where it provides a 'design for living'.[3]

This 'design for living' is fashioned collectively. It is constituted 'organically' over time, and passed on to new generations according to what has been proven to 'work'. A culture's 'design for living' is fashioned out of people's need to orient their own individual actions – at every moment of consciousness – in terms of both the social world they inhabit, and the meanings this social world attributes to action that allows the collectivity, and the individual, to survive. For a species for whom 'survival' requires collective and conscious social action, physical survival is intimately linked with a shared intelligibility of the world towards which that action is directed. Thus, as Clifford Geertz affirms, 'The drive to make sense out of experience, to give it form and order, is evidently as real as the more familiar biological needs.'[4] As Geertz goes on to observe, the whole complex of symbolic activities that follow – in religion, art, ideology and so on – are all, 'attempts to provide orientation for an organism which cannot live in a world it is unable to understand.'[5]

'Understanding' however resides only within the person's immediate fully coloured subjective world – where individual consciousness can engage 'here-and-now' with direct objects of experience.[6] All else is illusion or meaningless abstraction unless it can be brought into reach of the individual's subjective and inter-subjective domain. Thus the whole infrastructure of institutions, of social relations of production, of mores and symbolic systems has no meaning until its products are directly within everyday life. The apparent 'externality' and independence from subjective engagement that this infrastructure appears to embody, therefore only exists because its meanings are *lived* so deeply within subjective experience that they disappear behind the facade of everyday life into a screen onto which conscious intervention in the world is painted. Within the collectively assumed 'grammar' that this cultural background provides, the grammar is reasserted by people acting and living in their daily lives – in exactly the same way that the grammar of a language is reasserted by people speaking and communicating.

If we were to change the 'grammar' or structures of immediate lived experience, we would therefore change the whole symbolic system of the society, for this symbolic system is built on the foundation of everyday life and consciousness.

Culture cannot be separated from consciousness, and the manner in which consciousness is constituted, for it is *only* within consciousness that the carriage of meaning systems rests. Whilst the accumulated meanings of past generations may be 'objectified' in artefacts or totems which 'stay there' to be returned to even though thought and interaction may have wandered elsewhere, if there is no consciousness in the present about these meanings, the meanings simply *must* disappear. Thus the meaning of Aztec rope-knotting mathematics, the cultural salience of Stonehenge and the relevance of the 'appearance' of 'spacemen' in ancient aboriginal paintings, have evaporated into the mists of lost cultures along with discontinuity in cultural consciousness.

Consciousness is constituted in face-to-face interaction. It is here that we are linked directly with the subjective consciousness of others, and can thus draw into reach, respond, reformulate, mirror – *learn* to harmonise our own consciousness and subjectivity with that of others. As adults we experience people in *anonymous* encounters, that is, in relationships that are mediated by time and distance (non-immediacy), or by mode of interaction. For example, we experience and may well be influenced by authors of the past where our relationship is only through our reading of the text they wrote; we experience people in the present as disembodied television images, or as faceless bureaucrats at the end of a phone line; and we experience people of the future as imagined entities that surround the projected adulthood of our child-generations to whom we may feel responsible in present action. But, as with projections onto the future, so too with all 'anonymous' relations. They have meaning only because we can draw the person, or an image of the person's subjectivity into reach – experience 'similar' subjectivities in the fullness of face-to-face interaction. This process, the essence of construction of social meaning in consciousness, is described by Alfred Schutz as the 'reciprocity of perspectives' – the ability to learn only through aligning one's own consciousness with the experienced objectivations of the consciousness of others.[7] This inter-subjective relationship between 'thou' or the person in reach, and 'I' (initiator) and 'Me' (receiver) in constituting consciousness is basic to the 'symbolic interactionism' of George Herbert Mead.[8]

Subjective consciousness therefore emerges from being able to *read* the objectivations – in gesture, language, symbolic behaviours, and so on – that indicate the others' internal world. Evidence for the centrality of *inter-subjectivity* to interactive dialogue has emerged along with difficulties experienced in the recent advent of 'teleconferencing'. Intended as a device for full inter-subjective interaction, the medium has proved inadequate, because the fullness of the other person cannot be experienced in two-dimensional visual and one-dimensional aural transmission. The 'teleconferencing' mode allows effective transmission of 'information', but 'negotiation' is very difficult unless the teleconferencing participants meet each other on a regular basis between teleconferencing sessions – and can therefore 'fill in' the subjectivity that is missing when meeting 'electronically'. As an aside, the idiocy of technocratic solutions to cultural problems is revealed in one response to this observation, where a serious proposition was being considered for 'humanising' interaction through installing pneumatic hands at each station so that participants could shake hands remotely with each other.[9] Not even a smelly, chatty, hologram can replace full inter-subjectivity as the constitutive base for consciousness, and as the carriage of culture. This is written into the structure of consciousness itself.

The 'reciprocity of perspectives' that is basic to consciousness is largely *asymmetric* during early child development. It is in this asymmetry that one can see how unopened cultural baggage enters consciousness as a 'grammar' within which we read the text of direct interactions. As the 'reciprocity of perspectives' principle implies, we cannot read the text of external 'objectivations' until they can be accompanied by internal representations or significations in consciousness. As the research of Jean Piaget demonstrates, this mirroring cannot be achieved until approximately the second year of life, by which time the child has achieved two capabilities. The first is the development of adequate locomotive skills for the child to *intend* action and physically carry it out, as for example in grasping a desired object, or moving away from an unpleasant stimulus. The second capability is the development of at least primitive language whereby *absent* things can be represented symbolically in words, and thus correlated with thought, and signified as internal images that can be associated with action.[10]

Two observations concerning the link between consciousness and culture follow from the principle of asymmetry. The first is that of *sedimentation*. The cultural meaning system that rests as background to the immediacy of face-to-face interaction has already set the horizons and structures of consciousness before the child can be socially conscious. Cultural practices and saliences are embedded in the modes of response to the child by adults – even though they lie anonymously *behind* the adults' immediate response. The child cannot, without linguistic means of signifying, unpack these assumptions. He or she can only learn *within* them. During maturation the asymmetry becomes increasingly balanced, but the wider culture is permanently sedimented into consciousness before we can consider culture or cultural objects with any level of sophistication. As adults we experience the subjectivity of others within the cultural taken-for-granted assumptions that *frame* consciousness and the meaning of action. Thus cultural continuity and persistence in the meanings of experienced cultural objects follows. That is, cultural continuity persists *until* the very frame within which it is continuously asserted in interaction is directly threatened – as was shown to be the case in the Third World examples presented earlier.

The second observation that follows from the asymmetry principle is that consciousness only forms around *intention*. Consciousness forms as the person fashions desire into a plan which can be acted out to achieve the desired goal. This 'tension of consciousness' joining thought to action towards a 'pragmatic motive' parallels Marx's idea of 'praxis', where consciousness and labour are coterminous in transforming both the physical and political world.[11] In acting out goal-oriented behaviour and being successful, the person is therefore carrying the meanings of society that 'work' back into consciousness – asserting in consciousness the cultural reality principles that hold the society together as a whole. Consciousness and the meaning of 'reality' are thus joined in a progressive dialectic spiral. As 'reality' changes, for example through transformations of ecological horizons (as Lewis Mumford observes of the discoveries of the New World of the Americas), so too does consciousness change (as Mumford shows in the expansion of horizons of thought).[12] Equally, as consciousness changes, as for example in the expansion of horizons of thought, so too does 'reality', as objects of thought (for example inventions that reflect the new consciousness) are applied to objectify the new consciousness, and mediate the relationship between consciousness and the world it seeks to grasp.

In the two observations of *sedimentation* and *intentionality* as basic principles of the consciousness/culture interaction, we see an interplay between what Edmund Husserl describes as 'active' and 'passive' synthesis.[13] In 'active' synthesis, the object or objectivation is productively constituted in consciousness in relation to intention: consciousness *engages* in the world. In 'passive' synthesis, the person *receives* objectivations as givens. Active synthesis transmutes into passive synthesis when meanings are 'given' or taken-for-granted, rather than actively engaged. Habituated action, as in driving a car, leaves consciousness in automatic drive, not needing to pay attention to the actions of pressing pedals and steering. Without passive synthesis, consciousness would be overwhelmed by total overload of choice and stimuli. Without active synthesis, consciousness cannot open up 'received' meanings for scrutiny or scepticism.

The implications that follow for the interaction within culture between consciousness and technology are considerable. As I showed in Chapter 2, the direct experience of technological artefacts is set in passive synthesis of the systems that lay behind them. Active constitution of conscious engagement in transforming the world through industrial technologies is mediated through the 'passively synthesised' assumptions and cultural values that are embodied within the machines. Thus, the process of 'enframement' that Chapters 2 and 3 dealt with is a direct product of the way consciousness is constituted in an increasingly systematised, technologically-penetrated world. Reality is transformed *through* the assumptions, not independently of them. Consciousness is transformed *along the trajectory* that the sedimented assumptions that mediate the consciousness/reality relationship can allow. The dialectic spiral of interaction between consciousness/culture and 'reality' is therefore fundamentally constrained by the mediating assumptions of the industrial world.

As a consequence, what at a first level of analysis can be viewed as a 'cultural text' of technology – to be *read* with some degree of autonomy by the culture 'reader', becomes a cultural *frame*. That is, the cultural values of the 'text' penetrate consciousness itself, yielding a 'passively synthesised' set of assumptions and values that set the horizon *within which* the technology text *can* be read. The 'frame' is as the frame to a painting. The frame of a painting signifies to the viewer that what lies inside is separated off from the outside world and is to be seen as a work of art, with all the cultural values this implies. The 'frame' of assumptions and values that the technology text implies to consciousness signifies to the 'reader' that what lies inside conscious *experience* generally is to be read *in terms of* the technology text's basic values, not outside them. According to the level of alignment between consciousness, culture and the technology text's values, the person within a technologically mediated world cannot however see the edges of the frame. For the frame is contiguous with the meanings that *can* be constructed within. The 'frame' is therefore beyond conscious scrutiny, the same way that a child's prelingual cultural experience is beyond immediate conscious analysis.

This process of increasing *enframement* is exacerbated by the associated level of *anonymity* that is experienced as, with the 'ubiquity' of technological systems, the centrality of our subjective world shrinks in the wider context of received knowledge of the whole world outside. As Schutz demonstrates, consciousness grasps the world that is outside immediate reach through abstracting and typifying that which is glimpsed over the horizon of direct inter-subjective experience – through 'ideal-typical' construction.[14] Typified social types or cultural objectivations are malleable, or open to reflexive scrutiny (active synthesis), *only* to the extent that these typifications can be drawn into reach, into an immediate 'we' relationship that can be filled with content. Otherwise, that which is 'anonymous' remains rigid and enframing. Thus, as the salience of the immediate subjective world shrinks along with its increasing enframement and penetration by wider technological systems, the received meanings of the systems themselves expand in their power to enframe. This process stands at the core of what appears to be 'inevitability' of the technology trajectory, the basic premise of 'technological determinism'. Instead of the appearance of inevitability residing in the *machines*, this appearance therefore lies within the processes of *consciousness* engaging in a world that is transforming according to technological logic.

The process of enframement subsequently becomes a self-feeding spiral. As Thomas Luckmann and Peter Berger observe, when experience of the world is largely *outside* direct inter-subjective mirroring, the person must depend increasingly on more concrete objectivations – in which ideal-typical constructions of received cultural meanings are housed.[15] Therefore, increased cultural salience is awarded to 'objects' that house these meanings. 'Objects' – like cars, houses, consumer appliances and so on – therefore locate the person, their meaning system and status, within the sea of anonymity they confront. 'Location' extends both ways, for the objects mirror the meanings of the anonymous world to individual consciousness, at the same time as they can be seen in consciousness to *present* the individual to the world of strangers who wander past the locked front door of direct subjective engagement. The need for 'objectivation' amidst anonymity prepares a seed-bed within which increased penetration of subjectivity by technological systems can flower. Each new object that stands between subjectivity and the anonymous world widens the gap between the two. Each new object therefore prepares the way for the next generation of objects that can both protect the subjective world from anonymous intruders, and make sense of the subjective world in terms of objectivations of the world that (by its distance) is remote, scary and dangerous. Flowing as a tidal wave in front of the process of technological enframement there is therefore a clearing of the beaches for the wave to continue unhindered. At the level of the very processes of consciousness and culture constitution, the path for continued progress is smoothed by the need that technological enframement itself injects into social demand for objects that the system can produce.

It is therefore no wonder that the trajectory of industrial technology appears 'autonomous' and is expansionary. Equally it is no wonder that the trajectory's path of enframement is so powerful, or that the trajectory has had such a massive impact on vanquishing traditional cultures. For the power rests not in external control but in the processes of consciousness and culture within which the meaning of the trajectory is constituted and willingly accepted. The legitimation of external hegemony and the power interests that foster the trajectory follow naturally from this process.

Culture and Technology

The Holistic Character of Culture

The structure of culture in any society is built on the foundations of consciousness outlined above. The most basic assumptions of the culture provide a passively-constituted 'grammar' for lived experience. Shake these deep foundations and the entire edifice of meaning and purpose in daily experience crumbles: when the foundations are eroded, the domain of 'here-and-now' action becomes unintelligible, a deep existential threat, for the person cannot actively constitute meanings as there are no longer stable predicates on which to base them. As in the traditional society cases, the quest that follows in everyday life is for new symbols (particularly of modernist artefacts) that by their passive constitution of meaning deliver a new grammar for meaning.

Within the industrialising world, the cultural *frame* follows from dependence on produced object symbols to mediate subjectivity (where culture is constituted) and anonymity (from which culture is received). The object world provides both prop for inter-subjective poverty – in understanding and relating to the 'whole' – and at the same time is constituent of the cultural patterns that make sense of 'here-and-now' action. Thus, it is no-longer-established, inter-subjectively communicated folkways that structure consciousness, but anonymously produced *objects* that stand *for* the social whole of meaning. Shake the system that produces these objects of consciousness, and the whole system of culture itself is at risk, an existential threat of such magnitude that a progressively technologising society is wedded irrevocably to the technology system's trajectory. That is, the society is wedded to the trajectory *until* it is confronted by an inescapable 'new' reality, where, for example, the ecological destruction caused by system progression must be dealt with – and change to culture and consciousness follow. However, as the argument concerning 'enframement' demonstrates, even perception of crisis itself is mediated through the very system that creates it, and will therefore be resisted until absolutely *no* alternative except radical change is available. One potent example displays the depth of this resistance – where the reality of crisis of megalithic proportions stands immediately over the horizon of everyday experience, but is consistently denied for what it is. The example is that of the immediacy of the threat to the entire survival of humankind that is posed by the proliferation of nuclear systems of destruction. It is unarguably *real* that the people and the culture of Europe could be destroyed within four minutes of a single human decision, and the rest of the world not long after. But, response, particularly by the US government, is to stall arms-limitation negotiations until *technological systems* of verification of the 'enemy's' intention are developed. And, with more conviction, action is taken to deal with the shortness of reaction lead-time by placing responsibility for decision-making about when to wage war in the hands (or circuitries) of 'efficient' machines, whilst building super, outer-space, ubiquitous, technological systems of defence. The 'reality' of imminent annihilation of reality itself is therefore denied in favour of building more pervasive technological systems that symbolise safety or 'winnability'. The reality of potential annihilation is painted over with ideologically comforting colours of *our* technological mastery, a painting that thus obscures the reality that lies behind in the same way that an advertising billboard obscures the natural world. As in this example, enframement of the whole culture by a technological trajectory is very powerful indeed.

The power of technological enframement over the constitution of culture and cultural response is revealed further through exploring the nature of culture a little more. Culture is fundamentally predicated on survival – of a society that can deal realistically with its physical and social world. Yet the cultural mores that allow nuclear war to be a possibility threaten society with total self-destruction, a terrible paradox. As 'meaning-seeking' animals however, survival is not merely physical, but also to do with survival of a meaningful world without which we cannot act at all. Every intention and action 'here-and-now' is an engagement in making sense of the *whole* of experience. Therefore, inscribed within the cultural frame are depictions of the whole, not just of the myriad collection of separate bits – in an ontology, in an epistemology of how we can know what is real and worth taking note of, and in a morality that allows us to know how we *should* act within the received whole. Thus, everything that is not intelligible to a society – in terms of this holistic package – is either denied (as UFOs and mystical spirits are denied within industrial culture) or incorporated (as alien technological artefacts are incorporated into traditional societies).

Denial or incorporation are both predicated on the assumptions of the pre-existing *whole* cultural frame. Meanwhile, everything that *is* intelligible within a society aligns with the dominant cultural assumptions that prevail. Thus the *possibility* of nuclear war, or at least its full existential meaning, is denied. Or the existential meaning of *possibility* is hidden under the distorting rubric of militarist interests that claim minimal trauma through 'winnability', or of religious fundamentalists who see only the light of God's cleansing power in the darkness of Armageddon. For to assert the full meaning of 'possibility' by the ruling classes that control or the subservient classes that depend, would be to deny the basic holistic 'grammar' of the technology culture. It is this same grammar that produces not only nuclear threat, but also the objects of direct experience that make sense of the world, and make it comfortable (existentially) to live within.

Culture is a 'complex whole'. The overall package includes everything that has meaning, and that is everything we can perceive. As E. B. Tylor observes, culture therefore encompasses meanings of not only its *material* elements (from arrowheads to nuclear missiles), but also the *non-material* products of group life – mores, laws, customs, as well as significations of the salience of *meaningful relationships* – between the separate domains and institutions of the culture.[16] But, as in the link between nuclear war, economic 'progress', philosophy, ontology and existential security, we do not have actively to constitute fresh meanings for each of these separate elements. Instead, the elements of culture are organised as in a Chinese puzzle in terms of each other. The alternative of total chaos of disparate meaning systems would make human action impossible. In dealing with separate domains of meaning within 'here-and-now' action we therefore must have a means of relating to the whole in order to make sense of the immediate. 'Superordinate symbols' provide this means of integration. These are 'objectivations' that house the meanings of the whole culture, and direct our attention to their consequences in every element of experience. Superordinate symbols embody the highly abstract and reality-defining definitions of the culture – in any society. Superordinate symbols are 'sacred' in the sense that they stand apart from the 'profane' world of everyday experience, but through their 'contagiousness', command and penetrate the profane.[17] In a society where world views, structures of authority and ideology are commanded by religion,

Such religious symbols ... are felt somehow to sum up, for those for whom they are resonant, what is known about the way the world is, the quality of the emotional life it supports, and the way one ought to behave while in it. Sacred symbols thus relate an ontology and a cosmology to an aesthetics and a morality: their peculiar power comes from their presumed ability to identify fact with value at the most fundamental level, to give to what is otherwise merely actual, a comprehensive normative import.[18]

Clifford Geertz goes on to demonstrate the superordinate symbolism of the circle to the Sioux Oglala Indians:

The Oglala believe the circle to be sacred because the great spirit caused everything in nature to be round except stone. Stone is the implement of destruction. The sun and the sky, the earth and the moon are round like a shield, though the sky is deep like a bowl. Everything that breathes is round like the stem of a plant. Since the great spirit has caused everything to be round mankind should look upon the circle as sacred, for it is the symbol of all things in nature except stone. It is also the symbol of the circle that makes the edge of the world and therefore of the four winds that travel there. Consequently it is also the symbol of the year. The day, the night, and the moon go in a circle above the sky. Therefore the circle is a symbol of these divisions of time and hence the symbol of all time.

For these reasons the Oglala make their tipis circular, their camp-circle circular, and sit in a circle at the ceremonies. The circle is also the symbol of the tip and of shelter. If one makes a circle for an ornament and it is not divided in any way, it should be understood as the symbol of the world and of time.[19]

One has only to add, in keeping with the earlier Third World case studies, how fragile the wholeness of culture becomes when white man introduced square houses. The houses symbolised the encroachment of the invading culture on everyday life, at the same time as they symbolised the power of this invasion that was located within the guns and other powerful new technologies that supported homestead living at the frontier. Along with emaciation of the power of the circle came erosion of the wholeness of the Sioux Oglala culture.

Within industrial society religion has lost its power to define, for the wholeness of culture is based not on structures of religious experience, but on structures of industrial technological progression. Religion has thus become a separate and specialised domain that is 'secularised' – in relating doctrine to everyday life within industrial society, and 'privatised' in separating religious commitment from the anonymous world of external observers.[20] Religious symbols therefore fit into the superordinate symbolism of industrialisation, not the other way round. This is a direct product of the commanding enframement that the technological trajectory injected into society's cultural veins. By way of an aside at this stage, it also should be added that the rise of the superordinacy of industrialism's symbols grew out of prior transformations of religious symbolism – an issue I will take up in the next chapter.

The power of superordinate symbols however did not decline. For this power derives from a fundamental property of culture, not from the characteristics of a particular society. The 'sacred' symbol simply shifted elsewhere. As Durkheim observed, by representing God, religious totems represent the society's order,[21] by representing the dominant objectifications of the industrial order, 'leading objects' (as Henri Lefebvre refers to central industrial symbols)[22] represent (and command) an emergent trajectory of industrial society's order. Three examples display the picture.

An early superordinate symbol of industrialisation was the factory. Within the factory, the clock symbolised the discipline of calculated life that the factory's social relations of production and repressive discipline represented. However, the factory itself (with all that it symbolised for those who worked within) was plainly visible within the everyday life of all. Smoke-stacks and factory buildings belched their way across the landscape, and into people's consciousness from the late eighteenth into the early nineteenth centuries. The symbol of the factory smoke-stack represented all that was to come, a mechanised order that was at its birth strongly contested – in machinery sabotage, in philosophic questioning by elements of the middle classes, and in cultural patterns that referred back to the rural past rather than forward to the modernist future. But, according to its power to enframe, the symbol kept marching across the landscape of the economy and geography, and increasingly confronted people's immediate life-world with the permanence of industrialisation. What the smoke-stack symbol embodied was a quite new order. This was an order in which change was paramount, so it therefore threatened traditional values at their core. It was an order that implied quite new social relations of production – where technical systems and those who controlled them dominated the basic cultural grammar of rhythm, time and the centrality of humanly-constituted meaning. The order implied new statuses – displacing the power of the aristocracy and the church with the emergent bourgeoisie. And the order produced objects that had a new salience to culture, in that they were available to an increasingly large proportion of the population rather than an elite, and implied materialism and human control as an adequate replacement of God in controlling the order of things. The factory replaced the cross.

A second core example of industrialism's superordinate symbolism came later in the symbols that were furnished by the first very large-scale production of electricity. Just as the world was on the verge of organising life according to the newly invented electricity generation systems – between 1895 and 1901 – three enormous (for the day) electricity generation stations were installed. The first was erected at Niagara Falls in 1895, where three 5,000-horsepower two-phase turbogenerators 'signalled the coming of age of a new technology'. Shortly thereafter, in 1901, a 1,500-kilowatt two-phase steam turbogenerator was installed at Hartford Electric Light Company, and a 5,000-kilowatt steam turbine unit was erected at the Fisk Street station of the Commonwealth Edison Company in Chicago. As Thomas Hughes observed, these power plants 'opened an era'.[23] They were publicly very visible in the plethora of press coverage that accompanied their installation. Yet the power plants were remote from daily life in the suburban environments that fed from them – and therefore were symbols of the vast power of the *background* 'system' that commanded thereafter urban design,[24] and the seduction of the whole society into a world of consumer appliances. The new power plant symbols therefore conveyed the new order of technologically-systematised living, of 'object-centred' culture, and of social relations of consumerism (as, for example, was earlier demonstrated in the 'proletarianisation' of the middle-class housewife).[25] More than that they were *big* - in dominant command of both the landscape and the technological capabilities of humankind. Factories brought religion into productive life through their superordinate symbolism. The electricity-generation systems brought productive life into daily living through all that the symbols conveyed. And technology marched further into the subjective life of the society, conveyed as it was, by the symbols that replaced the old order.

Interestingly enough, the power of the symbol in the social order it represents, is demonstrated also in what was happening across the Atlantic Ocean at the same time. In England, steam power still ruled. English inventors had developed a number of the patents that were central to the burgeoning development of electricity generation, but had not capitalised on them, whilst the leading edge of change was being commanded by Germany and the US.[26] Meanwhile the design of factory steam engines was becoming increasingly influenced by the aesthetics of classical times – in alignment with the 'classics' (rather than technology) dominated education and ideological systems that still persisted, along with the decaying empire.[27] Anyone who cares to view the display of stationary steam engines in Munich's Deutsche Museum can see a progression of design towards machines where representations of Grecian columns provide supports and the moving beam. The symbol of the steam engine was becoming a symbol of past glory rather than present industrial reality, and represented exactly where Great Britain stood in the changing technological world of the late nineteenth century.

The third superordinate symbol in the present set of examples is that of the automobile.[28] The automobile symbolised the entry of the machine system into personal life. It conveyed images of individual power and status – through personal possession of the machine. It implied the whole of suburban life and consumerism; it implied progress – where each new model implied the future obsolescence-based series.[29] And, the automobile implied the whole assembly-line production *system* that stood behind it. The automobile stood for, and commanded, the consumer oriented phase of the twentieth-century industrial order.

The superordinate symbols of industrialism change, along with the changing order of the society itself. The leading symbols are connected in a progressive trajectory, where each emergent superordinate symbol implies those that went before. The symbols are 'sacred' as religious symbols are in a religion-dominated social order. This is so even though the objects are directly in and used within the profane world. The 'sacredness' (or setting apart from the profane) lies in the objects' 'opacity'. That is, the industrial symbols are set apart from the everyday world in that their content is a mystery for it embodies stocks of knowledge that are simply not accessible to the layperson, and imply obeisance of the layperson to the larger system in which 'ultimate' knowledge is controlled. Indeed, with increasing size, power, complexity, ubiquity and interconnectedness written into the object symbols, their level of opacity and therefore inaccessible 'command', is continuously increasing. As such, and in representing the social order and cultural meanings as a whole, along with the trajectory of change that is built into this order, the superordinate symbols command with increasing power. They make daily life intelligible in terms of the overall industrial order, and therefore lay claim to the whole of experience within the inter-subjective world, the domain in which the culture is constituted and reasserted every day of our lives.

Ideology, Power, Culture and Technology
The whole picture of industrial culture is painted on a wall of *enframement* that surrounds the domain of everyday life. The

technological system is assumed, 'passively synthesised', in every action that is cast within its shadow. The wall stands for the world beyond, and mediates the relationship between the subjectivity of here-and-now action and the anonymity of the *whole* culture that lies outside direct experience.

However the wall is not experienced as a separate entity, but lies inside day-to-day life. Superordinate industrial symbols are embodied *in* objects of experience, and stand for, and in front of, the entire order that lies behind. Yet the symbolic objects convey a sacredness, a separation of the ultimate meanings of the system order from profane living – through the mystery and opacity of the inner workings of the objects that stand in front of us. The symbolic objects therefore imply an order that is beyond active constitution in daily life, an order of inevitability.

In line with a culture-centred view, power to *do* only exists in a context of power to *define*. Thus, those who control the master symbols and their content control the social order. This is particularly the case in control over the means of productive interaction (the social relations of production) and communication – for it is from this base that cultural meanings are constituted. Where social relations of production appear to be determined by the inevitability of their technological frame – as is the case in the economic pragmatism that characterises most debates about technological unemployment in the 1980s – the interests of the ruling classes can remain unexposed, but powerful. Where means of communication are determined by technological possibility – as in telecommunications and the media – the means mediate the human message, and hide the power interests and values that lie behind.

As in any society, power cannot be maintained for any length of time by coercion that is regarded as illegitimate by the people.[30] Legitimacy persists as long as daily experience aligns with perceptions of meaning (and horizons of accepted privilege), and trajectory of the order as a whole. Thus, a ruling class's power is predicated on *alignment* between the legitimating ideology that the people accept, and the continuous constitution of the order and its meaning *within daily life*. (Ideology is seen here as the cultural system of beliefs as invaded by, and shaped according to, the vested interests of the ruling class.)[31] The people remain silent whilst they *see* through the filters of ideology. Existing power interests crumble when the people *see through* the ideology itself. The test lies in the alignment of ideology with daily life experience.

Thus, the ruling classes of industrial capitalism have maintained their privilege through maintaining hegemony over the means of production of ideas that could otherwise threaten the ruling interests' position of authority to command.[32] Hegemony is maintained through education systems that align with 'system' interests on which the ruling class's authority depends. The overt and covert role of education in feeding and maintaining early industrial capitalism is developed in the next chapter. Hegemony (particularly today) is maintained in media images that *assume* rather than expose the system and its contradictions. This is a hegemony over the 'grammar' of the cultural text, the content of which is subjectively experienced and reasserted in daily life. As Ralph Milliband observes, the capitalist class seeks to persuade society not only to accept its policies, but also the ethos, values and goals that are central to its way of life. Thus, the oppressive nature of capitalism is hidden behind the images of neighbourliness, innocence, parental love, security and reliability that characterise family television programmes: for the images disguise capitalist oppression in the immediate 'benevolent, public-spirited, socially responsible capitalist' who appears at home exhibiting loving care for his family.[33] Hegemony therefore lies in control of cultural grammar and the way in which it is constituted, rather than in coercive control of the people.

However, as with family television (where programmes persist only because the ratings remain high), the legitimacy of the ruling class is maintained ultimately because the people want it, or can see no alternative. The power of hegemony to legitimise therefore persists because it remains in *alignment* with what the people's own constructions of meaning tell them is true and desired. As Louis Althusser affirms, ideology is a structural feature of any society. Its functions are to cement the society's unity. In a class-based society, ideology keeps the exploitation by the ruling class 'opaque' to the subservient class, makes 'mythical' the representation of the world that is necessary for the maintenance of social cohesion.[34] Cohesion (ruling class interest) is therefore eroded as soon as lived experience conflicts with ideology, and in turn renders the interests of the ruling class transparent and illegitimate.

Thus, power and the horizons of ideology are themselves *enframed* within the main dynamic principles of the culture itself. As this chapter has shown, these principles are universal, but have assumed a particular shape with industrialism whereby a systems, object-centred, technology-penetrated trajectory has become the major frame within which culture is acted out. As I will show in discussing early industrialisation in the next two chapters, where ideology moves out of line with this trajectory frame, the ideology is demolished, and the power of the ruling class erodes – for the ideology is alienated from cultural experience at the core of the consciousness/culture process.

Ideology is housed in the society's superordinate symbols – maintaining its power to distort or define culture *in terms of* ruling class interests only as long as the symbols continue to represent the industrial system's trajectory and the people's experience of it. This is the case not only under the authority structures of capitalism, but also under the industrial order of communist or socialist states. As one example, Joseph Stalin erected a superordinate symbol to his regime in the aircraft industry he promoted during the time of his major political purges of the 1930s. But, although drawing on deep cultural and mythological roots of Russian society, the way he defined the symbol – in terms of the regime's power to prove its modernist lead over the world through achieving air records – did not align with the international technological trajectory of the evolving aircraft system.[35] The symbol was demolished (and thus served to erode Stalin's legitimation of the Soviet regime) when Hitler invaded Russia in 1941 and destroyed Russia's air defence system within days. The symbol was demolished because the meanings did not align with the technological trajectory that even Stalin could not command into his own ideological control.

The *power* of the superordinate symbol when it aligns with daily experience is demonstrated in Mahatma Gandhi's strategy to overthrow the British Raj in India. Central to this strategy was the way that Gandhi exposed the repression that lay behind two key symbols of imperialist control over daily life – salt and imported cloth. When, as a counter-demonstration to the arrival of the Prince of Wales in Bombay, Gandhi lit a great bonfire of the foreign cloth the crowd had been wearing, he was showing them that in buying foreign cloth they were supporting the British Raj. Similarly, when Gandhi led the great march from his ashram in Sabartmi to the sea at Dandi to make salt, and thus defy the iniquitous Salt Laws, he was showing the people that they did not *have* to accept the system's rule over daily life.[36] The level of public resistance that followed could not be contained by the full might of the British empire, and the Raj shortly thereafter withdrew, leaving India its Independence.

But, with the coming of Independence, Nehru's modernising policies soon erected India's own industrial symbols. India was inescapably a part of the industrial world, and Gandhi's village-centred symbols of, for example, the 'spinning wheel', simply disappeared under the onslaught of the new industrial, science and consumer symbols that represented the meaning of India's participation in the international technological trajectory.[37] Before Independence the industrial symbols represented external repression, and therefore aligned poverty-stricken daily experience with an illegitimate power. After Independence, the symbols represented India's quest for equality within the world's technologically determined economic frame, and therefore represented *escape* from the repression of experienced poverty in daily life.

As with all other elements of culture – the meanings of stocks of knowledge, social relations of production, means of communication, and so on – the power of ruling classes persists *only* whilst the class's hegemony and control align at the deepest levels with the cultural grammar of all society's meanings. As is demonstrated in the present chapter, within industrial society, the cultural grammar itself is fundamentally predicated on the trajectory of the technological system itself. Thus, power itself only remains shored up as long as the power centres retain alignment with the cultural grammar of the technological system.

What happened as society moved across the threshold of industrialisation, from the late eighteenth to the early nineteenth centuries, demonstrates the significance of this alignment – between the dynamic dimensions of technological systems when viewed as cultural forces, and the deepest structures of culture. Observation of this historic period shows the importance of this alignment for not only the assertion of ruling class power, but also for the formation of class, and in particular, for the shaping of the system's trajectory of enframement itself. For it was during this period that the values written into the 'technology text' emerged as a 'frame' within which wider culture was constituted. This is the subject of the next two chapters.

Part II
The Historic Drama of Industrial Society

6

Industrial Capitalism on Cue

The Entry of Industrial Technology

In one of the most remote corners of the world, an outer island of the Cooks in the South Pacific, the villagers decided that modern technology was too problematic. They took the one pick-up truck they had acquired three years before, conducted a traditional funeral ceremony, and they buried it.

This event occurred nearly thirty years ago. But its message is highly pertinent to the mood of resistance to modern technology that is spreading through the region today. In the Cook Island example, the people precipitously found themselves relatively wealthy in the wider cash economy when the world discovered and bought the pearl shell that the villagers dived for off their reefs. Subsequently, the people found that they had to do very little to maintain a relatively easy lifestyle. They imported alcohol and spent a considerable amount of time getting drunk. Health problems followed close on the heels of the hedonistic self-indulgence that ready access to cash permitted. Infant mortality, for example, grew to 50 per cent of live births. Sixty of the villagers pursued the benefits of wealth by taking a trip to the 'bright lights' of the capital, Raratonga. At the end of a spending spree they took home a number of gasoline-powered electricity generators and the pick-up truck. One year later however, in absence of technical capabilities and spare parts, none of the newly acquired technologies was working. The truck supplier was by this time marketing a new model and could not supply spare parts at all. Meanwhile, nothing of the people's village lifestyle had improved. Two years on, and they interred the rusting, immobile vehicle in a symbolic gesture of rejection of the fruits of modernism they had originally been seduced by.

As tiny island states standing at the far edge of modernist progress, islands of the Pacific have been late to enter the modern industrial world. The impact however has been profound. This is so first because their geographic and resource advantages made the nations highly vulnerable to the interests of high technology-based super power exploitation. And second, the impact has been profound because the seductive demonstration effects of the modernism that encroached – along with easier access to the international community – have 'burnt like a cigarette on a silken fabric' into the culture and traditional practices that have existed unchanged for centuries. The states are presently reeling under the social and economic dislocations that modernism has unleashed. But they are starting to find a voice of resistance. Unfortunately it is no longer as easy to get rid of the encroachment as it was for the Cook Islanders. The new technologies and lifestyles cannot simply be buried, and they won't go away.

On the surface, the traumatic and pervasive enframement of social life and adjustment appears similar to what happened in England as the late eighteenth-century Industrial Revolution marched across the social landscape. Many people then too sought to 'bury the truck' in smashing the machines that were identified with this encroaching industrial repression, or in seeking to have the industrial machinery exported to the colonies to leave England's pastoral lands untroubled. By the time that the nineteenth century matured however the technological frame of industrialisation had marched through the centre of proto-industrial society. As today in the Pacific, it had chained the people and their culture to the emerging machine system.

There are however fundamental differences between the situation of the Pacific nations today and the situation of England during the early Industrial Revolution in the way that technological enframement interacted with pre-existing culture.

In developing nations of the 1980s the people are confronted by a fully formed and articulated frame. Behind the immediate artefacts that are experienced lies an articulated background of factory, transport, energy, communications, market and knowledge *systems* that are complete. The steel prison has no escape hatch. In the late eighteenth century the enframing systems were just emerging in the form of the technology text. The prior feudal culture was adjusting and living alongside new and immanent technological alternatives. The iron prison appeared to have an escape hatch, but it was kept closed, at least at first, by direct coercive repression.

In developing countries of the 1980s the people are confronted by implied values and levels of technical sophistication that *directly* conflict with traditional values and technical capabilities. At the turn of the nineteenth century the emergent industrial society was building new culture–technology alignments on deep cultural changes that had gone before.

In developing countries of the 1980s the people are confronted by exploitation (and cultural transformation) that is operating principally through market and consumer demand mechanisms. At the turn of the nineteenth century exploitation was through direct coercion particularly of marginal, displaced men, women and children into a rhythm of factory labour.

The Pacific Islanders do not *have* to participate in an industrialised economy. Rather, along with the prior destruction of their own traditional ways, and along with the vibrant new images of modernism that are erected in front of them, they *want* to. The cost is only perceived later. Counter to this, in early industrialising England, the edge of cultural change was not seduced by consumerist attraction, but was enforced by productive might and exploitation of a labour force that had *no choice* but to participate simply to survive.

Thus, both present-day Pacific Islanders and late eighteenth-century English people stand on the edge of technological enframement, testing the shark-filled waters with their toes. But the difference between a completed frame and one that was emerging are significant. At the time of the Industrial Revolution, the cultural adjustments to technological change were emerging *within* rather than *against* prior systems of values and meanings. At least this was the case for the ruling classes of the time. Where the edge of adjustment was most in conflict with past ways – primarily for the subordinate classes – direct coercion was necessary to make the transition possible. Today, the subordinate classes are willingly following the ruling classes' lead.

Through exploring the difference between these two cultural dynamics we can therefore identify what it is that has made the contemporary technological text so powerful over cultural transformation. Consequently, this chapter seeks to explore the original emergence of an industrialised culture–technology alignment as a way of seeing where the cultural power of the technology text, and thence the technological text, came from in the first place. Later, in Chapter 9, I will explore the way in which the technology text came to rest in a mirror of production values within a consumerist culture, and therefore acquired the power of *seduction* over people's lifestyle preferences.

Conflict, Coercion and Adjustment

The Arrival of 'Calculated Life'
Charles Dickens, writing in the mid-nineteenth century, portrayed life in a town dominated by machine-based production. In his book *Hard Times* he described an industrial town as encompassing a society where everything was quantified, mechanised, calculated as 'so many hundred hands in this mill; so many hundred horse steam power', calculated in every respect except in terms of the 'soul of men'.[1] Life, he observed, was

dictated as by the piston of a steam engine which worked monotonously up and down, 'like the head of an elephant in a state of melancholy madness'.[2]

Karl Marx, writing at much the same time, looked inside the factory and observed the same dependency of productive life on dominating machine rhythms. The 'self-acting' steam engine, with its governing mechanism was, as Marx described it,

> a mechanical monster whose body fills whole factories, and whose demon power, at first veiled under the slow and measured motion of his giant limbs, at length breaks out into the fast and furious whirl of his countless working organs...[3] ... the labourer becomes a mere appendage to an already existing material condition of production...[4] ... the workshop may ... be considered as an engine, the parts of which are man.[5] [so that] ... labour ... [is] ...subsumed under the total process of the machinery itself, as itself only a link of the system, whose unity exists not in the living workforce, but rather in the living (active) machinery, which confronts his individual, insignificant doings as a mighty organism.[6]

The 'Age of Machinery' as Thomas Carlyle described it[7] had by the mid-nineteenth century gripped the heart of British society and commanded the rhythm of life, not only within factory work, but also in the supportive and burgeoning town systems that had grown up around them. By the mid-nineteenth century three generations of people had passed through the machine discipline of industrial capitalism. The Machine Age was an inescapable fact of life, a commanding force that could no longer be denied as it measured and controlled all aspects of social and cultural life. Society had 'adjusted' to this 'remorseless tragedy', but the development of factory discipline had by no means been a smooth and accepted transformation.

As Pollard observes, factory discipline 'was new, and called for as much innovation as the technical inventions of the age.'[8] The prior rhythm of agricultural labour and cottage craft was very different indeed. Agricultural and craft labour may have involved hard, grinding, bare subsistence labour, but it was organised against the rhythm of nature's harvests and planting times, the rhythms of the day, and against autonomous decisions to work when food or wealth was required but not when economic income was good. Thus, as Hobsbawn observed, 'cloth workers in particular had been notorious for lives of alternate spells of frenzied, round the clock labour followed by bouts of drinking, idleness, or work on their own farm plots.'[9] Industrial labour on the other hand had to abide by the rhythm of machine systems, not nature, or according to autonomous participation in a fluctuating economy.

The path towards industrialised labour started well before the first steam engines were hooked up to factory systems. By the time that Boulton and Watt integrated a steam engine into a factory at Papplewick, Nottinghamshire in 1785 and the 'balance was finally tipped in favour of large-scale enterprise',[10] the idea of industrialised time discipline was well established, though by no means well accepted amongst the labouring classes. Crowley's Iron Works in 1700 for example, developed a time-based organisational system which included time-sheets, timekeepers, informers, and fines that were based on an entire civil and penal code that sought to prevent workers from 'slacking off'. Workers were penalised for the slightest deviations from persistent work for the master's interest, following: 'calculations after, deductions for being, at taverns, alehouses, coffee houses, breakfast, dinner, playing, sleeping, smoaking, singing, reading of news history, quarrelling, contention, disputes on anything foreign to my business, any way loytering'.[11] Josiah Wedgwood introduced a time discipline that was widely approved by the emerging bourgeoisie into his ceramics manufacturing business through a 'clocking-in' system, and rewards for regularity.[12]

Labour patterns persisted in their irregularity however, for two primary reasons. The first was that the emerging industrial form was only one amongst several competing alternatives for employment of productive labour. The second reason was that it was not until the productive system was attached to external sources of power that the rhythm of labour in the foundry or factory was controlled by the technical system *per se*, rather than merely the exhortations and penalties of the bosses. With the industrial system growing up alongside traditional practices, people of the late seventeenth century often participated in *both* agricultural and industrially oriented employment. Cornwall tin-miners for example, were also pilchard fishermen.[13] Monday was often taken off as an extension of Sunday's free time, a practice that persisted into the subsequent full industrial period, where 'Saint Monday' became for a long time institutionalised as the day when work was 'put-out' or 'taken-in', or when machinery repairs were done.[14]

Idleness and personal autonomy of labour were against the interests of capitalist profitability. But, whilst the people had choices, the capitalists had little real power to impose discipline on a recalcitrant work force. Indeed as Stephen Marglin observes, 'The recruitment of the first generation of workers willing and able to submit to an externally determined discipline [was] a continuing obstacle to the expansion of the factory system.'[15]

Exercise of Social Power: Breaking the Yoke of Craft Production

Whilst the craft unions retained power, and whilst manufacturing activities could be conducted outside the direct supervision of the capitalists, the 'problem' of discipline remained. The reverse salient for capitalism therefore was the need to *break* this power and autonomy, as a precondition for the imposition of a discipline that was an anathema to the cultural ways of people who had yet to learn to bow down to the machine.

The path towards industrial discipline therefore started with breaking the power of the guilds. This was done more through political power and legislation than through more efficient economic competition. The early profits of capitalism permitted the influence of capitalists within the political realm. As a result of this influence, legislation was introduced to free up the markets for labour and commodities, along with strict rules of industrial discipline and harsh penalities for embezzlement (by employees). These were institutional arrangements that fostered capitalist power of accumulation at direct expense to the hegemony, apprenticeship discipline and market control that guild-based production was based upon.[16]

The early development of the eighteenth century 'putting-out' system, where the capitalist interposed himself between the market and cottage/family-based production, depended on these legislative changes. But the 'putting-out' system itself had major disadvantages as far as capitalism was concerned. These disadvantages arose particularly because the capitalist was unable to control 'embezzlement' and 'laziness' effectively when the manufactures were conducted at home. The capitalist was further disadvantaged under this system as he could not adequately tune the levels of output to market opportunity. Thus, having broken the power of traditional guild organisation of craft labour through legislating a free labour market, the putting-out system was but a transitionary phase in the progress towards a factory system where labour could be supervised, controlled and disciplined.

Consequently, as Marglin further observes, the development of centralised and hierarchically organised factory systems did not take place because of the system's technical superiority, at least in the first instance. Rather, the factory system better allowed capitalists to further their interest of accumulation through wielding tighter control of the *discipline* of the labour force.[17] *Technical superiority* did not provide the power to overwhelm the alternative cottage-based modes of productive labour until later. This technical power remained dormant until steam power was harnessed into the factory system. With the possibility of large-scale factory systems that steam power allowed, 'technical' superiority then slowly started to take command. It directly displaced the cottage industries of handloom weavers and so on, along with the opportunity that large-scale systems offered for intense division of labour (and therefore technical efficiency) and employment of a relatively unskilled (and therefore cheap) labour force.

Consequently, the power of the technology text (of itself) did not originally impose a new discipline on a feudalistic culture. Rather, it was the political and economic power associated with early capitalist accumulation that framed the choices and alternatives of the labour force, and required they abide by coercive, *socially* mediated discipline.

Exercise of Social Power: The Enforcement of Discipline
Two basic means of co-opting workers into the new factory system were applied. Both were repressive. But the level of repression that could be exercised depended on how much choice labour had. Exploitation was much less virulent where labour still possessed craft skills that the capitalists did not yet have the technical means to master or command. However, both for the sake of discipline and 'efficiency' the replacement of these skills that yielded labour autonomy was the next reverse salient of capitalist technological development.

In areas where a level of craft skill was needed, whole families were transmuted out of their cottage into the factory, thus retaining a reliance within factory labour on the former family patterns of authority and collective economic interest. In the early mule-spinning factories for example, adult males worked on a subcontract system that was primarily initiated by the capitalists because of the difficulties they experienced in recruiting and supervising factory labour. The burden of recruitment and supervision was shifted onto the operative spinner. The spinner had the advantage of a significant degree of control over the division of labour associated with 'his' mule, so he could hire and supervise his own children, and in some cases, his wife. Spinners retained this right whilst the technical proficiency of production could not displace their craft skills. Whilst retaining some degree of power, the mule-spinners were thus able to organise themselves, from 1779 onwards until the 1840s, as a strong union, able to resist changes to their work control.[18]

In areas where the technical system of the factory was less dependent on craft capabilities, the use of power by early capitalists to coerce and repress the workforce was significantly more naked. The profit interests of agricultural landlords, backed by coercive legislation that permitted the burning of 'crofters' cottages, and enclosure of common lands, had prepared the way for a labour force that either had to join the factory systems or starve. Therefore, for the most part, with the advent of (particularly large-scale) factory systems, 'factory labour consisted of the most ill-assorted elements: country people driven from their villages by the growth of large estates (that is, by the enclosure movement), disbanded soldiers, paupers, the scum of every class and occupation.'[19]

The early employment of women and children was resisted in factories where male-controlled craft unions saw the lower paid skills of females and children as a threat to their own autonomy and employment. But elsewhere, the lower paid and less skilled labour force was employed extensively. In the direct interest of capital accumulation, wages for women were typically half to two-thirds of the wages paid to men. But, also in the interests of capital accumulation, women and children could more easily be converted out of past feudal ways into the discipline of factory life. Women were considered more docile workers than men, less likely to take collective action, less likely to cause work slow-downs and stoppages.[20] *Discipline* of a marginalised labour force was the key issue for industrial capitalism of the time. As Reinhard Bendix observes, 'Country mills such as those of the Gregs, Ashworth, Drinkwater and Dales drew on indentured child, vagrant and family labour ... entrepreneurs sought to stabilize labour turnover through long contracts, and to discipline labour through autocratic mill communities.'[21] Discipline was therefore enforced not only within the factory, but also through capturing village life and culture into mill-towns where the capitalist controlled communal life and alternate opportunities as well.

As the more marginalised members of these communities, women and children could be controlled more effectively than men. Change to the rhythm of life that the factory system required was a deep cultural transformation of everyday life. Even with direct repression this conversion was difficult. As Andrew Ure commented some years later (in 1835) in the course of extolling the virtues of Arkwright, not for his manufacturing genius, but for his development of an effective means of fostering factory discipline, 'The main difficulty [in factory productivity], is in training human beings to renounce their desultory habits of work, and to identify themselves with the unvarying regularity of the complex automaton ... [thus], it is found nearly impossible to convert persons past the age of puberty, whether drawn from rural or from handicraft occupations, into useful factory hands.'[22]

Whilst this was a legitimate observation of the difficulties people had in adjusting to the grinding regime of factory work, Ure, as an apologist for early capitalism, was also presenting a legitimation for the seemingly boundless exploitation of children. 'They could adjust' the argument went, so children *should* be used for the good of longer term capitalist interests which sought a compliant workforce. What was being done to children was horrific. There is little evidence of intention to assist children to grow up as productive labour; and there is considerable evidence of unbridled slavery.

In the early industrialising period, large consignments of child paupers were drafted from the workhouses of large cities like London and Edinburgh, and sent to Lancashire and elsewhere 'to learn a trade'. 'Child-jobbers' 'scoured the country purchasing children to sell them again at a profit into bondage as factory slaves'. The children were gathered together and packed into waggons like livestock for the four to five days' journey to the factory. Children from the age of 5 years to 21 were then forced to work 14 hours a day, 6 days a week, and locked up on Sundays after an 84-hour working week so that outsiders could not see how wretched they had become. The original mills were erected close to the power source of running water in isolated locations, rewards were offered for runaway 'apprentices', and magistracies and town juries were co-opted so that coroners' inquests were rarely held, and if they were, usually returned a verdict on child death in favour of the millowners. The children had no escape.[23] As late as 1844, Lord Ashley, defending a parliamentary Bill that unsuccessfully sought to introduce 10-hour days for child labour, demonstrated,

> ... that many of the children employed in the spinning mills had to walk or trot distances varying from seventeen to thirty miles every day, their labour being increased by the strain of having continually to lean over the machine and return to an erect position no less than 4,000 to 5,000 times a day.[24]

Meanwhile 35,000 children in Lancashire printworks alone were working a 14- to 15-hour day, and being forced to work nightshifts as well.[25]

The burgeoning factory system required large chimneys to carry away the noxious effluent of the system below. Here, the worst conditions of labour were imposed on children. The Parliamentary Committee of 1817 reported evidence that children from seven or eight years of age were forced as 'climbing boys' (and that also included girls) up industrial chimneys no wider than 14 inches by 9 by 'cruel blows, by pricking the soles of their feet, or by applying to them wisps of lighted straw ... not unfrequently they were suffocated in the flues.' The children were sent up chimneys on fire to extinguish them.[26] As Lord Ashley reported in 1834, '... children were sent up the chimneys naked; they often passed the night naked on a soot heap, and the soot produced a most noxious effect on their flesh.'[27]

A Royal Commission in 1840 showed that some children employed as 'climbing boys', most of them orphans, were as young as four to eight years, and were trained to move up and down the long winding chimney passages by,

Pressing every joint of their bodies against the hard and broken surfaces of the chimneys; to prevent their hands and knees streaming with blood, the children were rubbed with brine before a hot fire to harden the flesh. The skin became choked in every pore, and 'sooty cancer', one of the most terrible formes of physical suffering, was very often the result. They began their day's work at four, three, or even two in the morning, were half-stifled by the hot, sulphurous air in the flues, often got stuck in the chimney, and would faint from terror, exhaustion, and foul air; and then if the usual remedy of lighted straw failed to 'bring them around', they were often half-killed, and sometimes killed outright, by the very means used to extricate them.[28]

All of these practices of child exploitation continued until at least the 1870s, when parliamentary legislation finally started to bite hard into the conditions of industrial child abuse. The practices continued for over 100 years, not just until the labour force had adjusted to the regime of factory employment. Meanwhile, Britain's industrial 'progress', built as it was on such exploitation, peaked in strength, and by the 1870s was starting to decline in the face of America's and Germany's mechanised competition. Certainly the children were able to 'adjust' as employed adults would not. However the children had no choice – from the age of four – but to bow down to the factory system's tyrannical logic of machine-fed greed.

That such abuse was able to persist so long reflects the power of the new profit-making capitalist elite to define the situation and either enforce legislation to maintain it, or forestall legislation that could have brought change.

The landlord interest was strong in Parliament, and outside there was far more sympathy for the rich, whose pockets were threatened, than for friendless little lads whose bodies were tortured, whose souls were debased, and whose lives were sacrificed under an iniquitous system.[29]

Sir Robert Peel, son of a millowner philanthropist, commanded Parliament as Prime Minister through the early nineteenth century in direct interest of the millowners. As Lord Ashley, a reformer, reported in his diary in February 1842, 'Peel's affinities are towards wealth and capital. His heart is manifestly towards the millowners, his lips occasionally for the operatives. His speech was a transcript of his mind – cotton is everything, man nothing.'[30]

Assertiveness of the Technology Text

Meanwhile however, the 'Machinery Question' was, for the populace at large, characterised by a sense of 'struggle, apprehension, excitement and unpredictability' that could only characterise a society that was experiencing for the first time in history an exciting and progressive, but technologically repressive, new order. The acceptance of the new order was not only because of coercive power of the capitalist elite, but because England as a whole was attracted, but at the same time concerned, by an order that promised millennial progress in equal measure to the repression that seemed to be necessary to make it happen. As Maxine Berg observes,

> For some who contemplated the prospects of wealth and power the machine might bring, the experience of technical change was a novelty and an excitement. But alongside an emergent industrial landscape large sectors of the economy remained traditional. And to many, the implications of the new machines were not at all welcome.[31]

Thus, at the same time as enchantment with machines was reflected in the substitution of models of machines for children's toys 'to rouse the faculty of invention, and confer the habit of pursuing trains of thought to a great extent' (in the 1790s),[32] machine-breaking mobs were mobilising across the English landscape.[33]

The capitalists saw their newly acquired power lay in the machinery that they controlled. Through the same access to Parliament that their profits and influence allowed in the sanctioning of child exploitation, they sought to retain hegemony over their machines. Thus, in the 1770s, restrictive laws had been passed on the mobility of both machines and machine artisans. These laws which reinforced the autocracy of the millowner were steadily extended through the first part of the nineteenth century, and only repealed after extensive debate in 1825. Still, restrictions on the export of machinery persisted until 1844.[34]

The debates over the control of machinery and artisans reflected however a conflict *within* capitalism rather than a conflict between the exploiting powers of capitalists and those who spoke for the exploited. The debates therefore had a very different outcome.

The development of the factory system was necessarily accompanied by the development of a new engineering and capital goods industry to support it, particularly following the advent of steam power and large scale factories. As this knowledge-based industry emerged, it acquired a large and specialised workforce, and its own product market based on home and international trade. The engineering sector therefore formed the leading edge of industrial change, which, by its independence from millowner control, displaced the direct power of the millowners to command technical advance to their own direct advantage. Both Parliament and wider public sympathy identified the growing industrial might of the British Empire with technical advance. Thus public subscriptions were raised for inventors who had not benefited from their inventions due to absence of patent protection, or through major applications that postdated the expiry of their patents. For example, a public subscription of £500 was raised around 1800 for Samuel Crompton, inventor of the spinning-mule. Parliament voted Crompton £5,000 in 1812, and voted Dr Edward Cartwright, inventor of the power loom, £3,000 in 1810.[35]

The debate concerning millowner hegemony was therefore a debate between 'progressive' elements of English society that could see that the source of British progress lay in technical and inventive mastery, and those who by capital privilege sought to hold onto their power. With the progressive expansion and intrinsic momentum of the technology text, the millowners lost. They continued to hold power over labour conditions, exploitation of children, and so on – conditions for *forcing* labour into service of capitalism. But they lost power over the technology text itself, as the cultural frame created by this text increasingly penetrated the life experience of the populace, and their visions of the future.

Also, during the early part of the nineteenth century, the emergent industrial technological system rested alongside alternative modes of production that had yet to disappear. The disappearance of past ways was by no means fully accepted. Thus, ranged against the millowner capitalists were conservative forces that wished to return to the old rural-based order. Tory 'radicals' wished for a return to a simpler peasant society, for a 'revival' of close bonds between the great lords and the people, whilst they attributed rural and urban poverty to capitalism and industrialism.[36] 'Chartists', the 'Owenist' movement and others took up the same cause. George Burges, addressing his remarks to the 'present generation' in 1831 wrote, for example,

Unrestrained machinery demoralises society – substitutes idleness for industry – want for competence – immorality for virtue. It has pauperised the peasant, – pauperised the citizen. It has abstracted capital from agriculture; capital from manufactures. – It has abstracted money from circulation, and drawn it into heaps. – *It has created taxes.* – It has destroyed domestic trade, – domestic consumption, – domestic industry.[37]

Until well into the nineteenth century (around the 1830s and 1840s), the industrial landscape stood alongside traditional forms of craft and industry. Indeed, some forms of technological advance created craft and domestic industries where they had not existed before, or alternatively, extended what traditional crafts were able to do. For example a number of industries expanded through the use of more labour and skill rather than through mechanisation. These industries included mining, quarrying, market gardening, food industries, building and construction, glass, pottery, woodworking, some areas of metallurgy, leather manufacture, shoemaking, glove and hatmaking and reinmaking.[38] So, whilst reaction was primarily against the rate of industrial progress, against 'unrestrained machinery' rather than industrialism *per se*, genuine economic and social alternatives appeared to persist. There were those then who simply wanted to remove further industrial encroachment from their landscape, to 'bury' it in much the same way that the Cook Islanders interred their pick-up truck. 'Burying' industrial technology in the early nineteenth century however meant exporting it. Richard Oastler (and others), writing to his member of Parliament, George Poulett Scope, in 1835, commented,

we will freely consent that you should take all this System of *unrestrained* Machinery and Capital to the 'outlying countries', and the fairer plains of Canada and Australia ... we resign the best parts of the Empire to such Scientific Gentlemen as yourself – leave us the secondary and less happy soils of the British Islands.[39]

Needless to say, the export of England's centralised control over industrial progress never happened. As I show in Chapter 8, where Australia's nineteenth-century technological progress is mirrored against what was happening in England, the colonies were seen – in much the same way as British pauper children – as resources to be exploited to power England's industrial might. In lieu of compliant labour, what the colonies were providing were agricultural and raw material inputs for Britain's progress, and consumer markets that Britain quite specifically refused to allow colonial industrial development to feed.

The US, on the other hand, was a force to be reckoned with, for it quickly developed a technological mastery that from the mid-nineteenth century started to threaten England's industrial hegemony very deeply indeed. In other words, the US started to take command of the technological text itself, and therefore wrested power over the international economy out of England's hands. This is reflected, amongst other things, in the move of prime economic and technological influence from Britain to the US that occurred in the colonies of Australia in the late nineteenth century. More on this later for this issue concerns the way that the technogical text, once formed into a frame for culture, can sweep aside international economic interest.

What is important to realise at this point is that even with the power of early capitalists to control Parliament and the legislature for their own privilege, the growth of technical advance that their capitalist interest had spawned overwhelmed the capitalists' own hegemony. Yet still, until the 1840s, whilst the industrial landscape was not yet all-pervasive in people's life experience, the 'Machinery Question' was alive, not resolved.

By the 1880s no such question remained. All that was seen by reformers and critics alike, was the need to redress the social inequities that had accompanied the system's excesses. The technology text had by then formed into a frame which was clamped tightly over cultural alternatives. William Preston, writing in 1889, for example, observed,

> There are few in these days sufficiently heretical to avow their disbelief in machinery. To it, by almost universal admission, we owe, in great part, our industrial progress and our national wealth. Yet the introduction of machinery was precisely what brought about the deplorable condition of things with which we are now concerned, and which ultimately compelled parliamentary interference.[40]

Resistance to the Technology Text

Up to the 1840s however, the Machinery Question touched all classes in English society. The content of the question varied according to the class position of the people asking it. For the aristocracy concern was with loss of the old order of their privilege. For the capitalists the question concerned creating the social conditions that were conducive to their newly established privilege. The middle classes were somewhat ambivalent, for on the one hand many were committed to progress, and developing the privileges that derived from their attachment to industrial sources of wealth; and on the other hand, there were many who were concerned about the negative effects on their lifestyle that were being caused by a burgeoning industrial landscape; or, there were those who sought to balance a religious world-view that asserted salvation through disciplined accumulation against a Christian concern with pauperisation and exploitation. But for the marginalised labouring classes, the question was one of survival and resistance.

Primary resistance did not come from the most marginalised elements of the labour force – the unskilled itinerants, women and children. They were indeed a 'docile' labour force, with no sources of power and no basis for cohesion within a dungeon of continuous, insecure, drudgery. Resistance came more from craftsmen or skilled groups who had a source of cohesion in a trade that was being displaced under the advance of mechanisation.

The handloom weavers were the largest group to experience unemployment over the first half of the nineteenth century. The Luddite resistance – in 1811-12 and 1816 – was formed primarily from the disenfranchised croppers and shearmen of the woollen industry, and the stocking knitters and handloom cotton weavers. The form of their resistance was to smash the machines that they were confronted by in factories as a way of preventing the machines' continuing encroachment on weaving employment. Similarly, the violent demonstrations and powerloom wrecking that occurred in 1826 and 1829 followed an increasingly desperate resistance to the weavers' descent into obsolescence and poverty.[41]

The mechanisation of agriculture was resisted in the riots led by Captain Swing in 1830-1, where fires were set among the hay ricks, and threshing machines were broken. By the time the Swing riots occurred, however, it was too late. Until 1819 the threshing machines had largely been confined to the North of England, locked away from sight of the majority of even the agricultural labour force. The riots broke out following the pervasive diffusion of the machines through the rest of England – through East Kent, Wiltshire, Huntingdonshire and Berkshire – when agricultural labour was confronted by an apparently immutable progress of mechanisation across their employment landscape.[42] By the time of the Swing riots, threshing machines were thus fully entrenched in the path of industrial progress, and with the power of agricultural capitalists, resistance was quickly suppressed.

Similarly, whilst the Luddite resistance of the 1810s occurred at a time when powerlooms were only just starting to encroach on handloom weaver employment (there were 2,400 powerlooms in England in 1812 and 200,000 handloom weavers), the march of powerlooms as an industrial force was inexorable. By the late 1830s, shortly after the powerloom wrecking incidents of the late 1820s, there only 50,000 handloom weavers left. The weaving process was almost completely mechanised by the 1840s. Given the mechanised displacement of the handweaving craft and the politically mediated shattering of the power and cohesion of its members, resistance was easily broken. This was particularly so because aligned against the weavers was an industry that drew its political and national power from a contribution of 5 per cent of total national output during the 1820s, 1830s and 1840s.[43] Thus, the seemingly inexorable march of the industrial technological text continued.

The story was much the same as mechanisation encroached on other forms of craft employment through the middle of the nineteenth century. Resistance to the use of moulding machines in brickmaking was one cause of the 'Manchester Outrages' in the late 1860s, whilst at the same time, wage reductions and unemployment of previously skilled cutlery tradespeople in Sheffield provoked union sanctions that sought to prevent further mechanisation of the industry.[44] In Stafford, during the 1850s, the agent for the new domestic sewing machine sought to give a public demonstration of the machine, but it was seen by the audience as a direct threat to female sewing employment:

> when the agent for Howe's patent went into the marketplace, and, in the presence of ten thousand women, sewed before their eyes, as they had never sewn, they were ready to tear him to pieces, and did, in fact, drum him out of town.[45]

But the dynamic that drove the technology text outflanked resistance and continued on its path of mechanising all aspects of productive life – in the interests of capitalist accumulation. Indeed, the very fact of resistance together with the difficulties experienced in creating a docile, compliant and machine-disciplined workforce out of skilled groups, who still retained some power that owners could not control, was a direct inducement for *accelerating* technological change.[46]

Strongly unionised groups such as the mule-spinners were able to strike persistently for better economic conditions – for example, to bring country piece-rates into alignment with those offered in Manchester, and to preserve male hegemony and wage conditions. Mule-spinner strikes occurred in Lancashire in 1810, 1818, 1825, 1830, 1834, 1836–7, and there was a similar strike in Scotland in 1837. But the strikes all eventually failed.[47] Technical innovation, and the enframing quality of the technology text, continued to encroach on the union's collective power to resist the force of capitalist progress. The 'reverse salient', to use Thomas Hughes' term for the focal point of invention,[48] was primarily *social* – concerning compliance and discipline – so that as Bruland observed, the millowners developed particular technologies specifically designed to encompass industrial conflict.[49]

The technological frame to culture that was delivered by the technology text of the early Industrial Revolution was thus informed by the twin perspectives of labour control *and* technological advance, not just by improved technological efficiency *per se*. The technological frame for industrialisation was therefore quite specifically based on drawing social and cultural forces into *alignment* with technical advance, all in the interests of fostering technologically-induced profitability.

Arguably the only case of protest that was successful, at least for a period of 20 years or so, occurred in the cotton-manufacturing town of Oldham. What is worthy of note in this protest was that the condition of its success lay in attack being aimed, not at the cosmetic appearance of capitalism, that is, the machines, but instead at the social and political forces that were enforcing 'social alignment' elsewhere in Britain. John Foster's comparative study of class struggle during the early nineteenth century in Oldham versus two other towns, South Shields and Northampton, is revealing.[50]

Oldham was a town based on cotton manufacturing. South Shields' economic base lay in shipyards, coal carrying and coastal trade. Northampton's economy was primarily based on sweated shoemaking. The extremely limited technological base of the early industrial period intensified trade booms and slumps across all three towns, leading to the ever-deepening nature of succeeding crises, the continuous fall in prices for cottage goods, and the lowering of wages by capitalists seeking to remain economically profitable. All three towns were subject to severe economic hardship, with South Shields and Northampton even more seriously affected than Oldham. However, successful class-based rebellion grew up in Oldham, but not in the two other, more hardship-depressed, towns.

What distinguished success from failure was the development of wider social solidarity and human relationships in Oldham that together aligned *against* attempts, both within the town, and from outside, to impose the interests of capitalist mechanisation.

In Oldham, the 'revolutionary vanguard', anti-capitalist philosophies of Jacobinism invaded the town from the previously marginal position of the doctrines in democratic deist chapels in the outparishes. The strength of the philosophies within the town grew with each succeeding economic crisis, until by the 1830s the social solidarity of the town was based on an anti-capitalist ideology that was fully integrated into trade unionism. The class solidarity was not however confined to the work sphere. It was reinforced more widely in urban neighbouring relations between trade groups and intermarriage between them. In particular, the shared anti-capitalist ideology was underlined by the approach to cohesive action which specifically sought to define and reinforce the social/neighbourhood/life-space boundaries of the populace's everyday life-world and culture. This was not the case in South Shields and Northampton.

Thus in the 1830s, the people of Oldham, instead of being involved only in fitful and reactionary actions of machine-breaking, seized collective control of the *social* and *political* processes of the town. They seized control of the vestry and police commission, so that the unenfranchised could sway elections, both local and parliamentary, through exclusive dealing and intimidation. The people shut off the town from external forces of authority, consequently providing extensive licence to unionists and radicals. The succeeded in effective confrontation for 20 years – in strike action, attacks on mills, machinery and manufacturers – through *coherence* of their continued mass agitation. With powerful social coherence and control over the whole social and political life of the town, Oldham therefore was able to confront the wider coercive powers of a capitalist-inspired Parliament, to resist the new 'Poor Laws' that were widely applied elsewhere, so that the laws remained unenforceable in Oldham for 13 years.

Eventually, around 1850, Oldham started to accommodate rather than confront the external reality of industrialisation and its politics. This occurred partly because the town's communal integrity was by then encircled by wider technological progress, and the town could not remain an island any more. The dissolution of community integrity against capitalism also grew from within: the very success of the Oldham movement attracted middle-class radical leaders who, with the best of intentions, eventually distorted the confrontationist politics of the Oldham working class into accommodationist philosophies of the bourgeoisie.

Oldham was an exception. The town's power to control its own destiny under encroaching industrial technological encirclement lay not in reaction to hardship, nor in worker resistance to machinery, but in the *ability to control the social alignment* of the community with capitalist technological forces. This did not happen elsewhere.

Oldham's insularity was eventually swept aside too, primarily because the encroachment of technological progress was starting to penetrate deeply into the culture and social lives of *all* English society by the 1850s. Oldham held out for a while, but could not remain insulated from wider forces of change forever. The middle-class transition in internal community ideology was part of this general process, a point of some significance that I will return to in the next chapter. What is important to realise at this stage is how deeply industrialism had penetrated the cultural and community life of England by the 1840s and 1850s. For it is in this cultural transformation that the full realisation of capitalism's power came into being.

Resignation to the Technology Text

As the earlier quote from Charles Dickens reflects, the culture of industrialism had deeply penetrated town life by the 1850s. The industrial towns were characterised by a philosophy of, and a dependence on, mechanised, calculable but 'soulless' life.

The people were enmeshed in change. As Clapham observes, the labour that people were engaged in was so different from the skilled and un-skilled labour of the late eighteenth century that the labourer of the 1850s was performing 'operations ... which would have made his grand-father gape.'[51] Yet, all this was in living memory. Industrialism, originally rest-ing quietly in the isolated valleys of northern England, thence alongside traditional craft industries, had spread its ganglion of smoke-stacks and industrial communities across the length and breadth of England. By the 1850s industrialism was widely visible, and had penetrated the conscious-ness of the people as symbols of its remorseless progress encroached further with each passing day into people's life experience.

Standing at the centre of this progress stood the steam engine that had made large-scale manufacturing possible. In 1800 only 490 Watt engines had been installed. But by 1850, 500,000 steam engines had been installed throughout Great Britain.[52] Standing at the centre of the economy were the steam-powered mills, where three-fifths of the workforce of Great Britain were employed.[53] The technological frame to the culture of industrialisation was inescapably in place.

Meanwhile, new sources of social solidarity were just starting to emerge. The bases for solidarity in craft unions and village life had been largely displaced as both the power and machines of capitalism had marched through the centre of proto-industrial communities. But new sources of solidarity were starting to be recognised within the *new* social alignments that were forged in industrial town 'villages'; an awareness was emerging that labour was a *necessary resource* of capitalism, so, *because* labour could be regarded 'as a commodity to be sold in the (new) historically peculiar conditions of a free capitalist economy,'[54] a collective strength of labour could also control its own commodity value. It was only on *this* basis that, after another 30 years of building industrially-framed solidarity, workers' strikes, based on class solidarity rather than craft exclusiveness, eventually started to have their first significant impact on capitalist interest – in 'new' unionisation of the 1880s and the Dockers' Strike of 1889.

Victory in the Dockers' Strike was a key symbol of labour solidarity. It led to widespread organisation among the gas workers, labourers on Tyneside in engineering and shipbuilding, the Birmingham metal trades and the South Wales tinplate industry.

Meanwhile, both capitalist and middle-class interests also adjusted to the new wave of unionisation. Capital interests sought to use technological innovation (particularly in the gasworks and on the docks) to dispense with general labour rather than make use of it. And the middle classes welcomed unionisation as a way of bringing greater order into society – greater regularity and discipline to the lives of the poor.[55]

However the *discipline* of labour that capitalism itself depended upon had also been a prime force in converting the machine-breaking mobs of the early nineteenth century into the disciplined unions that had power to reshape capitalism's yoke in the latter part of the century[56] – as 'calculated' and disciplined life became the cultural property to which all had adjusted. This 'discipline' started to enter the organisation of workers around the 1830s, as is reflected in the 'Union Club Oaths' written in 1830. The oaths asserted, for example,

> I will never work any work where an obliged brother has been unjustly enforced off for standing up for his price, or in defence of his trade.
>> So help me God.

> I will never take any more work than I can do myself in one day, except necessity requires me to do so; and if I do, I will employ none but an obligated brother, and will pay him according to the master's price, or according to his work.
>> So help me God.[57]

Thus, in spite of the continued *enforcing* of 'adjustment' on pauper children, the workforce as a whole had already *adjusted* – over three generations or so. Or, perhaps more accurately, the workforce had become *resigned* to the mechanical regime of factory life, and were defining life and access to power *within* this frame.

The 'remorseless tragedy' of technological society had therefore begun, so it was no longer as necessary for millowners to use overt exploitative repression over the marginal and powerless, the strategy which shook people out of their feudal cultures and into the fires of the Industrial Revolution. That this change had occurred is reflected, amongst other things, in the success that at this time started to be experienced in Parliament by reformist movements. That the change was a change in culture, rather than merely resistant obeisance to repressive sanction, is reflected in what evidence there is of a transition in fantasy life of the people during the 1840s.

One indicator of this change in fantasy life is the change in the main themes of penny novels. During the 1840s the previous primary theme that centred on rural domestic plots was displaced by stories of heroines combating powerful patriarchal odds through virtue.[58] This transition in attention reflected a turning away from nostalgia for rural and family-based life, a mode of living that had been broken – both economically and socially – by the remorseless, changed, industrialising world of everyday experience. In its place was a focus of attention on super-heroic individual morality in a world of industrial repression and immutable machine subservient discipline.

Given the price and distribution of literacy, the penny novel was probably appealing more to the middle classes (who were also more likely co-opted into a social alignment with capitalism) than the working classes. However, it is likely that the same shift in cultural attention pervaded through the working classes as well. Literacy was generally low throughout the working classes, though some had developed basic reading (though less so writing) literacy.[59] But the desire to participate in a reading culture was strong, for in cultural alignment with technological progress, the 'spirit of self-improvement ... was a leading characteristic of nineteenth century social development'.[60] Charles Shaw described what it felt like as an illiterate child in 1840 to be confronted by a literate person. At the age of eight, Shaw, a mould-runner in a factory, experienced seeing a young man who had the time and means to be 'reading of his own free will', as follows:

> I felt a sudden, strange sense of wretchedness. There was a blighting consciousness that my lot was harsher than his and that of others ... I went back to my mould-running and hot stove with my first anguish in my heart.[61]

With knowledge and literacy being seen as the path to improvement, the working classes had developed their own bridges for participating in a literate culture. Workmen would take on additional work so that they could release one member to read to them while they worked; public houses would employ professional newsreaders; and reading to families was a common feature of home life.[62] As a consequence, the popularity of penny novel themes is likely to have spread even where literacy had not yet been able to penetrate.

The inevitability, the possibilities and the fears of accepting industrial progress were expressed in what was arguably the most potent novelistic allegory of the time, Mary Shelley's *Frankenstein*. As a metaphor of the Industrial Revolution, Frankenstein, an aristocratic man of science, possesses the world's greatest power – the ability to create life through the joining of science to machine. But he only fashioned a monster. 'Man', with the greatest power to solve any problem and to create Utopia through applied science and machines, created instead a hell on earth, the nineteenth-century industrial town. Humanity became slaves to machines, in turn giving birth to the proletarian 'monster' that capitalism most feared and sought to repress. The monster in *Frankenstein* was pursued into the Arctic, but whereas Frankenstein perished of cold in the pursuit, the monster, searching for death and release, simply disappeared – one day to return again.[63]

Thus, the culture of the mid-nineteenth century had been dragged, thence co-opted, into alignment with its emergent technological frame. Though, as David Landes observes, the British economy and society of 1851 may not have seemed very different to that of 1800, but 'Beneath this surface, the vital organs were transformed; and though they weighed but a fraction of the total – whether measured by people or wealth – it was they that determined the metabolism of the entire system.'[64]

Interestingly enough, it was only as this culture–technology alignment became relatively complete that the level of technological innovation did start to beat to a different metabolic rate. As John Lienhard demonstrates, there was a dramatic shift in the doubling rates of technological innovation (as indicated by key technical efficiency measures for core technologies) in the mid-1830s, a doubling rate that thereafter remained constant until the present day.[65]

Conditions of Cultural Transformation to a 'Calculated Life'

The emergence of the technological frame for industrial society was a process of cultural realignment. The frame of 'calculated life' took three or four generations to achieve, as English society slowly shook off the cultural habits of feudalism and took on the mantle of industrial rhythm.

The cultural habits of feudalism were however deeply inscribed into work practices and the social relations of production that supported them. Industrialism required a fundamental realignment of labour, away from craft- and family-based autonomy over the means of production, and towards dependency on the control of life-rhythm by machine-systems. Given the depth of this transformation in the meanings of life-experience, merely offering new forms of employment could never have seduced the populace into what was tantamount to a new form of slavery. The Industrial Revolution therefore did not take off because of newly invented technological arrangements. Rather, the Industrial Revolution was predicated on the new breed of capitalists shattering the social relations of production that had gone before so that the people had no choice but to participate in the burgeoning industrial system.

Thus, industrial capitalists were able to feed from the dislocation of the feudal agricultural order that had already been caused through the greed of landlords who, through political power, enclosed the commons and drove excess labour off their lands. The itinerant and marginalised workforce that resulted was grist to the mill of industrialism, for they had little choice but to participate, or starve.

Through their own emerging political power, the industrial capitalists were able to enact further legislation that shattered the power of the craft guilds, and therefore allowed the interposing of capitalist interest between cottage labour and the market place. This was but a transitionary phase however, for it did not offer adequate control over labour discipline or productivity, essential ingredients for the required culture of capitalism. The factory system offered direct supervision and control. But for the system to work required the direct *imposition* of discipline, an imposition that those with any level of power resisted.

Capitalism therefore targeted its early development on the powerless. Again, supported by parliamentary legislation, capitalists took the pauper children from the workhouses, bought them from poverty-stricken parents, and then enslaved them from the age of five years into a daily regime that was controlled by both direct cruelty and the enforced requirement to abide by the rhythm of machines. For those who were subject to less direct exploitation, capitalism erected mill-town communities that generalised the level of control within the factories into autocratic control over all social life and alternate opportunites. Again, legislation was employed to limit the mobility of people out of these towns, particularly of machine-artisans that the system could not do without.

The basic social dynamic for the development of an industrial culture was therefore direct *social* coercion, legitimated and enforced through alignment with ruling class interests in Parliament. As with all regimes however, the ruling class's power to continue its path of coercion could

not last *unless it was accepted as legitimate or inevitable by the people.*
It is evident that this occurred, but not until near the middle of the
nineteenth century.

Such an alignment of the meaning systems of the people with those of
the industrial system is a deep cultural transformation. There were
several important ingredients which contributed to this happening.

The first ingredient was the power of the technical *system*. This
power was unleashed, much like Frankenstein's monster, as soon as
efficient steam power linked its tentacles of motive energy into the
factory machines. Large-scale factories could be developed, and the
dynamic of system properties – increasing 'complexity', 'scale', 'power',
'ubiquity and interconnectedness' – was unleashed across the productive
landscape. The 'system' offered new means of social control, for it
offered the unrestrained expansion of technical invention to replace the
craft skills that permitted the workforce some degree of control over
conditions of production. The 'system' also offered the possibility of
continuously spreading, taking over its previous 'environments' and
drawing them into the ordered world of system control. Economic
advantage was associated with capitalising on these properties.

Traditional crafts rested alongside the expansion of the industrial
system over the first part of the nineteenth century, and at times were
offered opportunity *because of* the spread of industrialism. However,
these craft-based modes of production were steadily encircled and
incorporated. Craft-based resistance resulted. The people smashed the
machines of industrialism. But this form of resistance was only to the
cosmetic appearance of system power, not to the basic dynamic of the
system itself. Invariably rebellion was swept aside because the
technological text, supported as it was by political power, continuously
outflanked the protesters. It incorporated their crafts, destroyed their
employment, and therefore their sources of social solidarity and power.
The economic base, and therefore the social relations base, for a culture
that did not align with industrial capitalism, were therefore
undermined. The only case where protest was successful, at least for a
time, was where the people of Oldham seized power over the social
alignment itself, and therefore were able to exercise some degree of power
over the system. But eventually this too was swept aside, as the culture of
industrialisation invaded from within, and the frame to social and
economic life imposed by the technology text, invaded from without.

The cultural power of the technological text that capitalism had
created was however a monster that even the ruling classes could not
control. With its base property lying in technical knowledge and
ingenuity, attempts by the millowners to contain technical advance in

their own interest were also swept aside as the leading edge of technical advance expanded outside their control – into engineering companies, into wider areas of the British economy, and eventually into international competition from other national powers that developed greater mastery over the leading edge itself. The technology text created new social relations of production in an emerging self-conscious proletariat, and the sources of solidarity that followed were ranged against and retarded subsequent capitalist interest.

However, the self-conscious power of the proletariat did not emerge out of collective perception of repression (for that had been there all along). Rather, it emerged *within* the technological frame *once the culture of the people had been drawn into alignment with acceptance of the technology text into everyday life.*

Here, the second ingredient of cultural transformation is important. Precisely because of the 'system's' intrinsic dynamic of spreading, of increasingly ordering its former 'environments' into system-connectedness, the technological text, once unleashed, penetrated daily life and consciousness very deeply. The superordinate symbols of the factory system, the smoke-stack, the giant brick buildings and the industrial towns, penetrated every corner of the English landscape. The people were confronted by a seemingly immutable march of highly visible permanent change, change that implied new meanings, new social relations of production, new ruling class statuses, and also new 'millennial' horizons for the future.

The industrial towns enclosed the experience of many to nothing but the town's physical reality rather than the natural world that lay outside the boundaries of industrial life. Charles Kingsley, writing in 1848 for example, advocated the use of 'picture-galleries' that depicted the nature to which people no longer had access, as a means of 'refreshment' that a walk through nature would otherwise have provided:

> There, in the space of a single room, the townsman may take his country walk – a walk beneath mountain peaks, blushing sunsets, with broad woodlands spreading out below it; a walk through green meadows, under cool mellow shades, and overhanging rocks, by rushing brooks, where he watches and watches till he seems to *hear* the foam whisper, and to *see* the fishes leap; and his hard-worn heart wanders out free, beyond the grim city-world of stone and iron, smoky chimneys, and roaring wheels, into the world of beautiful things.[66]

The superordinate symbols of resolute industrial progress therefore were erected *in front of* the natural world that symbolised the past, and an alternative. For the town-dweller, this 'other' world was captured into a substitute reality that could be experienced *within* industrial town life.

Along with acceptance of the permanence of these symbols, and the industrial town life they implied the culture of the people *had* to adjust to a new reality, to the implied meanings for all of daily life that the superordinate symbols presented. Adjustment at this deeper level was not a product of repressive coercion. Rather, it was a property of radical change in the objectifications of culture itself. The immutability, the 'sacredness' of the symbols was enforced through the opacity of the 'text' that the people could not read, as its meanings were already buried under a sedimented complexity of technical knowledge to which they had no access. The culture, and along with it the consciousness of the people, therefore moved into alignment with the new reality that was emerging.

Thus the 'Machinery Question' was alive and well during the early decades of the Industrial Revolution, expressing a cultural ambivalence to both the prospects and repressions of industrial capitalism. But the 'Question' disappeared into reactions that were *framed* by the technological system from the mid-nineteenth century onwards. The 'system' was accepted as inevitable, and reformers' attention was directed towards cleaning up its dirty side.

Emergence of industrialism is therefore the emergence of technological enframement over culture. The transition could only be achieved in its early days through direct coercion and exploitation. But once set in place, the technological frame to culture itself became a superordinate reality that set the pace and content of cultural transformation thereafter. The power of the technology text to create this frame was not actualised however until it aligned with the wider culture of the people, and their everyday life experience. By then it was too late to 'bury the truck', for the process of seduction had begun.

Burning deeply beneath the embers of these fires of change were two other forces. The first was the development of ideological legitimation for the changes people came to accept. The second was the development of alignments of knowledge with the system itself. Both forces were essential to actualisation of the culture–technology alignment that came to rest in the mid-nineteenth century, an alignment that thereafter accorded technology a dominant culture-defining power. To complete the story of the emergence of the technological text as a dominant cultural force, we therefore need to explore these dynamics – of evolving ideological and knowledge alignments. This is the subject of the next chapter.

Ideological Choruses

The 'Morality Play' of Schooling

The move in cultural alignment into the technological frame of industrialism was not merely a product of enforced co-optation. Working deeply at the centre of morality and legitimation were the interests of the middle classes, who feared disorder on the one hand, and God on the other, but who also spanned the chasm between capitalist exploitation and labour repression.

For over a century before the steam-powered factory system appeared, primarily interstitial group interests had been involved in education and religious instruction of the poor, in 'uplifting' the working classes. Though partly aimed at moderating the excesses of the early emergence of capitalism, the latent function of schooling was to *adjust the morality of the people to the mechanical social order* that was yet to come. The 'morality plays' of schooling continued throughout the early part of the nineteenth century, but by the 1850s had assumed a different face with the attachment of morality to the new 'political economy' philosophy (or the 'dismal science' as its detractors described it) that was a *direct* legitimation of capitalism.

Prior to the start of the eighteenth century the poor had virtually no access to education. Public grammar schools provided a classical education for the gentry. These schools were then supplemented by a number of private schools that taught a wider range of subjects, but being expensive, were still attended almost exclusively by the sons and daughters of the wealthy.

The unsettling influences of ascetic Protestantism were starting to be widely felt however. On the one hand Protestantism had already overthrown the shackles of hierarchical Church control over knowledge and order, and on the other hand, ascetic Protestantism's assertion of the obligation for disciplined conduct of secular affairs threw the order of society back onto the responsibility of the individual. As a horizon of change started to invade the early eighteenth century, the emerging middle classes started to become concerned about the possibility of anarchy if individual morality was not maintained. They identified that the problem lay with the religiously uninstructed working classes. Thus, the instruction of the lower classes in articles of the Christian faith became a priority.

Charity schools, supported by public subscription, were founded, particularly in the latter part of the eighteenth century, with the primary intention of providing moral and religious education for the poor.[1] The emphasis of these schools was on the moral self-discipline that was required of ascetic Protestantism, a discipline that was enforced both in doctrine and in student control. For example, John Wesley, founder of 'Methodism' (that literally meant, 'husbandry of time', and was informed by the doctrine of 'buying up time from Satan'), addressed Kingswood School in 1786 on 'The Duty and Advantage of Early Rising' in the following terms: 'By soaking so long between warm sheets, the flesh is as it were parboiled, and becomes soft and flabby. The nerves, in the meantime, are quite unstrung.'[2]

At about the same time the Reverend William Turner of Newcastle spoke of Raikes' charity (Sunday) schools, quite specifically associating their moral order with the emergent order of capitalism. Turner described Raikes' schools as 'spectacles of order and regularity', and, referring to the use of children in hemp and flax manufacture, observed that the schools had exerted an extraordinary influence. Through the exhortations to punctuality and regularity that were written into the school rules, along with the schools' rigid discipline and military form, Turner saw that the schools had produced children who were, 'more tractable, more obedient, less quarrelsome and revengeful'.[3]

The order of religious education was therefore the order of the discipline of mechanised capitalism that was emerging. This was so, not only in the doctrinal assertion of the legitimacy of accumulating profit, but also in the assertion of the discipline required of the subservient classes to make profit possible. With profitability at the centre of the affirmation of 'salvation' through disciplined use of time, the schools therefore mirrored the adage phrased by Benjamin Franklin on the other side of the Atlantic, 'he that is a prodigal of his Hours, is, in effect, a Squanderer of money'.[4]

By the early nineteenth century, many schools had been established by the two rival societies – the National, and the British and Foreign. In both, the syllabus was elementary. In the British and Foreign schools, emphasis was on instruction of elementary literacy and numerical skills; the National schools, 'founded largely in anxious reaction to the potentially seditious and morally ruinous effects of godless education, retained a measure of moral and religious education'.[5] Schools were also attached to workhouses and industrial factories, but in all cases – for both day-schools and Sunday schools – where poverty often got in the way of school attendance, the schools were characterised by irregular attendance. This was particularly the case in schools attached to factories where employers were often unwilling to allow the children the time for 'instruction'. Still however, the influence of Raikes' (Sunday) schools was widespread, with the number of (irregularly attending) students growing from 750,000 in 1785, to 1,550,000 in 1833, to 2,400,000 in 1851.[6]

Education therefore touched the lives of poor and working-class children during the early days of the Industrial Revolution. However, as was demonstrated in the last chapter, the schools fostered only limited levels of literacy or opportunity. Instead, what 'school' represented – for both those who attended, and those who were not given the opportunity – was an association between participation in the culture of the times and the rigid discipline and morality that was seen to be necessary for participation in industrial life. Schools acted as an institutional bridge between the interests of capitalism and the deeper religion-based world views that both preceded and were associated with the industrial order. Most importantly, the bridge was symbolic. For the existence and spread of schooling for the poor presented the legitimating expression of moral concern on the face of a social system that lived through the oppression of its most marginal and powerless human elements.

The association between morality and disciplined labour that underscored capitalism was not, however, a mere ideological invention of the ruling classes. Instead, the philosophy evolved out of deep existential concern for eternal salvation that was no longer guaranteed once the authority of Catholicism had been undermined. Max Weber's *The Protestant Ethic and the Spirit of Capitalism* deals eloquently with the transformations in religious ideology that followed.[7] I shall not discuss such a familiar thesis here. What are worth adding, however, are the recent observations of George Ovitt concerning the transition between *prior* religious views of labour, and those that characterised the secular world views that were associated with the eighteenth-century culture that allowed capitalism to take off.[8] Ascetic Protestantism's assertion of the role of individual labour in morality was derived from what had gone before; it was not in opposition. So, the evolution of ideology behind eighteenth-century schooling represented a smooth transition in world views as society adjusted against a changing landscape, rather than the erection of a new capitalist-related belief system.

The Benedictines (in whose monasteries the original mechanical devices for measuring time were invented) had very similar views to those of Protestantism concerning the potential sinfulness of a non-disciplined life. For Saint Benedict,

> Leisure (*otiositas*) is the enemy of the soul, and for this reason the brothers must spend a certain amount of time doing manual work (*in labore manuum*) as well as the time spent in divine reading (*lectione divina*).[9]

But, although the philosophy of the Benedictines (or of the Irish Saint Columbus for that matter, who viewed labour as 'penance') stressed the potential sinfulness of being idle, the philosophies did not support notions of productivity and efficiency for their own sake. As George Ovitt observes,

> Until there is a cultural consensus supporting notions of productivity and efficiency for their own sake, there is no incentive within a social system – any social system – to concentrate on developing techniques for the tedium of labour. Early medieval Europe spiritualized daily life, including daily labour, but until a clear-cut distinction could be drawn between acts performed for spiritual ends and acts performed for secular ends (such as profit), there could be no rationale for technological advancement.[10]

In an apparent paradox, it was this association between spiritual morality and obeisance to the discipline of capitalism *for the sake of secular profit* (objectification of the wise use of 'talents') that attached the meaning of 'spiritual' labour to its end rather than its intrinsic performance. The ascetic ethic of Protestantism fostered this rationalist transformation of the meaning of labour. But the schools systems and their symbolism *actualised* it in socialisation practice. As demonstrated earlier, the education institutions grew out of prior systems for religious and classics enlightenment of the gentry, and were stimulated by the fear of change and disorder that loomed over the horizon of the eighteenth-century world. But the orientation of the schools towards the poor, and the encouragement of secular discipline that mirrored the evolving machine age was an *adjustment*. This was an adjustment of religion to a burgeoning secular order that was itself catalysed (or at least, legitimated) by the individualising catharsis of Protestant guilt and insecurity. Thus, as Ovitt observes,

> Christianity was not itself responsible for creating the conditions

under which change occurred ... Christianity should perhaps be seen as having adjusted itself to a world being altered by technology rather than as being the decisive force behind such alteration.[11]

Indeed, John Wesley had himself been influenced by 'industrial' discipline when he founded the ascetic disciplinary doctrines of Methodism. Wesley visited and studied the Moravian settlement of Herrnhut in Saxony in 1738. His journal record of their rules and systems of life demonstrates the relationship between Methodism and the factory system.[12]

As the technological text progressed in its enframement of culture, religion continued to adjust, as did its influence as a basis for secular education. By the late nineteenth century, religious instruction was increasingly being displaced – in England – as was attention to the classics, by elementary science education. In 1875 Mr Percival, the Headmaster of Wellington School, told of the recent introduction of science into the curriculum. Science was taught for six hours per week, six hours were spent on mathematics, two on geography. He still felt it necessary to justify the introduction of science as, on the one hand, having an 'undeniably good effect', and on the other, not displacing the classics (still taught for 18 hours per week), an act that would be seen as 'a fatal mistake, which men of science would certainly never advocate'. Religion, by this time, had disappeared from the curriculum, for it was assumed that this would be taught on Sunday.[13]

The morality of discipline was however now deeply entrenched in the popular consciousness. For example, a poem published in the same year (1875) entitled 'Of Industry and Idleness', mirrored a common theme of the time:

... Is it not a duty, a religion,
Still to energise and do, though doing be not much?
It is given unto few men to achieve, it is lent to none to
   perfect
A labour worthy of their lives, industrious to the end;

... Labour hath sweet uses, labour sanctifieth all
   things,

... Idleness ever hath its peril, in stagnation and
   corruption.[14]

By the mid-twentieth century, Bishop Robinson declared 'God is Dead!', or at least seriously displaced from His pedestal at the centre of rational secular life.[15] And religion was individualised, privatised and marginal to the structures of both education and secular authority and morality.[16] For morality is by now directly in service of capitalist interest, and needs no religious support to legitimate abiding by the technological frame of the social order. This is an issue that I will take up further in Chapter 9.

Returning to the early Industrial Revolution, what is important to recognise is that the interaction between past world-view legitimations and an evolving technological frame were at an early stage of synthesis and adjustment. But the deeper religious adjustments to, and legitimation of, the evolving capitalist form, were deeply woven into the cultural transformations that the schools systems actualised and symbolised. Thus the patterns of *adjustment* to capitalist discipline, and the cultural consequences that followed – actualised around the 1840s – were deeply sedimented into cultural progress within an evolving technological frame. From the 1840s, the frame took over. More on this shortly.

What else was happening with middle-class involvement in education of the working classes is particularly important. For other initiatives of the middle classes represented a translation of the secularised religious discipline into direct ideological support for the capitalism that was emerging – that is, in fostering the acceptance of 'political economy'.

The 'Ideological Play' of Technical Education

The middle-class reformers of the late eighteenth century were firmly convinced of the need for 'scientific' education of the artisan, the building of a *direct* bridge between capitalism and the labouring class. Enlightened by the prevailing ideology of the time concerning 'self-improvement', the initiatives that followed were a translation of prior concern for the moral and disciplined education of children to socialise them into the evolving industrial order.

By the late eighteenth century the structures of technical knowledge that were required of artisans were undergoing quite radical change. Traditionally-acquired skills were simply not adequate for the machine-system to progress. For the majority of the eighteenth century, engineering skills were integrated into the person of an all-round skilled craftsman, the old corn millwright, and the early millwright engineer. The craft was highly exclusive, following the model of traditional crafts where the trade was passed on within the family. Thus, the millwright, though a 'jack-of-all-trades' had to be 'born and bred a millwright' to be able to enter the trade.[17] With the emergence of a high demand for millwrights as the new factory system developed, and particularly along with the linking up of steam engines to the factory system, two things happened. The first was that many of the craft skills were standardised as the dimensions of early factories became uniform enough for the production of 'builders' manuals'. Thus, the skills of many millwrights were levelled to those required of 'ordinary apprentices'. The second effect was that those who were better able to be involved in design started to 'professionalise' as engineers. To assert this newly acquired status, the engineers initiated hegemonic control over their position through creating 'professional societies' such as Smeaton's Society of Civil Engineers, established in 1771, and the subsequent opposition to this Society, the Institute of Civil Engineers, established in 1818.[18] Thus the position of the traditional millwright was split as the need for more specialised design knowledge arose, and the need for more widely accessible and standardised technical knowledge progressed. Both trends aligned with the social separation of design and implementing skills that thereafter characterised the link between technical skill and production under industrialisation.[19]

As with former trade or craft societies, the new professional bodies were exclusive and hierarchically organised according to age. They sought to distance their status from artisan-based trade societies, of iron forgers, steam engine makers, millwrights and so on, through appeal to 'mental' rather than practical skills. The advent of professionalism therefore represented an evolving alignment of a technical knowledge system with the changing face of industrialisation. Professionalism was a social product of the evolution of technological crafts out of the traditional craft structures of hegemony, and into the new structures of hegemony that aligned with capitalist interest. The power of professionalism lay in the increasingly central role now starting to be played of large-scale machine workshops, foundries and engine factories in servicing industrial progress.[20]

A key product of the professionalisation of engineers however was that, by separating 'mental' activity from implementation, it allotted the burgeoning number of new artisan skills that were required by industrialisation, to the status of 'labour'. This was labour that was dependent on the relatively standardised practice of crafts, the dimensions of which were dictated by the newly emergent breed of 'thinkers'. Such an alienation of thought from practice directly aligned with capitalist interest of the time in employing a less skilled, interchangeable and docile workforce.

The middle-class reformers saw this gap emerging along technical knowledge dimensions, and identified reform with putting improved technical knowledge within the hands of the lower classes as a means of 'self-improvement', of benefiting from the fruits of capitalism (and therefore being more committed to its progress). Thus, as a means of bridging the gap, the 'Mechanics Institute' movement was brought to life, a philanthropic effort ostensibly oriented towards the development of 'scientific education' for artisans. The 'movement' was diverse, consisting of a myriad of local societies with widely varying structures and constitutions. Some societies were genuinely artisan-based, seeking to provide 'mutual instruction' as a means of alleviating shared poverty and ignorance. But the majority of Mechanics Institutes were dominated by provincial middle-class (often Whig-Liberal) elites.[21]

The shared philosophy of the Mechanics Institute movement directly legitimated the interests of capitalism. The philosophy claimed that industrial transformation was conducive to harmony and stability; that science was an appendage to (rather than the centre of) the technical knowledge that was required to power industrial transformation; and that economic wealth was derived from an *optimal combination* of science and skill. Thus, within this ideological doctrine, the key purpose of the Mechanics Institute movement was to foster the development of a thinking artisan (the ideological subtext of which was, a person more committed to the order of industrialism) rather than an imitative tradesperson. As a consequence, encouragement was provided for disciplined observation of the workplace, and in some instances for patenting, as an incentive for artisan thought. The Wakefield Mechanics Institute, for example, took steps to develop (in 1825) a joint stock company to foster inventions made by Institute members.[22]

These ideological intentions of the movement did not however align with the reality. For the artisan members, the key advantage of the Institutes was that in a fluid labour market, where trades employment was now free of kinship or guild obligations, the Institutes acted as a labour exchange for workmen who could claim superior technical abilities by their membership. For them, the Institutes thus acted as buffer against the job displacement consequences of industrial advance that were widely perceived as having a principal effect on the less skilled workers. Institute libraries also provided a source of reading material that was very difficult to acquire at low wages, and so fed the widely felt desire of the illiterate classes to acquire reading skills, seen to be essential in participating in the culture of the time.[23] Neither stimulus for working-class membership contributed to advancement to economic wealth. Rather, they consolidated the position of members as a class set apart from the unskilled, but not members of the bourgeoisie.

The technical discoveries that led to economic wealth did not come from the workshop, nor from science. This was the case even in the early days of the Industrial Revolution. Instead, technological mastery of the productive processes was largely in the hands of the capitalists who controlled the means of production, and those that controlled the production of engineering designs – through capitalist engineering design companies. Apart from the very early days of industrialisation, the widely fostered image of the self-made man rising from the artisan class was very little more than a myth.[24] I will return to this point later in the present chapter. For now, it is simply worth noting that the intentions of the Mechanics Institute patrons to foster the rise of artisans to positions of wealth through scientific instruction were doomed from the start.

Meanwhile, the reality of the reasons for middle-class commitment to the movement lay less in the expressed aims of improvement of the lower classes, than in the subtext of creating a more ordered society. The production of work (and social) discipline, the production of the belief in opportunity, the production of a technical skill-based status, all served the interests of capitalism. For each of these goals directly aligned with capitalism's rapacious need for compliant (rather than powerful and resistant) sources of artisan expertise. This capital-serving subtext may not have been visible even for the most perceptive of the middle-class reformers. But nevertheless it was there, for it expressed the collective ideological alignment that was growing up alongside the emergent technological frame.

Thus, the reality of the Institutes – both in the product of the objectives of membership for artisans, and in the covert influence of their middle-class patrons – was the production of greater numbers of skilled and adaptable workmen, and the creation of new social and economic hierarchies that stabilised the contribution of skill to industrial progress.[25] The opportunities for rising to the ranks of the bourgeoisie were outflanked by the role of technical knowledge in industrialisation that had already been set in place even in the early days of the assertion of the technological frame.

There are a number of ways in which the covert intentions of the middle-class patrons were expressed.

Science was presented as the path for individual improvement. What was drawn from science into the Mechanics Institutes was not its specific application to produce wealth, but its *method* – of disciplined observation and contribution in the workplace. The Institutes had little chance of forging a bridge between science and industrial wealth, for even in knowledgeable scientific circles, the bridge between science and industrial practice was loose and highly tenuous. More importantly, what was drawn from science was an ideological product. It was used to show (in keeping with its Baconian roots) the *moral* advantage to be gained from disciplined observation and knowledge. Such discipline would 'fit men more wisely to direct their own conduct in whatever situation they may be placed in (by implication, disordered, anarchistic, metropolitan) society'.[26] This was an ideological use of science that aligned with the middle classes' fear of disorder in a rapidly changing world, a fear that had stimulated the development of schooling for poor children some years before.

The use of science as legitimation for order was not an accidental product of middle-class ignorance of the reality of the way technical knowledge was actually used in production. Rather it was a quite specific intention of the philanthropists who patronised the Mechanics Institute movement. Again, because of the alignment of their interests with the legitimation of capitalism, the philosophies of wide currency at the time amongst the middle classes 'explained' capitalism's power and progress. The Mechanics Institutes provided a central vehicle for popularising the new creed of capitalism, guised in the raiments of science, namely 'political economy'. This philosophy was a 'science' that *explained* the triumph of British industry, and Britain's economic supremacy through *natural laws* by which economy and society intrinsically operated. The 'science' of political economy explained away the social problems that were associated with capitalist progress in terms of violations of these natural 'laws', by those who intransigently refused to follow them. The philosophy therefore encouraged the view that submission to the laws led to infinite progress – an ideological position that directly fitted the claims of the middle classes to superiority in a millennial future of English society, at the same time as 'tranquilizing the popular mind and removing from it all those delusions which are the main cause of popular disaffection'.[27]

Thus the Mechanics Institute movement grew largely out of the particular interstitial alignments of the middle classes in the late eighteenth century. The middle classes were concerned on the one hand to preserve and legitimate the order from which their class advantage was nourished. And on the other hand, the middle classes were concerned to redress the imbalances in this order that they believed were potential signals of disquietening anarchy in a world of change where traditional constraints on order were breaking down. The movement was based on similar premises to those of the earlier interest in establishing charity schools, that is, 'education' to upraise the morality and discipline of the lower classes. In both cases, the middle-class intervention fostered the machine-disciplined order, into which – at this stage – capitalism was beating society into submission. The movement met the interests of its artisan members for it offered a labour-market advantage by which they could separate their skilled superiority from the downtrodden and easily unemployed depressed classes.

Consequently, the Mechanics Institute movement aligned with both the social conditions and trajectory of early industrialism, and also provided a means of 'selling' legitimation of capitalism's ideological rationale. But, paradoxically, the movement was itself enframed within the emerging trajectory of industrialism, and could *only* achieve aims that fitted an alignment with the technological frame itself.

The movement's evolution was fundamentally predicated on the level of penetration (and separation) of labour skill demands, that in the late eighteenth and early nineteenth centuries were basic to industrialism's accelerating power. Thus, instead of building an educated, morally compliant working class who were enthused with the 'laws of political economy', the Mechanics Institute movement *widened* the gap between skilled workers and common labourers. This was so because the movement allowed the skilled labourer a new status, and erected an intervening class between the unskilled working class and the middle classes – as the demand for *new* skill formation progressed. But the new 'skilled' class did not have means of access to middle-class status. They were stuck there, in limbo, as a buffer between the lower classes' aspirations and bourgeois opportunity. Consequently, the Mechanics Institute movement, unintentionally as far as the ideologues were concerned, *limited* the mobility of labour into the middle classes rather than promoted it.[28] The trajectory of technological enframement was calling these class formations and boundaries into being as it increasingly enframed skill into productive enterprise, and nothing the middle-class reformers could do could change it.

By the late 1840s the philanthropists recognised that they were not reaching the masses, whose disorder they most feared. The Chartist, socialist and radical movements were a direct threat, for these movements addressed the interests of the working class more directly. They taught a more radical and popular set of subjects than political economy – encompassing, for example, politics and music. More insidiously, as far as the Mechanics Institute ideologues were concerned, the alternative movements offered *entertainment* – through tea parties and dancing.

The political-economy-inspired philanthropists sought to adjust by upgrading the philanthropic and entertainment image of the Mechanics Institutes. But these moves were unsuccessful in co-opting the lower, less skilled classes. In final recognition of the permanence of classes lower than those that the Mechanics Institutes sought to target, the middle-class philanthropists then shifted focus towards the establishment of the *Lyceum*. These were organisations that sought to co-opt the lower classes into the order of political economy through their greater emphasis on entertainment and elementary education, offered as cheaply as possible.[29]

The intentions of the middle-class reformers in creating the Mechanics Institute movement had therefore failed. The class formation they were dealing with was a direct product of the emergent technological frame, not of ideological intervention that was out of alignment with this frame.

The concern to promote 'political economy' continued, though it had little impact on the working classes whose daily lived experience did not align with the exhortations and doctrines concerning 'natural laws' they *should* abide by. Meanwhile, as the US wrested technological leadership out of the hands of the British, they also exposed the ideological text of political economy that linked 'natural laws' to Britain's industrialism. An excellent example of this arose at the time of a technological advance that *linked* England with the US, in 1875. At that time a duplicate set of stereotype plates of *Chambers Encyclopaedia* was sent to Messrs Lippincott, of Philadelphia, so that the work might be simultaneously printed and issued in the US. The American company however altered the text, still publishing the Encyclopaedia under its British imprint. The alterations specifically contradicted the English view of political economy, and led to considerable conflict between William Chambers, the original publisher, and the American counterpart. The contradictions are expressed in three extracts, concerning 'free trade', 'protection duty' and 'Victoria I':

Free Trade:
   English Edition: This term, when used so late as twenty years ago, expressed a disputed proposition, and was the badge of a political party; it now expresses the most important and fundamental truth in political economy ... it has in reality been established (as an axiom) as the result of a double experience – the one being the failure of all deviations from it, the other the practical success of the principle during the short period in which it has been permitted to regulate the

commerce of the country.

American Edition: A dogma of modern growth, industriously taught by British manufacturers and their commercial agents. For many years certain political economists have laboured to establish this theory upon a reliable basis, and have asserted that the doctrine represents an important truth; but no nation has attained substantial prosperity except by protection to native industry, whether avowed or disavowed. The sophistries of free trade are put forth to lull the suspicions of the deluded purveyors to the wealth of England, and are advocated most strenuously by agents of British manufacturing houses and foreign residents in our cities, whose chief aim is the accumulation of wealth by extensive sales of foreign products, regardless of the injury they may inflict on American interests.

Protection – Protection Duty:
English Edition: In Political Economy, terms applied to a practice, now in disuse in Britain, of discouraging, by heavy duties and otherwise, the importation of foreign goods, under the notion that such a practice increased the prosperity of the country at large.

American Edition: In Political Economy, terms applied to a practice, found necessary in the United States, of discouraging, by heavy duties and otherwise, the importation of foreign goods, it having been proved that such a practice increases the prosperity of the country at large.

Victoria I:
English Edition: The progress made by the nation in the various elements of civilisation, especially in that of material prosperity, has been unparalleled (See Great Britain); and perhaps during no reign has a greater measure of political contentment been enjoyed.

American Edition: The progress made by the nation in the various elements of civilisation, especially in that of material prosperity, has been unparalleled (see Great Britain): but a growing discontent under her unequal institutions, and a progress towards Republicanism, are plainly apparent.[30]

As the US took command over the leading edge of technological progress, according to principles that were at variance with English political economy, the final nail in the coffin of political economy ideology was hammered in. English workers had only to look across the Atlantic to see that there was nothing absolute at all about the English ideology. It was an ideology that stood out of line with where the technological frame had evolved to, and the ideology therefore fell in its influence even within Great Britain.

Conditions of Connection Between Knowledge and the Technology Text

Scientific education, as a vehicle for acceptance of political economy, failed. It failed principally because it did not offer the opportunity promised for the artisan to rise through improved scientific knowledge to self-earned wealth. Thus, the associated doctrines of political economy and discipline had little meaning in terms of the life-experience of members of the Mechanics Institute movement. The reason that scientific education *could not* offer such an opportunity escaped the middle-class ideologues. They did not realise that almost from the start of the Industrial Revolution, the connection between wealth and knowledge was not commanded by either inventors or scientists. Instead, the locus of power in extracting wealth out of technical knowledge lay firmly in the hands of the capitalists. Inventors were essential to the process of capital accumulation, but in general gained very little from the wealth that it generated. *Science* contributed a methodological discipline and basic well-established principles, but *scientists* contributed virtually nothing directly.

In the very early days of the Industrial Revolution, there was a chance for the ambitious and determined artisan to become a successful entrepreneur. This remained the case whilst the technological nature of British industry remained relatively primitive, and whilst the fixed capital requirements of the first industrialists were small.[31] Such opportunity disappeared however in direct proportion to both the rise in capital requirement and technical complexity of the emergent technological frame. At the core of this capital/technical nexus lay the inheritance from the logic of science noted in Chapter 2, that is, the logic of *systems*. What allowed this inheritance to take command of industrial invention and design was the application of steam power as motive energy of the factory systems. For along with the scale, complexity and autonomy (from human motive energy) that steam power offered, the system of factory organisation could expand at a rate that could not even have been envisaged a few years before. The level of capital required for establishing competitive factories grew accordingly.

Boulton and Watt's steam engine factory at Soho was a paragon of the systems that were emerging. The system was not only of technical integration, but also of social alignments and work flows that were required to make the system work. The Soho factory, established in 1799, consisted of a series of specialised foundries and workshops – concerned with separate functions of 'drilling', 'heavy turning', 'heavy fitting', 'nozzle production', 'general fitting', 'special fitting of parallel motions', 'working gears and governors', 'light fitting' (of safety appliances, throttles and stop pipes), 'pattern making', 'castors' and 'smithing'. The shops were all carefully positioned for the efficient delivery of goods from the yards, for the provision of steam-powered energy according to where it was needed, and for the necessary direct communication between functionally related shops.[32]

This form of technical/social organisation was increasingly mirrored throughout the whole factory landscape. What was spreading was a complex technically determined system of interrelated, specialised parts, all organised towards maximum productive efficiency, and beating to an organisational rhythm that labour had to abide by. For innovation to be introduced required fitting technical ideas into a complex established system that linked technical knowledge with direct commercial advantage. Few of the early inventors had either the capital to establish such systems or the breadth of technical and commercial knowledge that was required to put the whole system together. Contemporary scientists, whose focus of interest was in the sacred laws of nature rather than the profane world of commerce, were even further removed from practical technical or commercial knowledge. Even James Watt, as inventor of the core technology of the age – the steam-engine – remained an unsuccessful entrepreneur until he teamed up with the commercial acumen and capital of Thomas Boulton. Consequently, the idea of the 'self-made man', popularised by Samuel Smiles in the 1850s and subsequently perpetuated by historians such as T. S. Ashton, C. H. Lee, François Crouzet and Sidney Pollard, was a myth – a myth that underlay the ideological stance of progress for the masses of the Mechanics Institutes, but a myth nevertheless.

Katrina Honeyman exposed the myth in her comparative study of three representative sectors of the early British industrial economy – leadmining, cottonspinning, and lacemaking. Honeyman demonstrates that tremendous obstacles confronted the 'small man' entering the ranks of industrial entrepreneurs. With rare exception, those who did become entrepreneurs were unable to remain there permanently. Whilst some degree of upward mobility was evident in all three industries that Honeyman studied, in general the rising entrepreneurs were forced back into the milieu from which they had temporarily risen.

What the rising entrepreneurs confronted was the unexpected burden of raising working capital, the crippling market fluctuations that characterised the British economy in early industrialisation, a lack of managerial skill and experience, inadequate credit facilities, and expensive demands for utilising technologies that were no longer stable, but evolving with increasing rapidity.[33] The would-be entrepreneurs also confronted the wealthy, better established families, whose competitive greed is evidenced in the vigour with which they fostered the exploitation of the poor and the young as demonstrated in the last chapter. This elite had also acquired power to control the available labour force through establishing mill-towns over which they could exercise the autocratic power of a feudal lord. They also enjoyed enough political power within the changing face of Parliament to employ strong legislative influence to restrict both the movement of artisans and machinery out of their direct hegemony.

Thus, the entrepreneurs who survived generally came from these wealthier, better established backgrounds. They were frequently members of an hereditary mercantile elite whose roots of capital and influence were deeply planted in the proto-industrial economy of the seventeenth and eighteenth centuries.

As a consequence, the early (successful) inventors of cotton machinery such as Kay, Wyatt and Paul, and Hargreaves were men of 'some social standing and good education'. Samuel Crompton, inventor of the spinning-mule, who rose from an artisan background, died a pauper – in spite of a parliamentary vote of £5,000, and a public subscription of £500 – all of which was lost in business. Similarly, Dr Edward Cartwright, inventor of the powerloom, an exception in being an educated amateur-scientist, failed in business, and only survived poverty through an inherited country living. [34]

The system-based technological text therefore implied a particular relationship between technical knowledge and capital accumulation. The text's *capital intensity* implied prior wealth. The text's technical complexity implied *organisation of specialised knowledge*. The text's hard economic edge and organisational discipline implied *commercial and managerial acumen*. Whilst the independent inventors may have possessed specialised knowledge in some areas, only those with capital possessed power over the *organisation* of separate specialised knowledge areas *in commercial practice*. And the independent inventors had little access to the other capabilities and resources that were implied by the technological text itself. As with all the other aspects of the dynamic forces that created and maintained capitalism that this book has dealt with, the technological *frame* to culture grew out of what had gone before – in particular, the pre-existing powers of a commercial ruling class. Social and economic power *fashioned* the frame out of the technology text, and thereafter, both society and the power interests themselves adjusted to what had been unleashed.

The story of science during this period is the story of unconnectedness with industrialisation that, virtually for the same reasons, characterises the national science/industry nexus in developing countries today. It is a story of exhortation and interest, but not of application. At least this was the case primarily until later (that is, in the twentieth century), when *industry* needed science, and built institutional bridges to capitalise on it.

There was some interest in practical invention on the part of scientists during the early industrialisation period, and there are a number of associations that were formed between scientists and inventors of the time. The dynamic however for both interest and association was more one of 'curiosity' than practical intent. Michael Faraday, for example, struck up a continuing relationship with Henry Maudsley, inventor of early machine tools, but the basis of their relationship was mutual curiosity.[35] In the case of Faraday, his lack of concern with commercial invention mirrored an elite attitude amongst scientists of the time that sought to distance the 'purity' of their science from the mundane world of commerce. For example, Faraday, the son of a blacksmith, when first writing to Sir Humphry Davy seeking employment within his laboratory, asked to be able to quit trade, which he thought 'vicious and selfish'; later in life, though professing warm affection for his father's blacksmith occupation, Faraday was disturbed by the clattering noise made by the sculptor Noble who was chiselling Faraday's bust. Faraday said the reason for his agitation was that 'the noise reminded me of my father's anvil and took me back to my boyhood'.[36]

Consequently the scientific societies remained aloof from industry. When the first direct attempt was made to establish a closer working relationship between scientists and industry – in the establishment of the British Association for the Advancement of Science – the move was initiated, not by scientists, but by the middle-class philanthropists who were seeking to widen their ideological base for fostering 'political economy'. The Association brought together intellectuals, politicians and businessmen to promote science, based on the premise that economic improvement went hand in hand with scientific progress. Scientists who became involved saw wider markets for their research publication and influence, and saw that they could be more closely associated with the leading edge of 'progress' in British society – industrial development.

Industrialists who became involved found legitimation in membership, as it provided a higher level rationale than that provided by economic gain for the technological choices they made (including those that specifically disenfranchised labour), and for expansion of enterprises.[37] In both cases of scientists and capitalists however, the reason for Association membership was oriented towards status and legitimation, not towards practical commercial linkages. For industrial patrons, commitment was limited, for the utilitarian value of the Association to them was minimal: they did not see direct commercial advantage in it, but a social status that could equally be acquired in other cultural activities concerning music, art collections, antiquarian societies and so on.[38] Thus the Association, similar to many national research institutions in developing nations today, produced many papers (on for example, the steam engine, the railroad and fuel saving), but no applications. The sum of £500 was allocated in 1836 for research into Cornish steam engines, the strength of cast iron, railroads and steamboats, but very little effort beyond rhetoric was made to put application into effect. And,

> for the most part, neither the British Association nor the many provincial literary and philosophic societies (that the middle-class patrons had established with similar ideological intent) were able to demonstrate the existence of a relationship between scientific theory and any practical technological advance.[39]

Scientific advance therefore did not power the Industrial Revolution. Nor was it substantially associated with the development of industrialism's technological frame that followed immediately thereafter.

Perhaps the only real exception was the introduction and use of the electric telegraph. Paramount in the reasons for its commercial success however was that as an invention fostered by science, it stood outside the capital demands of the factory system, but *inside* the demand that was being generated for the *interconnection* of the wider technological system of society.

Inventions that spawned the electric telegraph were publicised as early as 1753, and from there on, practical inventions emerged in parallel with interests amongst scientific circles in the phenomenon of electricity.[40] But, more than anything else, the telegraph offered to later scientists, particularly William Cooke and Charles Wheatstone, a means of pursuing their curiosity. As Jewkes, Sawers and Stillerman observe,

The telegraph was an invention which revealed to physicists an application of their work and also provided new phenomena for them to study. For this reason the improvements to the telegraph and its extension to undersea uses were largely the work of scientists.[41]

What turned the inventions of Cooke and Wheatstone into widely distributed practical reality was that the technological system had reached a point where telegraphy was necessary for continued progress of the system as a whole. Thus, 'the stimulus for the development of telegraphy was not provided until the 1830s, with the expansion of the railway network in Britain.'[42] Associated with expansion of the railways was the need for immediate distance communication, so the invention was taken up by the Great Western Railway company who could progress in their capitalist interests only once this reverse salient was rectified. High levels of capital and technical complexity were however absent in the integration of the telegraph system with industrialisation. It was effectively an add-on innovation that was associated with (rather than *technically* integral to) the high capital railway system that was emerging. The scientists therefore presented an innovation whose 'time was right' for the continuing expansion of the technological frame of industrialisation.

It was not until a considerable time later that science started to play a direct role in industrialisation itself. This occurred when *industry* of the late nineteenth century confronted a reverse salient that only scientific enquiry could solve, and the first 'science-based' industries were born. The market in new colours within the dyestuff industry was by that time fiercely competitive, as the consumer appeal of fashionable apparel spread increasingly throughout the whole society, rather than the smaller elite who had enjoyed the primary benefits of the textile industry's earlier progress. The creation of new colours required new chemicals, a process that was simply too inefficient without the direct use of science to go exploring amongst the elements of chemical knowledge. Bayer in Germany, the nation that was by that time leading the field, therefore conducted chemical research amongst the compounds that were likely to produce new colours. His quest was successful, and led to his firm creating industrial research laboratories that institutionalised research *within* the company – and therefore drew the more sophisticated end of the society's technical stock of knowledge inside the boundaries of organisation practice. Based on the demonstration of successful industrial innovation that this research on colours unleashed, the laboratories within Bayer expanded up to the time of World War I, as the company grew and diversified its production to include pharmaceuticals, heavy chemicals, photographic laboratory supplies and synthetic polymers. The corporation, as a direct result of incorporating research into production, therefore grew from a minor slot in the industrial ratings to become market leader, a demonstration effect that other companies did not fail to notice.[43]

Science did not however offer the leading edge of industrial progress until after World War II. Existing markets for capitalist expansion were saturated. And the 'demonstration effect' of 'planning' science during the war showed that science *could* be planned for the achievement of practical ends. Thus, the leading growth industries of the post-war period (with growth rates of 10 per cent or more per annum) were born. These were in the areas of electronic consumer and capital goods (video, television, communications equipment), consumer durables (passenger cars, washing machines), synthetic materials incorporated in household goods, toys and packaging materials, drugs (antibiotics, tranquillisers, the Pill), and petrochemicals and agricultural chemicals that increase the energy and food resources on which general consumption depends. All of these industries rely on complex technical knowledge and the incorporation of new scientific and technological advances into corporate structure.[44] However, as I will show in the next chapter, the direct incorporation of science into corporate development also depended on a steady progression of prior engineering knowledge *within* the firm, and *new organisational structures* that allowed the construction of direct bridges between science and industrial practice.[45] Without these prior adjustments within the practical knowledge application resources within corporate enterprise, and without the direct demand – for the sake of competitive advantage – for *new* scientific knowledge, science, to this day, remains relatively unconnected to the technology text of industrialisation.[46] This is generally the case except where large capital-rich corporations command the leading edge of the technological progress.

Therefore, throughout the entire history of industrialisation, the 'technology text' and its direct association with the assumptions of capitalism *commanded* science, not the other way around. In the early days of the Industrial Revolution, science provided an ethos for disciplined technical observation; it provided a way of thought that encouraged the development of technical and social *systems*; it acted as ideological legitimation for the burgeoning interests of the classes that ruled (and were nourished by) capitalism, and that were nourished by progress in the frame to culture that an ever-expanding technology text provided. The resulting technological frame commanded the transition in craft and technically-based social formations that were associated with industrialisation. The technological frame called forth new skills and classes that fostered the system's further development. The technological frame called forth the *use* of science when no other means of progress were available. But equally, the use of more sophisticated knowledge could only occur when the organisational and social structures that surrounded the technological frame were drawn into alignment with the frame itself. This is not a technological determinist view of progress. Instead, this is a view of the development of technology's impact on (and relationship to) society that arose out of *alignment* between technical and social forces and ideologies.

The Subservience of Knowledge, Power, Ideology and Culture to the Technology Text

Following Louis Althusser, ideology is a structural feature of any society. Its functions are to cement the society's unity. All that is different in a class-based society is that the ideology makes opaque the exploitative interests of the ruling class.[47]

Ideology therefore provides a grammar for the social order. The myths that yield the ideology's *absolute* definition of the situation are constructed and reconstructed within daily life *inside* this grammar. And, as soon as the grammar of itself is questioned for falling out of line with experience, the ideology loses its power to define order, and to legitimate those interests that have most to gain from the way things are. Thus ideology can not be merely imposed by a ruling class, and be expected to survive. Rather, ideology makes sense of the *whole* order in which all classes participate, and it legitimates for the exploited classes, the 'natural' position of authority of their masters. The society as a whole needs order in its meaning system, not just the ruling class.

This chapter has shown the support structure on which the early capitalist ideology of social order rested. The grammar of the ideology was embodied in the wider frame of science. For, during the eighteenth century, this grammar increasingly made sense of a world of change and 'progress' in a way that religion could not. The *ideological* order of science was not however imposed in opposition to the religious order that went before. Rather, it *grew out of* religion, as religious world views continuously adjusted to a reality that would not stand still. Religion-based morality prepared the way – particularly through the vehicle of schooling – for a moral discipline that aligned with a factory-based industrial order that was just emerging. Wider appeal was to the natural and universal laws of God, but the final resting place of the ideology was *in* the morality of daily labour *in* daily life. This religious position itself had grown, in ascetic Protestantism, out of what had gone before in the moral concept of labour within monastic Catholicism. In the eighteenth century however, as the reality that people confronted was increasingly a product of human *rational* systems, God adjusted further and put on the raiments of science. The morality remained the same, but God's laws dictating disciplined obeisance to industrial discipline transmuted into Science's laws of nature. Based in the Baconian moral perspective (that nature's laws were accessible only through disciplined observation), appeal to science's laws equally implied obeisance and discipline. The ideology of science therefore took up where religion left off, and co-opted the exploited classes into the 'mythology' that millennial progress and national power depended on 'natural laws' (of the 'science' of political economy) that implied the authority of capitalists and the necessity for the lower classes' own exploitation. Both authority and exploitation within the prevailing order could be legitimated through science's ideology in terms of the disinterested laws of reality that science itself embodied.

The main observation that follows is that the scaffolding of ideology on which emerging industrial society rested did not stand still, but was in a process of continuous adjustment. Even though the moral core of daily life *appeared* to be the same, the wider contextual meaning in which the morality was set was hooked onto a continuously reconstructing scaffold of legitimations. As with any culture, the society had to deal with the *reality* it confronted in a whole and meaningful way. It therefore *had* to adjust at the deepest of ontological levels as the reality was transformed. What is particularly interesting to note from the early Industrial Revolution is that the main vehicle for carriage and transformation of ideology lay, not so much amongst the wealthier elements of the mercantilist and capitalist elite, as in the middle classes.

The wealthier ruling classes did not have the same need for finding legitimation. The ruling capitalist classes grew out of a pre-existing mercantilist elite, and continued a tradition of power to exploit. Their exploitation was direct and repressive for they continued to stand on a pedestal of privilege that was supported and legitimated by the congenially resonant political power of coercion. The lower classes, for them, were intrinsically unequal human beings, who, as John Stuart Mill said some years later, needed to be disciplined to remind them of their place, and who were without 'any taste for amusement, or enjoyment of repose' anyway.[48]

The middle classes however confronted an entirely different legitimation crisis. They emerged out of new social alignments that were being called forth by the changes in the productive order of the eighteenth century. The middle classes stood in an interstitial location *within* the superordinate and subordinate social order, and had greatest need of legitimation of an order, the trajectory of which was unclear, but to which their interests were directly wedded. Thus, the emerging middle classes played (and continue to play) a critical role in *balancing* the interests of the exploiters against those of the exploited. They sculpted the shape of ideological legitimation whilst tenuously seeking to maintain this balance.

It was the (principally) middle-class reformers who, in the interests of order, created the schools system for the poor that symbolically bridged the order of superordinate and subordinate interests in the society. It was the middle-class reformers who established Mechanics Institutes, and promoted science as a means of proselytising and legitimating the 'natural laws' framework of political economy. These were not cynical exercises in co-optation. Rather they were the well-intentioned acts of groups that most desperately needed to define and find the order on which their social location depended.

Thus, legitimation of the order of capitalist industrial 'progress' came from *within* the society rather than from the exploiters at the top. Capitalist interests continued their path of direct exploitation (as is evidenced in their use of child labour until the late nineteenth century) until overt exploitation was no longer so necessary. This became the case when the society was so embedded in capitalism's technological text that continued progress and capitalist profitability were guaranteed. The capitalists lived more comfortably in their privilege under the legitimations that the middle classes fostered, but they were less the instigators of *balance* on which acceptance of ruling class authority by the lower classes fundamentally depended in the longer term.

What is also of particular interest to note from the early Industrial Revolution is that the technological text itself developed its power as a frame to society by increasingly commanding the basic values assumptions of both culture and the legitimation of power.

In the eighteenth century, and even the first part of the nineteenth century, industrial technological systems stood alongside craft-based alternatives. Industrial production experience played *a* part in the cultural negotiations that produced both order and its legitimation. But progressively the role of the industrial technological system took over the centre field of these cultural plays. By the 1840s, the culture had moved largely into alignment, and all definitions and legitimations, as well as protests and reforms, were formed *in terms of* the technology text, not independently of it. By this time the technological text had moved from being a player in a cultural game of equals, to being the referee, a 'frame' within which culture was constituted.

The *power* of the technological frame came from its culture-*defining* properties. Capitalism would have been powerless without this *cultural* command of technology. The technological frame of industrialism injected into society a continually shifting *reality* to which (as in all cultures) the society had to adjust. The technological frame injected new social relations of production and obligation – originally through direct *social* coercion, but subsequently by demands of the frame itself. The frame injected new modes of communication and cohesion in a social/geographic landscape that was in constant movement, but which was dictated by technological system requirements. The frame erected new superordinate symbols to the reality of industrialism that could not be avoided in daily life experience, and which communicated what society was really about, and where it was going. In other words, the technological frame attacked the culture at the level of the *basic premises* from which cultural meanings are constituted in *any* society. As the frame increasingly confronted the life-world with its inevitability and ubiquity, it therefore set the grammar in place for subsequent cultural adjustment, and the socialisation of consciousness into its command.

These culture-defining properties all depended on the basic *technical* properties of the *system*. The concept of the system itself had however, like ideology and class alignments, grown out of the cultural roots that had been planted before.

The *idea* of the technical system, as with ideology and morality, grew out of Baconian science's view of the aesthetics of the cosmos – as a smoothly integrated, interconnected reality, external in its laws to human intention. The *application* of the technical system to human affairs aligned with the shift in eighteenth-century ideological grammar, which, adjusting to reality, displaced God (and the autonomous human) in favour of rational thought (and the dependent human) in defining the ontology of life and the cosmos. This move, which put humans at the service of technical ingenuity rather than technical invention in service of human play, was symbolised in the employment of Jacques de Vaucanson in factories in the 1740s rather than in the creation of mechanical ducks, a case presented in Chapter 2.

The basic premise of 'systems' that was drawn from these cultural transformations was the concept of *order*. The technical properties of systems, and therefore their culture-defining properties all follow.

Technical systems increase order through centralised control over the smooth integration of specialised parts, which, according to the necessity of integration, implies standardisation. Order is therefore increased by greater complexity of the integration of more highly specialised (but standardised) sub-components. Order is increased within this field of complexity through greater conceptual and co-ordinative control at the centre. Technical systems increase order by internalising and ordering the environments that lie outside the pre-existing system. Order is therefore enhanced by increasing power and scale, and by increasing ubiquity as the system spreads and interconnects with other standardised systems. With increased order of productive arrangements comes efficiency and predictability in transforming the natural world, basic premises for increasingly profitable extraction of wealth out of technical transformations.

It was the dynamic of increased system order that powered the expansion of the technological frame throughout nineteenth-century society. The property of complexity brought forth new artisan technical skills that nourished the implementation of more complex systems. At the same time, the property of specialisation allowed previous skills to be digested *into* the machines. The shifting face of social status and class formations and solidarities have followed this moving balance between skill creation and incorporation. The property of control brought forth professionalism, in particular of engineers who, in seeking a social status that aligned with the system, also fed the separation of concept from execution, an alienation that has underscored work design ever since. The properties of scale and complexity taken together have implied capital wealth as precursor to participation in system control – and therefore have implied exclusion of those without capital from the benefits of system progress. The twin properties of scale and complexity also imply a critical role for specialised knowlege, not in its isolated specialisation, but within *organisation* of specialities and application of a coherent whole to the practical issues concerning the system's technical arrangement. The power that is derived from knowledge is therefore not in the knowledge itself, but in the organisation of knowledge – a power that is not accessible to individual inventors or scientists, but to those who have capital power to employ and translate separate individual contributions. This is so except where the specialised knowledge directly *fits* within the parameters that are already set by the system, and where the knowledge answers a critical reverse salient to the system's progress, as in the case of the use of the telegraph. Power was therefore in the hands of the system controllers, not in the hands of individual scientists and inventors, right from the start of the Industrial Revolution. Science provided the leading edge *only* when the system of knowledge incorporation – through intervening engineering skills – had been digested *into* the system, and the reverse salient of future expansion required organisation of *new* knowledge into the system. This demand for science (particularly after World War II) was however stimulated by consumer markets that had burgeoned as a direct result of cultural changes that the productive system had itself injected. I will return to these cultural transformations in Chapter 9.

The properties of the technological system, with their associated culture-*defining* power, have therefore commanded culture since they were *sedimented* into a social alignment with technical properties in the mid-nineteenth century. Ideologies and legitimations (for example, through political economy) were swept aside or transformed as they moved out of alignment with the spread of *system*atic ordering throughout all social relations and communications experience. (This is a topic I will take up in more detail in Chapter 9.) For daily life, once out of alignment with ideological definitions of order, irrevocably leads to the demolition of the ideology. Equally, ideological transformations have continuously readjusted in alignment with the system's trajectory. And both economic and political power have been maintained only whilst their sources and legitimation aligned with the social order of a technologically enframed culture.

Meanwhile, the 'written text' of the technological system becomes increasingly opaque by virtue of its 'non-phonetic' complexity. The 'oral text' of daily life is fashioned entirely within this written text. The written text thus commands a passive, non-participative culture whose meanings are created within the system's grammar, but not actively constituted outside it. This may be a culture that tolerates protest, but protest and rebellion are framed within the system. So it is not a culture that can transform the system itself at the level of its basic grammar.

Consequently, the culture of industrialism is the culture of the technological frame. Its assumptions and values were sedimented into the culture-technology alignment that was forged out of prior cultural alignments in the early nineteenth century, and persisted thereafter.

From an analysis of the *emergence* of the technological frame we can then see the power of what it is that traditional societies and developing countries confront today. For what they confront is the finished product. Traditional cultures are not involved in the negotiations and transformations that gave rise to the original social alignment. Instead, they are confronted by a complete and systematically related set of fully articulated cultural assumptions that are sedimented *into* every modern artefact that people experience.

Behind the artefact stands the whole *background* frame of factory, transport, energy, communications, market and knowledge systems – a contextual grammar that must be accepted for an industrial artefact to be used or to make sense. Sedimented into this background text are the *developed* cultural assumptions of order that the system implies – concerning capital, power, ideology, knowledge and morality – all smoothly integrated into an aesthetic that puts active human constitution of meaning (and therefore control) at service of the technological frame itself. And the trajectory of the technological frame (though not its properties) is controlled by capital interests with a rich international power base to which a developing nation can never have anything but dependent access.

Sedimented into the background text are the very properties from which culture can be constituted – concerning communication modes and practices, social relations of production, and superordinate symbols of an order that by its powerful imposition of change, destroys the roots of a culture that is static in an unvarying reality niche. As a deeply inscribed written text, the technological frame is therefore 'context-blind' to the non-aligned cultures into which it penetrates. And traditional cultures must give way to the internationalised 'superculture'[49] that marches in as soon as the first modern artefact arrives. The only ones who benefit are those who have the capital and adjustment power to switch into alignment with the technological frame and its associated superculture the fastest.

Finalisation of the script of the 'Tragedy of Technology' requires that I tell two more stories. Both concern powerlessness that is experienced under an illusion of power. The first story is of imperialism. It is the story of what was happening in Australia at the far end of the British imperialist empire whilst the Industrial Revolution was getting under way and maturing. Australia was intentionally, as far as Britain was concerned, an outpost that fed Britain's burgeoning industrial might, and a dumping ground for those most intractable elements of Britain's industrialising society who did not accept its authority. But what was exported to Australia was not only Britain's convicts. What was also exported was an ideology that centred on Britain's imperialist might to define the cultural situation in terms of Britain's interest. The product was a 'cultural cringe' that persists to this day, caught in a time-warp of the nineteenth century. The product also was an impoverished technical base for a society that, seduced by the wealth it acquired in the late nineteenth century in service of Britain, remained inadequately prepared for entering the technologically led society of the twentieth century. This result is still being played out today in Australia's susceptibility to the neo-colonialism that marched in with local cultural bands playing tunes of willing acceptance, immediately after World War II. I will tell this story in the next chapter.

The second story concerns the way that the 'superculture' of modern consumerism came into being. As the opening metaphor of Chapter 10 expresses, it is the story of Echo and Narcissus. The superculture is the culture of image. It is the culture of a morality that is based on image. And the images were set in place as the cultural properties and assumptions of the technological frame were translated into *mirrors* in subjective life during the first part of the twentieth century. As with Echo and Narcissus, active constitution of meaning in modern culture is atrophying under the definitions of reality that these images imply. For the mirrors imply a passive culture, the morality and direction of which is dependent on the technological frame. The people feel powerful, but this is a power that is not determined by them, but *for* them. The social alignments that result are less ones of bourgeoisie and proletariat, and more ones of 'cognitariat' (to use Alvin Toffler's term to describe those whose 'thought' is captured into the technological frame)[50] and 'spectatariat' who watch the world go by under the command of the technological frame, but feel powerless to change it. This is the final social product and social alignment that the technological frame to culture has brought forth to this day.

Waiting in the Colonial Wings

Marginalisation of Industrial Development[1]

In August 1786, one year after Boulton and Watt installed their first condensing steam engine in a textile factory in Nottinghamshire, the King of England decreed an 'Order in Council' that New South Wales be established as Britain's new penal colony.[2] With the proximity of these two historic events, the birth of contemporary Australian society directly coincided with the technological start of the Industrial Revolution. Australia was formed however as an outcropping, not a participant in industrialisation. The colony fed Britain's need for agricultural products and minerals, and in turn was fed by Britain's cultural products. The colony fed Britain's need to dispose of the most intransigent elements of its lower classes, and was in turn fed by ideologies and institutions that maintained its dependence on Britain. And, both by design and because of continued industrial dependence on Britain, Australia developed only that minimal level of an industrial base as was necessary to foster Britain's imperialist interest in the nation's products and markets. As a direct result, Australia has remained on the margins of industrialisation ever since, crouched in a mendicant cringe to the technological fashion leaders of international capitalism.

Throughout the nineteenth century, whilst Britain surged forward to industrial might, Australia sat complacently in the background watching it all go past – either basking in Britain's reflected imperialist glory, or resting languidly in the shadow of its own sheep. In the first instance this was the direct design of Britain's imperialist strategy. In 1822–3 Commissioner Bigge, in his Reports to the British House of Commons, specifically discouraged colonial manufacture of goods which could be imported from Britain on the premise that 'only agricultural labour was likely to reform convicts'.[3] This ideological position only thinly disguised the vested interests of Britain's emerging bourgeoisie, for they had very little interest in reforming the lower classes, and considerable interest in marketing. The usefulness of Australia's colonies to Britain's nineteenth-century bourgeoisie is demonstrated in import statistics (for the colony of New South Wales) when statistics started to be collected some 30 to 40 years later. Between 1860 and 1870, 69 per cent to 70 per cent of *all* imports into NSW (except those from other British colonies in Australia) came from the UK. The percentage rose to nearly 80 per cent by 1880, before declining (to 61 per cent by 1901), as Britain's influence at the centre of international manufacturing started to atrophy.[4]

During the period when Britain's influence over colonial imports was strongest, from 1860 to the 1880s, Australia was one of the wealthiest countries (or collection of colonies) in the world. None of this wealth however was drawn from industrialisation. Instead, in keeping with its colonial status and servicing of British interests, the nation was basking in the foreign trade philosophy of 'tonnage-out'/'technology-in'. Thus, by 1860, across the colony of NSW, the manufacturing works covered only the fairly basic needs of a colony that was so remote from Britain. That is, there was a small number of food and provisions manufacturing establishments, whilst a large percentage of other provisions and household goods were imported. Meanwhile, the major concentration of manufacturing was on the production of agricultural machinery (38 per cent of all factories), and ship-building and repair – the lifeline of the colony. Indeed the dominance of the industrial structure by agriculture persisted through the remainder of the nineteenth century: 70 per cent of industrial establishments in 1876, for example, made agricultural machinery.[5]

Thus, as the nineteenth century drew to a close, the industrial base in Australia was very poorly developed. The result was that when new *core* technologies were introduced they had nothing like the impact they had overseas where they bedded into an industrial structure that was prepared – in terms of opening up whole new infrastructures of economic and social opportunity, and in consolidating a technological base for further development.

This was the case right from the start of the colonies' histories. Sydney's 'first mechanical engineer of substance', John Dickson (who had learnt his trade directly from James Watt), brought the first steam engine into the colony of NSW in 1813. The innovation of steam power did stimulate the development of *basic* diversification in the local economy, and a basic shipbuilding industry (the only transport link between the colonies). But steam power did not stimulate the development of an industrial sector as Boulton and Watt's engine had done in Britain 28 years earlier. Local markets were very small, and Dickson, like the rest of the free settlers in the colony, had his head turned towards open plains and exports rather than indoor machine systems.[6] Even towards the end of the steam era, by 1901, when the separate Australian states federated, and after a post-Gold Rush manufacturing surge, 41 per cent of all Australian factories used *only* manual labour, and had no power-driven machines.[7]

Similarly, the core technology of railways was introduced into Australian colonies in the early 1850s, not long after the diffusion of railway systems throughout Britain, Europe and the US. But railways did not act to service the interconnection of industrialisation, even though railway systems spread rapidly throughout the Australian continent. The first steam-powered railway was constructed by B. H. Babbage in 1852, over a few miles from Adelaide to Port Adelaide within the colony of South Australia.[8] By 1861, 243 miles of track had been constructed throughout the continent; ten years later, 1,030 miles of track had been laid; by 1881, 4,192 miles of railway tracks were in place, a distance that rapidly expanded to 10,394 miles in 1891, and 13,497 miles by 1901.[9] However, this rapid diffusion of the technology had very little relevance to the development and interconnection of an industrial base. Instead, railways provided a quicker means of getting crops to the seaports to send to Britain, and a faster means of transporting imports (from Britain) from one colony to the next, as well as of moving people between the isolated metropolises. The enormous boom in wealth that characterised the same period was based on primary production and urban construction, not on railways-led manufacturing, a situation at complete variance with what happened in the US.[10]

The only basic engineering factories that were stimulated by railways (and by the need for agricultural machinery) were those that fed these technologies directly. In NSW by 1876, 158 factories were operating as iron and tin works; iron, brass and copper foundries; lead works; machinists; engineers; and type foundries – compared with 119, nine years earlier. However, most activity was in service of agriculture and railways, not of other sectors of industry.[11]

The story of what happened with the introduction of the subsequent core technology, electricity, appears on the surface to have been quite different. For electricity generation did have an immediate impact on the expansion of secondary industry. In NSW in 1893, prior to the introduction of electricity, 96 per cent of all installed energy-producing machinery (by horsepower) was powered by steam (the rest by gas and water). The percentage of energy supplied by steam power dropped slightly in 1893 (to 93 per cent) – in favour of water and gas power – and remained stable until 1901 when electricity generation was widely introduced. Still, at that time, nearly 10 per cent of the energy used in the 'heat, light and power' industry was produced by *water* power. Just five years later however, electricity was a rising force, and the use of steam power was dropping – to 84 per cent of installed machinery power in 1906, and 81 per cent three years later. There had been a growth in the percentage of power generated from electricity generating stations from 11 per cent (in 1901) to 32 per cent (in 1906), a percentage that continued to rise to 53 per cent by the start of World War II. But most importantly, directly coinciding with the five-year growth in electricity application, there had been a growth in the total installed energy capacity for industry by *270 per cent*. The effects on manufacturing industry were immediate. As noted earlier, in 1901, 41 per cent of all establishments used *only* manual labour and no power-driven machinery. But by 1906, this percentage of factories without mechanical power had fallen to 35 per cent – thence, to 29 per cent in 1911, and 5 per cent by 1939. Between 1901 and 1906 there was a 50 per cent increase in the number of manufacturing factories, accompanied by a 64 per cent increase in employment in secondary industry.[12]

Thus, the early twentieth-century take-off in manufacturing industry in Australia was facilitated by centralised electricity production. However, without the prior industrial development, and without the orientation to *use* heavy industry, take-off in manufacturing followed the path of light industry for wider diversification of consumer products. Industrialisation was not concerned with heavy industry development. The contrast to what was happening in Germany and the US was enormous. Both countries had been strongly expanding and concentrating in the heavy industry base that Australia lacked. Krupps, the steel manufacturer in Germany, employed 16,000 people by 1873, rising through the early twentieth century (with the advent of electricity) to 70,000 people in 1914. This was a pattern of growth and concentration that was mirrored in France's 'Schneider-Dreusot', Britain's 'Vickers Armstrong' and the US' 'Carnegie' corporations.[13] The Krupps labour force exceeded the total manufacturing labour force of NSW in 1901.

Meanwhile Australia was importing steel, trade that accounted for 5 per cent of total imports in 1901 – imports across enormous distance from the US and Europe. As an import, steel was only surpassed by machine tools and implements (13 per cent), textiles and dress materials (26 per cent), 'drinks, narcotics and stimulants' (11 per cent), and staple 'vegetable substances' (6 per cent).[14] This pattern of imports revealed an economy that still fundamentally depended on European and US society for its lifestyle, technology and heavy industry, the substance of the twentieth-century economy. Britain had been displaced from its central command of Australia's imports – providing 61 per cent of imports in 1901, a 20 per cent decline from two decades earlier.[15] But Britain had left the legacy of its 120 years of rule that was visited upon Australia's move into urbanisation and consumerism, a legacy that had produced a technologically weak industrial structure, a legacy that Australia is still living with today. Australia had not participated in the laying down of the capabilities and technologies of an industrialising technologically-based society.

As a result, whilst Europe and the US in the late nineteenth century were vying with each other for industrial dominance, Australia remained content to bask in the glory of its agricultural wealth, living off primary industry in metropolises that were largely oriented towards services, not industrial development. Thus, as Barry Jones observed, Australia jumped across the development of a manufacturing base to become the first 'service-based' economy in the world. Unlike Britain, the US and Western Europe, manufacturing was *never* dominant in the employment of the Australian labour force. Instead, as Figure 1 shows, services replaced agriculture to become the largest employer towards the end of the nineteenth century, some 30 years before the manufacturing sector surpassed agricultural sector occupations as the second largest employment source.[16]

The consequence is very important indeed. The relative predominance of primary and tertiary industries led to an economy that was based on relatively low skilled enterprise. When the *international* economy later crossed from manufacturing to service sector dominance, the service sector was linked into a highly developed technical infrastructure. This was not the case in Australia, where the predominant skill of nineteenth-century service industry employees was household management. Domestic servants constituted 16 per cent of the entire 1891 non-primary producer labour force.[17]

It was at this level, of constraining development of the technical knowledge base within the technological structure of the economy, that Britain's ideology had its most insidious impact. Not only were the ideologies that supported Britain's imperialism accepted; not only was Britain's command over lifestyle and values accepted. More importantly, Australia accepted Britain's ideologies concerning education and science.

The British example was characterised by disconnection between education, science and industrialisation, as was demonstrated in the last chapter. At the turn of the twentieth century, as the internationalised technological trajectory started to slip from Britain's command, this lack of alignment of education and technical knowledge development with industry was directly at fault. Thus, Australia was left with an

FIGURE 1 CHANGE OVER TIME IN OCCUPATIONS WITHIN AUSTRALIAN LABOUR FORCE

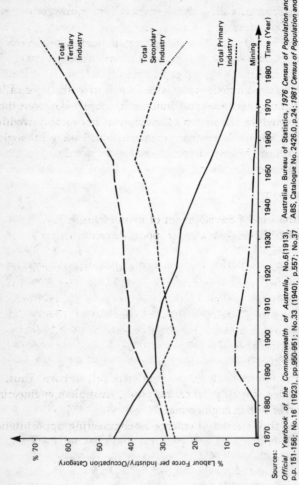

Sources:

Official Yearbook of the Commonwealth of Australia, No.6(1913), p.p. 151-156; No.16 (1923), pp.950-951; No.33 (1940), p.557; No.37 (1946-47), p.1291; No.43 (1957): CCWA, April 1911, Vol III, 'Detailed Tables', pp.1284-1285.

Commonwealth Bureau of Census and Statistics, *Labour Report, No.51* (1964), pp. 183-184; *Labour Report No. 53* (1961), pp.150-152, *No.58* (1973), (ABS, Canberra), p.14.

Australian Bureau of Statistics, 'Labour Statistics, Australia 1982', ABS, Catalogue No. 6101.0, p.27; 'Labour Statistics, Australia 1983', Catalogue No. 6101.0, p.46.

Australian Bureau of Statistics, *1976 Census of Population and Housing* ABS, Catalogue No. 2426.0, p.24; *1981 Census of Population and Housing*, ABS, Catalogue No. 2452.0, pp.56-57.

Australian Bureau of Statistics, *The Labour Force, Australia, August 1984*, ABS, Catalogue No. 6203.0, p.27.

ideological inheritance that was out of keeping with the direction in which the technological trajectory of industry was moving in the early twentieth century. Yet, the nation continued to adhere to Britain's example, even after Britain took its imperialist power home and whilst Britain steadily dropped off the international economic map. Between World War I and World War II there were some technologically sophisticated entrepreneurs in Australia, and even some interest amongst politicians in technology-led industry. However, it was only when confronted by the reality of technological isolation during World War II, and by the reality that wealth was no longer safe in agricultural and raw material production, that the Australian stocks of technical knowledge and educational culture started to align with those called forth by an advancing technological frame elsewhere – but even then, only slowly. Meanwhile, the nation's lifestyle was irrevocably wedded to the burgeoning 'superculture' that the internationalised technological frame had called forth, but which local technical knowledge alignments could not feed, but according to tradition, had to import.

Marginalisation of Technical Education

In parallel with the lack of development of manufacturing industry in colonial Australia, there was a very poor development of local technological skills.

During the nineteenth century, Australia drew its population of engineers almost exclusively from Britain. From Angus Buchanan's analysis of the *Australian Dictionary of Biography*, 71 people could be classed as engineers in Australia during the period from 1788 to 1850, and all but two were immigrants from the British Isles. Of the 138 engineers listed for the period between 1851 and 1890, whilst 6 per cent had emigrated from other major industrialising nations than Britain (the US, Germany and France), still, 80 per cent were British born. Thus, as Buchanan concludes, 'for all practical purposes, Australian engineering was an extension of British engineering'.[18]

Some independence started to emerge as engineering opportunities appeared in the late nineteenth century, and Australia started to organise engineering as a profession, and to train its own engineers. The Engineering Association of New South Wales was founded in 1870, and the Victorian Institute of Engineers in 1883. University courses began at the University of Melbourne in the 1860s, and at the University of Sydney in the 1880s. However, following the educational priorities of Britain, engineering education grew very slowly. By 1915 only 200 engineers were enrolled in university engineering courses in Australia – compared with nearly 1,000 medical students and 1,300 Arts students.[19]

This low level of concentration continued. As H. J. Brown concluded shortly after World War II: 'except for expansion brought about by its importance in time of war (engineering) education has plodded along at much the same level between the war periods of 1918 and 1939'.[20]

Meanwhile, across the Pacific in the US, between 1890 and 1938, the number of professional engineers had escallated by a factor of *10* – from 25,000 to 250,000 people.[21] Australia had established independence from importing British engineers, but engineering itself was not treated as a central concern to Australia's development.

Part of the reason for Australia's poorly developed engineering structure clearly lies in the colonially-inspired industrial structure of the nation. More important, however, was Australia's emulation of British educational practices at a time when the mother country was losing its grip on the technological edge of world industrial competition.

In Britain, 'technical education' was very slow to develop. Engineering in the first instance grew out of practical need from a population of artisans, mechanics, millwrights, instrument makers and stonemasons.[22] There was little official support and a general apathy on the part of the hard-nosed 'machine men' of industry to the application of science, and to technical 'education', as I showed in the last chapter. Universities, on the other hand, were intentionally unconnected to the 'base' interests of industrial practice and commerce. The universities were largely theological and classics-oriented in character and hostile to the new philosophies of science. As I observed earlier, it was therefore not until 1894 that *mechanical* science (engineering) was introduced at Cambridge.

Whilst technological education was accorded low prestige, and was disconnected from higher education in nineteenth-century Britain, this was not the case in Germany. Great prominence had been given there to technological education since the early days of industrialisation. It was also not the case in the US where technological faculties were given prominence at various institutions since their establishment between 1850 and 1870. By 1938, the US had *twice* as many full-time engineering *staff* in universities as Britain had *students*, and was spending five times (per head of population) the outlay of Britain on engineering education.[23]

The effect on Britain was to impoverish the knowledge base from which it could retain a grip on the leading edge of industrial development as industrial leadership increasingly depended on more complex technical systems, and on the application of scientific knowledge. Consequently, although Britain had since the 1850s made some very important industrial inventions relevant to late nineteenth-century industrial transformation, the nation did not have the structure of engineering resources to apply them before their international competitors. Britain's knowledge base had moved out of alignment with the leading edge of technological progress. The nation's industrial shortcomings were only revealed when World War I's conflict with Germany undermined the roots of British complacency.[24]

The effect in Australia of *copying* British educational philosophy was equally disastrous, but the cost did not become apparent until a quarter of a century later, when World War II isolated the nation from its technological sources. When a National Register of professional engineers was developed towards the end of the war, it was discovered that 50 per cent of Australian engineers had neither a university degree nor a technical college diploma.[25] In educational terms, Australian engineers were literally getting by as if they were still in the early nineteenth century. Consequently, as H. J. Brown, Professor of Electrical Engineering at the (then) NSW University of Technology, concluded in 1945:

As in England, we have failed to realise the importance of soundly trained men in industry, and have failed, therefore, to make full use of scientific developments. Whilst America and Continental countries have been trraining more and more engineers and industry has been making full use of their knowledge, we have stood at a standstill.[26]

Marginalisation of Technological Invention

It is hard to escape the conclusion that the poverty of Australia's industrial and technological skills can be attributed directly to national obeisance to Britain's imperialist intentions and ideologies. Because of this poverty of skills, where technical invention occurred in Australia, it often died because the knowledge base to adopt and bed it into industry simply did not exist. Shortly before World War II for example, only one-third of the 4,000 or so engineers in Australia were employed in private industry. The rest were working primarily on government public works programmes.[27] Add to this the relatively small size of domestic Australian markets, and the distances from the main metropolises of the world, and local innovation faced very considerable difficulty. An arid local industrial knowledge base, competing with an efficient, higher scale, international, knowledge-rich technological frame, has often resulted in Australian inventions either being bought out by international firms or just never quite making it into successful production.

It is not as though Australians have not proven themselves to be inventive. The nation's history is characterised by some quite extraordinary genius, often with a very particular national flavour to it, that is, developing inventions that have an 'improvising-battler-against-the-environment' style about them. During the nineteenth century, the 'tyranny' of Australia's distance from the centres of European invention meant that often there was very little choice but to innovate. This was particularly demonstrated in the quite extensive inventiveness of Australians in agricultural machinery. Inventiveness of people like John Ridley and James Morrow allowed the development of unique agricultural machinery that could handle the harsh Australian climate, an environment that Britain's machine-men had no interest in.[28] Many of the older farm sheds of today contain an archaeology of now disused improvisations that farmers had to make in order to keep producing. The centrality of agricultural inventiveness is demonstrated in the patents that were registered in NSW towards the end of the nineteenth century. In 1895 for example, 50 (6.4 per cent) of patents registered were for agricultural implements and methods alone.[29] And as a result, Australia's main technological export item in the early twentieth century was agricultural machinery – the principal export (worth £31,847) to Argentina in 1906.[30]

An ideal type of the Australian inventor was John Robertson Duigan, who built the first successful Australian aeroplane in 1910. Working from a book on the principles of flight and a photograph of the Wright brothers' plane, Duigan built a working aircraft in a makeshift corrugated iron lean-to on his property at Mia Mia, 80 miles away from Melbourne. Duigan had to improvise most of the components, and many of the tools. The airframe was made from ash and red pine, cut from the property. The aircraft had piano wire for stays. Old steel bands from wool bales were used for sheet metal fittings. The engine was designed by Duigan, built in Melbourne, but modified by Duigan on his property using tools he specially machined for the task. The 9 foot 6 inches propeller was sculpted out of wood from the property, and when affixed to the 24 foot-wide frame, it was, as one contemporary observer noted, a toss-up as to which revolved. But the plane flew – over a distance of three-quarters of a mile before an admiring audience in Victoria. Duigan only gave up flying his plane and developing it further when he ascended high enough for him to realise that he did not know how to fly, and went off to flying school in Britain.[31] By the time he came back, aeroplane technology had advanced considerably, and he moved into industrial engineering.

Australian inventiveness fitted Australia's needs whilst it still remained a subservient agricultural resource to Britain. But it was ill-prepared for the late nineteenth-century evolution of the international technological frame. The takeover of Australian inventiveness at that time can be seen in the early history of patenting in the colony of NSW. The patenting system was established in NSW in 1854, following the first Patent Act two years earlier. In 1855 three patents were registered, but this number steadily grew to 32 new registrations in 1870, thence to 89 in 1880, and 203 in 1886. By 1887, 408 patents were registered in the colony, 78 per cent of which were registered by Australians (either from NSW or another Australian colony). At this stage, overseas interests started to impinge more heavily on the NSW patent system. By 1890 only 67 per cent of patents were registered by Australians, and by 1895, 62 per cent. This was the start of a trend that continued in parallel with overseas industrial development, so that the percentage of patents registered to Australians dropped to 58 per cent in 1900, thence to 56 per cent in 1903.[32]

The international technological frame had started to impinge heavily on Australia. To look further at the reflections in Australia, in 1893, 17 patents were taken out in NSW related to the new industrial energy source, 'electricity and magnetism' – inventions that aligned with the evolving dynamic of the core technologies of the international technological frame. Just two years later, the number of patents had nearly doubled, shortly before the major revolutionising effects of electricity were introduced into the Australian economy. But the electricity systems introduced were all imported.

Also, the patent records of the time are testament to the changing locus of international power over the evolving technological frame. In 1887, 48 per cent of NSW patents registered to overseas interests were for UK interests, and 19 per cent for US interests. By 1895, only 36 per cent of NSW patents registered to foreign interests were attributable to Britain, whilst 25 per cent were registered in the name of US concerns.[33] This trend continued up to the present day, so that in 1981–2, Australia paid 3.5 times as much for US-based technical know-how as it did for British.[34]

The fact that it was not inventiveness that held Australia's technological development back, but inability to participate in the creation of the wider technological frame, is classically shown in attempts by Australian inventor-engineers to enter the automobile market. One of the very first successful automobiles in the world was developed by an Australian foundry apprentice from Melbourne, Herbert *Austin*. However, this was after he had returned from the colony to Britain in 1893, having been befriended by the car-maker, F. Y. Wolseley.[35] The history continued. Colonel Harley Tarrant and

Howard Lewis built a two-cylinder powered car in Melbourne in 1899. Felix Caldwell invented a four-wheel drive power-train in Adelaide in 1907. William Wege designed a radical valveless petrol engine which he displayed at South Australia's first Automotive Show in 1920. But the Australian market was dominated by imported automobiles, particularly Henry Ford's T-Model. It was not until World War II had forced the establishment of a heavy industry-base in Australia that it was practicable to develop mass-produced, locally-manufactured automobiles. By that time, American car manufacturers were firmly entrenched in the Australian economy, so the 'Holden', 'Australia's car', was designed by American engineers according to American automotive thinking, and produced for American profit.[36]

Technical invention in Australia thus tended to be an improvising response to the nation's distance from the technology centres of the world, and often involved considerable ingenuity. Not only, however, was it alienated from industrial enterprise because of industry's skills-deficient base, it was also alienated from the development of scientific research in the country. The ideological hand of British imperialism had been laid on that enterprise as well.

Marginalisation of Scientific Research

The Australian scientific research system was fashioned towards improving agricultural and pastoral productivity. Until very recently, it has never been substantially linked into the development of manufacturing activity. This orientation is directly in line with the imperialist models that informed the inception and growth of science, not only in Australia, but also in other colonial outposts of Britain.

The organisational model for British colonial science was Britain's Department of Scientific and Industrial Research (DSIR). DSIR itself however was the product of an experiment conducted first in the 'safe' 'laboratory' of one of the colonies, India. India was the only part of the British Empire to which laissez-faire economics did not apply[37] The colony therefore provided a good opportunity for Britain to use India as a testing ground for political and economic policies (particularly concerning state intervention and planning) that were later transported back to Britain. Within this ideological housing, the experiment conducted in India was the establishment of a Board of Scientific Advice (BSA) as an agency that sought to advance and apply science in British India from 1898 to 1923. As Roy MacLeod points out, the BSA was an attempt by the British government to test the idea of a 'council of scientists', the idea of an organisational framework to co-ordinate research activities throughout the British Empire.[38] The idea was re-exported back to Britain in the development of an Advisory Council for Scientific and Industrial Research (ACSIR), created in 1915 (which evolved into DSIR a year later). ACSIR (thence DSIR) was a transmutation of the colonialist planning experiment that Britain adopted when the nation confronted the wartime technological superiority of Germany. Once established at the head of the British Empire, the model was then re-exported back to the colonies and former colonies – to New Zealand, South Africa, Sri Lanka, India and Australia.[39]

Basic to the science organisation model was a principle that directly aligned with Britain's traditional separation of 'elite' science from practical commerce. This was a principle that safeguarded the organisation's scientific autonomy. The principle was established at the end of World War I as DSIR made the transition to peace-time organisation, and was based on recommendations of the Committee of Inquiry into the machinery of government held in 1917 under the chairmanship of Lord Haldane. Under the 'Haldane Principle' that became generally accepted, scientists were guaranteed a relatively independent relationship with political administration, and therefore, as it eventuated, from direct commercial or political accountability.[40] Britain's lack of connection of science to industry was therefore exported throughout the entire colonial empire.

Sagasti and Guenero observe the process whereby imperial science was used as a means of controlling peripheral colonialist economic development for the advantage of the imperial metropolises. As they observe, science was a means by which 'dependent economies were manipulated to increase colonial integration through world markets and in which the extension of knowledge, through education, remains dependent on the metropolis.'[41] As Roy MacLeod continues, referring to Australia specifically, as a result, the objectives and programmes of research in Australia were 'determined by the interests of the imperial power.'[42]

In keeping with a colonialist model, Australia's research effort, oriented largely towards agriculture, was primarily government funded. Very little effort was put into promoting technology for industry, a situation in direct contrast to the US and Germany, which in the late nineteenth to early twentieth centuries provided extensive research patronage to industry.[43]

Thus when the Council for Scientific Research (CSIR) was established in 1926 to promote Australian science and its application, it was based on the British research model as a centrally funded organisation, was oriented towards agriculture (but not agricultural technology), and, following the British 'Haldane Principle', emphasised freedom of scientists from government control or industrial responsibility. The fierce defence of scientific freedom by CSIR's founding chairman, Sir David Rivett, set the organisation on its path towards scientific excellence, but disconnection from industrial application and orientation.[44]

The Commonwealth Scientific and Industrial Research Organisation (CSIRO), as it has now become, holds the centre stage in Australia's present scientific effort. But, whilst having made some important contributions to agricultural productivity (through improved seed varieties, and so on), it has done little for agricultural technology, minerals exploitation technology or manufacturing industry.

Australia's knowledge-generating capacity in the 1980s has been fashioned from its colonial seeds, and in particular, the British disconnection between scientific knowledge and industrial practice throughout the nineteenth century. The explicit belief in research freedom has followed, as has the associated expectation that undirected research excellence *per se* would one day spin off into positive economic growth. Moreover, until the recent establishment of 'Sirotech' as a commercialising arm of CSIRO, and the development of science and technology 'parks' in several Australian states, the British-inspired Australian model assumed that the bridge between knowledge creation in government and application in industry is an easy bridge to cross. No such assumptions have ever characterised the research systems of all the major industrial nations of the twentieth century (except Britain) – the US, Germany and Japan particularly. These nations primarily conduct their research and development in industry, where it is embedded in a framework of expectations that emphasise commercial relevance rather than research excellence.[45] That is, research in these nations is more closely aligned with the technological frame than in either Britain or Australia, and the 'cultural' expectations within research laboratories are equally as closely aligned.[46] In Australia, over 77 per cent of research and development is in government or higher education institutions, that is, remote from industrial demand and application.[47] In this sense, Australia is more similar to agriculture-based developing countries than it is to the industrialised First World.[48]

When, under enforced isolation, the nation finally did realise that an integrated and heavy industry base had to be developed, the government aimed the development of manufacturing industry primarily at replacing products that were imported. With a poorly connected science base, and the need for a relatively uncompetitive production system (marketing for small internal markets), little appropriate research and development was either available or required.[49] The technologies could be imported. And there was considerable resistance amongst the scientists to a practical commercial orientation in their research after the exigencies of war had subsided.[50] The inheritance remained very strong, of both dependence on the import of the technological frame, and the persistence of an internal research culture that had been derived from colonialist ideology.

Furthermore, from the lowered stance of crouching behind high trade barriers, there was little incentive to *develop* the capacity to compete, whether in terms of price or quality, for export markets. Consequently, whilst the US, Germany, Japan and the rest of the industrial world put massive investment into new technology for the post-war leading-edge high-technology industries – petrochemicals, synthetics and electronics – Australian research concentrated on isolated scientific excellence. Managers, government officials and politicians became increasingly confirmed in a generally conservative attitude to the need for new ideas and products.

Australia's relative deficit in knowledge resources, compared with other OECD countries, is thus not merely a product of relative size of expenditures (1.05 per cent of total OECD R&D expenditure in 1981, versus 46.33 per cent for the US, 17.04 per cent for Japan, and 9.87 per cent for West Germany).[51] It is also fundamentally a product of the nation's orientation towards a colonialist past rather than a technologically-competitive future that aligns with the post-war technological frame.

As a result, although commercialised innovations do flow from the Australian science system (such as scientific instruments like 'atomic absorption spectrophotometry', the 'Interscan' airport system, or 'Sinrock' for burying nuclear waste), these innovations are more the exception than the rule, and often have great difficulty achieving commercial success. The occasional high technology success obscures a generally low level of development of technology. Ron Johnston, observing the commercial fruit that have been harvested from Australian science thus concludes, 'under the present conditions of the manufacturing industry, the research system irrespective of its deservedly high international reputation, can contribute relatively little to the effective development of technology in Australia'.[52]

This is shown most forcefully in data on the relative contribution of Australians to international scientific publication versus patented knowledge. Australia ranks ninth in the world in output of scientific publications, but owns only 0.65 per cent of the world's patented knowledge. Whilst the publication rate per patent is somewhat similar to that of Canada (also heir to British colonialism), it is very much higher than the rate for the most powerful industrial nations. The same conclusion can be drawn from a comparison of the ratio of US patents per year to the number of publishing *authors*. Again, Australia fares very badly, with a ratio one-tenth that of Japan, and one-sixth to one-seventh that of Germany, Switzerland and the US.[53]

Neo-Colonial Dependency on the International Technology Text

The result of such a poor connection between knowledge generation, inventive activity, technological skills and industrialisation is that as Australia embarks on the last couple of decades of the twentieth century, its economy is at a major disadvantage in relation to international capitalism. The nation never laid down the succeeding technological infrastructures and capabilities that are preconditions for the successful development and rapid application of high technologies today. The nation is therefore fundamentally dependent upon new technologies supplied from elsewhere, dependent on neo-colonialising influences of the latest technological fashion leaders.

The comparative position of Australia is revealed very clearly in recent calculations by the OECD of relative technological dependence of OECD countries – assessed as a ratio of the nation's technological payments/R&D (research and development) expenditures of business enterprise. Of the 15 OECD nations, Australia is the *fourth most dependent*, being surpassed in technological dependency only by Portugal, Spain and Finland.[54] Australian companies pay to the US alone 26 times the amount for technical know-how that is paid to other Australian interests.[55] Furthermore, as an economic presence in the world market, Australia is still back in its colonial history – as a primary producer. Of the nation's exports, 74 per cent are of relatively unprocessed agricultural and mineral products;[56] and 64 per cent of Australia's imports involve trade goods that embody a high technology component (compared with 11 per cent of exports), a percentage that has risen steadily since the start of the 1970s.[57]

Australia's colonially-inspired technology deficit is a direct result of the nation's exclusion from participation in fashioning the evolving technology text both by imperialist policy and by acceptance of Britain's nineteenth-century ideology. A position of double jeopardy follows as the nation now seeks to participate on a more equal footing in drawing economic benefit from the technological frame of the late twentieth century.

Australia's position is jeopardised on the one hand because in the leading-edge industries of the late twentieth century the nation must continue to import both the technologies and products as well as pay for the royalty privileges of using foreign technologies in Australia. These costs can only continue to increase.[58]

The national position is doubly jeopardised because the nation also sold out its ability to compete in the international technology markets: foreign interests were able to gain control of the leading edge of knowledge-generating resources in the country.

This outcome is a direct sequel to the technological marginality that was inherited from the nation's colonial history. To follow the nation's post-war import substitution and industrialisation strategy meant inviting foreign control as down-payment on imported capital and technology. The nation simply did not have the technological capacity suddenly to jump into a major new industrial infrastructure. The effect was strongest in the development of the minerals industry where very heavy machinery was required to exploit massive potential export wealth. Foreign ownership of Australia's minerals increased steadily from after World War II to cover 57.8 per cent of the industry during the 1970s, along with very high levels of concentration.[59] Foreign control also significantly penetrated the manufacturing sector, touching most deeply into the heart of industry where the demand for sophisticated technology is highest. Therefore, whereas the overall level of foreign control in Australian manufacturing industry stood at 34.6 per cent by 1981, the level of control in the very high technology sectors was radically higher: 93.8 per cent in the 'synthetic resins and rubber' sector, 81.3 per cent in the 'organic and inorganic chemicals' sector, 74.5 per cent in the 'pharmaceuticals' sector, and 70.1 per cent in the 'radio, television and electronic equipment' sector.[60]

These are also the industries which are most in need of continuing and adapting research. Thus, associated with the highest technology industry sectors is not only foreign control, but also the nation's highest research concentration.[61] Furthermore, these are also the sectors where there is greatest need for international flows of technology, so, as the evidence demonstrates, where there is highest research concentration, there is also the highest import of technical knowledge, and most importantly of all, by far the majority of this technical knowledge flows from a *related* enterprise. Of all overseas expenditures on technical know-how in both manufacturing and mining made by Australia 75 per cent do not even cross organisation boundaries, but are made in-house to related companies.[62] Within the late twentieth-century technological frame, technical knowledge is so tightly aligned with capital interest that it is extremely difficult (as it was for nineteenth-century inventors) to break in from outside. All that is different to the nineteenth century is the level of scientific sophistication of the technical knowledge that is aligned.

The result for contemporary Australia is that in the high technology sphere there is relatively easy flow of technical know-how across national boundaries – but via multinational corporations. But the flow is two-way, as it is largely contained *within* organisations for which nationality is no boundary. So, to look at the evidence of flows *into* Australia the other way around, research done in Australia in leading high technology areas is itself caught up in the internal corporate transfers of knowledge *out* of Australia. As a result, even if Australia were to become more successful in generating industrial technology, particularly on the competitive high technology front, the nation faces the very real danger that this technology will be siphoned off privately overseas, rather than distributed for the benefit of national wealth across industry in Australia. In this way we come to the position of double jeopardy. Because of the impoverishment of industrial technology resources created by colonialism and its inherited ideology, the nation is forced into persistent dependency on the neo-colonialist knowledge metropolises that are now more closely aligned with the evolving technological text. Thus, marginality became double-marginality to the driving force of late international capitalism, that is, control of the latest technical knowledge.

Culture and the Technology Text in a Colonial Society

Australia today stands somewhere between the situation of a developing country and that of a fully industrialised society. The nation's economy is like that of the Third World in being predicated on the export of raw materials and commodities that are converted into advantage for those who hold power over the leading edge of technological change elsewhere But the nation's culture and lifestyle is one that has steadily adjusted over the last 200 years into alignment with the modernised culture of the industrialised world.

Australia, throughout its history, *fed* the development of the international technology text, but only through providing raw material resources that allowed its expansion. Meanwhile, Australia has been *fed by* the technological frame that the text provided – in terms of material lifestyle and cultural expectations. But Australia has been an outpost to the development of social alignment with the technological frame since the nation's colonialisation started in direct coincidence with the technological start of the Industrial Revolution.

Australia was always an outpost. Its people came from Britain originally (that is, when white society took over from the aborigines). They looked to Britain to define for them their culture, their institutions and their future horizons, as the mother country commanded the world in its imperialist nineteenth-century might. And Britain defined the situation for Australia just like its capitalists did for poor English children – that is, in terms of direct, exploitable advantage. Australia had a major advantage over the Third World colonies that Britain had annexed however. It had the ability to generate wealth whilst it bowed in obeisance to Britain's economic and political interests. This was not the case in India or the other Third World countries that Britain commanded. As a result, Australia never had a revolution against imperialism, for, to its largely British-stock people, it was the 'lucky country'. Instead, the nation languidly accepted a gradual transition in its ownership, as Britain descended the international economic ladder through the non-alignment of its stocks of technical knowledge with the late nineteenth-century technological frame.

In keeping with an outpost mentality, Australia did not develop an independent technological text of its own, at least, not until well after the sun had gone down on the British Empire's influence. For the whole of the nineteenth century, the nation's technological development and inventiveness were oriented specifically towards the sources of wealth it enjoyed by subservience to Britain's technological frame. Australia's late nineteenth-century attempts to develop a manufacturing base were thus oriented, not towards laying down the heavy industries that were fundamental to manufacturing independence, but towards developing consumer industries that fed the lifestyle that Britain had left it with. The Australian nation's development entirely depended on importing its technologies. And, even though it imported the core technologies of industrialisation, these never bedded in as they could elsewhere – because Australia's technological text remained dependent, first on colonialism, and subsequently, on neo-colonialism.

Meanwhile, the outpost mentality had ingested Britain's ideology concerning education, and the connection of technical knowledge with industrial progress. This was an ideology that was originally associated with the reflected glory of Britain's might, and therefore of its 'superior' culture. But it was also an ideology that found itself increasingly out of alignment with the progress of the international technological frame. Yet, the ideology persisted. It persisted in priorities accorded to engineering education. It persisted in priorities accorded within scientific research and its organisation. The ideology persisted whilst Australia enjoyed its acquired position of relative wealth and, therefore, whilst the culture's reality was not under direct threat. It is only today, over eight decades after the independent nation of Australia was formed, that the non-alignment of Britain's colonially-inspired technical knowledge ideology with the technological frame of the international economy is being recognised. Recognition has flowed from a culture now confronting a new reality principle, where unemployment and cost to a consumer lifestyle are visited directly into the people's life-world experience. Meanwhile, as a direct product of the nation's colonial history and ideologies, Australia is in a severely weakened position within the international economy. It has not laid down the succeeding technological alignments that nations with contemporary industrial power have put into place as a platform for late twentieth-century competitiveness.

The culture of Australia retains some elements of larrikinism and lack of respect for authority that were sedimented into its meaning system from its penal servitude roots. But the Australian culture is largely the internationalised culture of the urban metropolises. The growth of Australia as an urbanised nation started early. In 1860, only 25 per cent of the population lived in cities, but this was already increasing as a percentage of the whole population at the rate of 5 per cent to 6 per cent every 20 years. By the time of federation in 1901, over 35 per cent of the Australian population lived in cities, a percentage that now stands at over 86 per cent.[63] The nation dipped in the trough of agriculture and minerals for its wealth. But its people lived largely in cities. Thus, railways served more to connect the people and lifestyles within the separate cities than to develop an integrated industrial structure. Electricity served to develop consumerism rather than a heavy industry base. Employment, outside agriculture, was primarily involved in servicing urban lifestyle rather than manufacturing. And the cities were all built after the Industrial Revolution had touched the metropolises of the industrialising world, and mirrored the culture that these 'modern' cities represented – particularly in the post-automobile age.

The modernised urban lifestyle of Australia is therefore a mirror to the 'superculture' of the rest of the industrialised world. It is aligned with the culture of the modern technological frame, but non-aligned with the technological institutions and resources that support the metropolis elsewhere. As a result, the culture is heavily dependent on what is defined for it within the culture fashion houses overseas. When colour television was introduced into Australia in the late 1970s, the market was saturated within six months. The introduction of video followed the same path. Some independence has been established for the Australian film industry. But the people largely watch *Dynasty, Dallas* and American police movies for their enjoyment. Some independence has been established for Australian visual arts, but over three-quarters of artists seen to be at the forefront of the Australian art movement are either overseas-born and educated or have spent most of their lives studying and living abroad.[64] And Qantas, the national airline carrier, has its staff uniforms designed by a French couturier rather than by an Australian. Each of these observations is but a moment in the whole cultural fabric. But the overall picture is woven from the same dependent thread. The culture of Australia is dependent on the superculture of the world, in direct alignment with the dependence of its technological frame.

The roots of dependency are to be found in Australian dependency on Britain's nineteenth-century imperialism. But the twentieth-century take-over of culture aligns with the take-over by the technological frame of the culture of the world. Chapter 9 tells this story.

Part III
The Contemporary Drama of Consumer Society

Winning the Audience

Consumption as a Health Problem for Industrial Capitalism

With the 'Great Crash' of Wall Street on Tuesday 29 October 1929, capitalism came to a new realisation. As Jean Baudrillard expresses it:

> The bourgeoisie knew how to make the people work, but it also narrowly escaped destruction in 1929 because it did not know how to make them consume. It was content, until then, to socialize people by force and exploit them through labour. But the crisis of 1929 marked the point of asphyxiation: the problem was no longer one of production but one of circulation ... mobilised as consumers, their 'needs' became as essential as their labour power.[1]

It was not as though people did not wish to be mobilised as consumers. Nor was it that people did not wish to purchase 'commodities' for their 'exchange' value, their fashionableness, or their social rather than 'use' meaning. Nor was it that people had not been responding to advertisements or popular trends that were based on novelty or social status. For 'social' consumption (for an increasingly larger proportion of the population) had been directly associated with urbanisation since the genesis of modern cities some 300 years before.

In the seventeenth century for example, the English gentry were seeking to outshine each other in their construction of ostentatious houses.[2] 'Social' consumption was revealed in a sudden and steep increase in the number of dress regulations.[3] 'Trivial' consumption was apparent throughout Europe. The Dutch, for example, shipped over three million pieces of Chinese porcelain to Europe in the first half of the century. Spanish Castile soap was sold all over Europe. 'Tulip mania' spread through Holland in 1636 and 1637. Crazes for perfume spread. Queen Elizabeth I led the way when she ordered 'a perfumed cannon to be fired while she entertained the Duke of Anjou'.[4] And the original mass media advertising – which appeared with the first newspaper advertisements in 1658 – sought to stimulate an appetite for the exotic, the latest fashion, the 'curious' in selling, for example, 'ear-trumpets', 'rejuvenating hot baths', 'teething necklaces' and 'grave markers'.[5]

Indeed the very basis for the factory system of the Industrial Revolution was an existing demand for textiles and apparel. The most fundamental reason for America's subsequent success in taking over command of the technological frame was that it had developed standardised, mechanical means of production that could cheapen production and make its products more generally accessible throughout the whole society. Thus, clocks and watches that had been only in the hands (or front parlours) of the relatively wealthy at the turn of the nineteenth century were available from America for one dollar each by 1850.[6]

Thus, the 'time was right' at the time of the Great Depression of the late 1920s. But three social inventions had to be put in place for the purchasing ability and desire of consumers to be brought into alignment with the technical system that produced for them. The first was the invention of consumer credit. The second was the invention of obsolescence built into commodities. And the third invention was that of 'marginal differentiation' of commodities so that their symbolism for the purchaser could reflect individual social status, whilst production could remain based on mass production principles.

Consumer credit had already been set in place before the Great Depression. Indeed, the over-extension of credit for automobile purchases was one key cause of the Depression itself. Some expensive household items such as pianos and sewing machines were sold on time-payment before 1920. However, 'it was time sales of automobiles that set the precedent during the twenties for a great extension of consumer instalment credit. By 1926 time sales accounted for about three-fourths of all automobile sales.'[7]

With a market approaching saturation, the finance companies became concerned and started to diversify, encouraging instalment purchases of many other commodities. The ideology that legitimated consumer credit was, by this time, well in place. Walter Engard, for example, wrote in *Motor* just before the Depression,

Higher standards of living are built up through the millions of individual extravagances. To keep America growing we must keep Americans working, and to keep Americans working we must keep them wanting; wanting more than the basic necessities; wanting the luxuries and frills that make life so much more worthwhile, and instalment selling makes it easier to keep Americans wanting.[8]

Credit was however over-extended during the 1920s, and was very heavily concentrated on a commodity that was very expensive, and therefore highly susceptible to changes in income levels throughout the economy – the automobile. When the economy therefore started to slide, the impact of overextended credit was to precipitate this descent into the Depression. However, by now the 'idea' had been established, that is, the idea that people could invest their future into the purchase of expensive commodities in the present.

At the centre of widespread acceptance of this 'idea' was the consumer object, the automobile. As Henri Lefebvre claims, this was the 'Leading-Object' of the culture of the time.[9] The automobile represented the ingenious technical advance of the productive 'system' brought into daily life. It represented personal power. And the automobile was expensive, thus implying a series of other interconnected social and financial obligations that were binding on everyday life and earnings. The symbolic power of the automobile was deeply entrenched in American society by the time the Depression confronted them. Thus, during the 1929–33 period there was a drop in the number of *new* cars sold, but only by 10 per cent. But people desperately hung onto their cars no matter what their economic circumstances. 'While ... people were riding in progressively older cars as the Depression wore on, they manifestly continued to ride.'[10] For car ownership stood for a large share of the 'American dream'. A contemporary report by the Lynds of the people of 'Middletown' observed, '... they cling to it as they cling to self-respect, and it was not unusual to see a family drive up to a relief commissary in 1935 to stand in line for its four-or-five dollar weekly food dole.'[11]

As leading-object the automobile therefore led the way into the social invention of 'obsolescence' that powered economic recovery out of the Great Depression. As James Flink observes,

Increasingly in the 1930s, capital investment in the automobile industry was being stimulated much more by the demands of planned obsolescence and the dictates of style than by basic innovations in automotive manufacturing technologies.[12]

The cost of annual model changes in the American automobile industry accounted for 25 per cent of total costs from this time, to the point where expenditure on novelty *per se* in automobiles alone was $10 billion in the US in 1972. As a demonstration of the symbolism of image over function that powered the acceptance of automobile fashion, the cheapest and shortest standard automobile models grew almost a foot per decade – from 185 inches in 1938, to 197 inches in 1948, to 208 inches in 1960, to 217 inches in 1971.[13]

As with consumer credit, the 'idea' of obsolescence was housed in wider ideological legitimation. This legitimation quite specifically aligned wider political and cultural justifications to the technological frame itself, and identified the driving dynamic of this frame in terms of 'obsolescence'. Harlow Curtice, President of General Motors, coined the phrase 'dynamic obsolescence' in 1956, as a central tenet of not only technological and economic progress, but also of democracy and freedom as well. In his speech at the opening of General Motors' Research Center, Curtice laid out the ideology:

> Continuing emphasis on change, on a better method and a better product, in other words, on progress in technology, has been the major force responsible for the growth and development of our country. Some call this typical American progress 'Dynamic Obsolescence' because it calls for replacing the old with something new and better. From this process of accelerating obsolescence by technological progress flow the benefits we all share – more and better job opportunities, and advancing standard of living – the entire forward march of civilization on the material side ... The promotion of the progress of science and the useful arts is of crucial importance ... [but] there is a *far more* vital consideration. I refer to the importance of technological progress in assuring the continuance not only of American leadership in the free world, but of the democratic processes themselves.[14]

Both consumer credit and the marketing of obsolescence were directly connected, and collectively housed in an ideology of progress, economic and personal power, and national prestige. Both inventions aligned directly with the expansionary property of the technological system, and its values support within the institutions of capitalism. But, in ways that I will come back to shortly, the culture of the time was increasingly placing an emphasis on individuality, and privatised possession of unique status symbols, rather than on collective consumption. This would appear a paradox to the technical properties of systems that emphasise standardisation and uniformity in production processes and products. The third social invention, of 'marginal differentiation', solved this paradox. In marginal differentiation, the body of the technical system remains standardised, but minor variations are allowed at a cosmetic level as far as the product is concerned, and at the latter stages of production. Thus a standardised system can produce 'personalised' commodities without the massive expense that personally-oriented fabrication would otherwise imply. Again, the 'leading-object' of the automobile provided the model for other commodity producers to emulate. Jean Baudrillard provides the example of marginal differentiation of Mercedes-Benz cars, where seemingly endless personalisation is available with only marginal impact on the smooth turning of the wheels of *mass* production: 'According to your desire, you can choose your Mercedes-Benz from among 76 different colours and 697 assortments of internal trimmings.'[15]

These three social inventions represent a critical phase change in social alignment with the technological frame that characterised industrial development from the 1920s onwards. However, it is essential to realise that they would not have had an impact at another time in history. The success of the three innovations critically depended on a culture that was already prepared via a series of prior realignments with the evolving technological frame. The success also depended, within this specific cultural context, on the functions of the social inventions in evoking quite specific psychological needs and aligning their satiation with the technological frame itself. At the heart of this process – where consciousness, culture and the technological frame are drawn into alignment – stands the mechanism by which the subjective life of the person came to mirror the values and demands that are inscribed into the properties and assumptions that are sedimented into the technological frame itself.

Social Mechanisms that Prepared the Way

The automobile drove the international economy into the late 1920s Depression. With fashion and obsolescence newly written into its paintwork, the automobile drove the economy right out again later. For, as leading-object of the time, the car heralded in what could be termed an 'Age of Waste' which, spawned by saturated markets for existing products, led to the use of entirely new technologies to produce commodities that people had previously not even conceptualised. Thus, the post-World War II development of consumer-oriented synthetics and petrochemicals industries was based on the prior acceptance in the market place of an ideology of obsolescence that the automobile had helped set in place.

By the time of the Depression however, the car had already had an enormous impact on the societies into which it had been introduced. In particular it had taken over the shape of urban life. Robert and Helen Lynd reported the difference in the midwestern town they studied at the time between the pre-automobile age, and the period that followed around the 1920s. The Lynds reported a 'Middletown' housewife who remembered life before the automobile:

> In the nineties we were all much more together. People brought chairs and cushions out of the house and sat on the lawns evenings. We rolled out a strip of carpet and put cushions on the porch step to take care of the unlimited overflow of neighbours that dropped by. We'd sit out so all evening. The younger couples perhaps would wander off for half-an-hour to get a soda but come back to join in the informal singing or listen while somebody strummed a mandolin or guitar.[16]

By the 1920s this kind of direct contact, and sharing of interests with neighbours, had largely disappeared. Largely because of the mobility afforded by the automobile, the Lynds observed that,

> instead of a family's activities in getting a living, making a home, play, church-going and so on largely overlapping and bolstering each other, one's neighbours may work at shops at the other end of the city, while those with whom one works may have their homes and other interests anywhere from one to two-score miles distant.[17]

The automobile privatised life. It broke the social cohesion between work, play and living domains. Social networks became scattered across the territory that automobiles could reach, rather than being located within the immediate neighbourhood. As Donald Schon observes,

> Automobiles led to the creation of suburbs which in turn changed the prevailing theories of the function of cities (no longer as places to live *and* work) and set in motion a broad-ranging pattern of decentralisation of virtually all services and supplies. The belts and rings around our large cities gave rise to new concepts of industrial location and development which tended to isolate those still living in centre cities.[18]

Estates grew up in the suburbs, transforming the nature of neighbourhoods. This was particularly the case as urban settlements increasingly developed in corridors or strips along new road transportation routes. Use of public transportation radically declined – by 64 per cent in the US between the end of World War II and the 1960s – as a result of the enormous increase in the use of private automobiles for commuting to and from work.[19] The automobile commanded the structure of cities through the demand it imposed on road infrastructures and service facilities. By the 1970s, it was estimated that 82 per cent of Los Angeles – as archetype of the automobile city – consisted of space allocated for the moving, servicing and parking of cars.[20]

Streets ceased to be places where people met, and became commuter territory – except for the remote dark lanes where the young could park their private lounge-rooms. As John Steinbeck, the novelist, commented somewhat tongue-in-cheek in 1944, most of the children in the 1920s and early 1930s, 'were conceived in Model-T Fords and not a few were born in them'.[21]

However, the car did not do this by itself. Instead, its impact occurred because the artefact *aligned* in both the automobile's symbolism of the value of commodity-possession, and its implied structure of social life, with other forces producing this same alignment. The *system* of electricity production and distribution had already prepared the way.

The advent of electricity as an energy system distributed power not only to the industrial centres, but also to the home. Electricity generation therefore on the one hand allowed the development of 'full mechanisation' within production, and on the other hand, offered energy to consumers to capitalise on the products of mechanisation. As Siegfried Gierdion observed of the period from the 1910s to the 1930s,

> more appliances grew into household necessities than had been introduced in the whole preceding century ... [they] ... capture the fantasy and arouse the acquisitive instinct of the public to an astonishing degree ... [and] ... absorb an unprecedented share of space, cost and attention.[22]

Thus, fans, irons and toasters became popular after 1912, the electric vacuum cleaner after 1917, the electric range after 1930, and the electric refrigerator after 1932.[23] By 1935, to take Denver City as example, virtually everybody had a radio, and for the middle- to high-income groups, over 50 per cent had an electric refrigerator (rather than mechanical refrigerator or icebox), 50 per cent to 60 per cent of people had washing machines, and the percentage of people who possessed vacuum cleaners increased along with level of income – from 36 per cent amongst the low income groups, to 95 per cent among the high income groups.[24]

The electricity distribution system made producing consumer appliances for the home practicable. But the profitability of doing so, and thus the commercial drive behind the burgeoning consumer market, was directly associated with the alignment of suburbanisation with the impact of automobiles. The choice about producing *for the home* rather than developing food, laundry, or child-care services to take away these functions, '... was made between 1907 and 1916 when large capital investors found a profitable outlet for the automobile'.[25] Thus, 'associated residential dispersion made many group services unprofitable compared with such technologies as appliances and convenience foods which fit the atomized pattern'.[26]

The alignment of the automobile with electricity impacts on suburbanisation and associated consumption patterns also depended on what electricity had done for the centralisation of labour. Across the Atlantic in Germany for example, where electricity was making similar inroads on production trends, between 1880 and 1914,

> the number of small industrial plants, employing five workmen or less, declined by half, while the larger factories, employing fifty or more, doubled; in other words, the number of industrial units declined, but those that remained were substantially larger and employed no less than four times the total of industrial workers recorded for 1880.[27]

The scale of centralised manufacturing employment that was permitted by electric power, together with the mobility of the workforce permitted by automobile transport, enhanced the separation of work from 'suburban' home life. Together, the two brought forth electricity distribution systems that aligned with and perpetuated the trend. In the case of Kansas City for example, in the mid-1920s the DC (Edison) system of electricity production and use was more efficient than AC current for industry – particularly for high-torque, variable speed motors such as industry used. But DC current was very expensive to transmit over distance as it required enormous investment for substation equipment. The Kansas City Power and Light Company therefore centralised the DC distribution system – and as a consequence fostered the centralisation of industry. However, the competing AC current system could be distributed over larger distances more cheaply. The company therefore built (in 1926) a 92 mile AC service loop along the major thoroughfares and key public transport routes (the shape of which had largely been determined by automobile transportation). But, planning ahead, they built the service loop well beyond the present urban complex to cater for future suburban estates that were likely to develop. The result was that the AC distribution system established the *subsequent* suburban and strip-development shape of the city. The new estates, as well as commercial firms, particularly retailers, established themselves where the electricity infrastructure was available. But industry, up to the 1940s, remained near the centralised DC lines.[28]

The electricity system therefore commanded urban design – through its encouragement of industrial centralisation, of suburbanisation, and of the support for suburban lifestyle through accessibility to electrically-powered consumer appliances. But the use and development of the electricity distribution system, as well as the new inventions (for example concerning AC current) that were called forth, were only possible because they aligned with the cultural changes that were related to automobile technology. The alignment was not only a technology-system alignment however. Instead, both technical alignments bedded into society, and transformed it, because ideological alignment made the trajectory of urban design and consumerism a cultural pattern that the people wanted. The ideological alignment was a product of what had gone before.

With the increase in employment opportunities that electricity-inspired industrialisation fostered, it became difficult shortly after 1900 to find household servants. Their wages had risen, their numbers had fallen. Houses started to be designed without maids' rooms; kitchens were being designed for housewives rather than for servants.[29] Between 1900 and 1920, the percentage of household servants dropped by nearly half (from 10 per cent to 6 per cent of the United States population).[30] There was a *need* for consumer appliances to ease the burden that the absence of servants imposed upon middle-class households. To capitalise on this need, however, required that the producers had to get the housewives committed to consumption as a deep psychological need. Availability of appliances was not enough, because the early 1900s' housewives had not yet learnt to consume, for much of the basic purchasing had previously been done by the servants.

Thus, as Ruth Cowan points out, much of the early twentieth-century marketing sought to appeal to housewives through 'guilt'.[31] This was a guilt that arose from the women feeling that the onus of responsibility for child-nurturing lay now on their shoulders rather than on competent nursemaids. The guilt arose from the need to make sensible choices about household purchases and management. As in the early nineteenth-century proselytisation of political economy through appeal to the ideology of 'science', the new marketers found a wider grammar also in science. Advertising strategies capitalised on the discovery of the 'household germ'. The 'science' of Freudian psychoanalysis provided guidance and legitimation for marketers to capitalise on, and seem to redress, anxiety and guilt.[32] Consequently, as Ruth Cowan observes from contemporary women's magazines, whilst before World War I household tasks were seen as 'trials' to be endured until qualified servants were found, after World War I housework was an 'emotional trip'. Laundering to whiteness was an act of love. Feeding was an artistic activity that allowed encouragement of family loyalty and affection. Changing diapers was a way of building baby's sense of security and love of mother. Cleaning sinks was the act of a protective maternal instinct. The emotional magnitude of the tasks could no longer be trusted to servants. This ideology was not only the province of marketers. The ideology aligned with housewife culture and was quickly accepted into it.

Readers of the better-quality women's magazines (during the 1920s) are portrayed as feeling guilty a good lot of the time, and when they are not guilty they are embarrassed: guilty if their infants have not gained enough weight, embarrassed if their drains are clogged, guilty if their children go to school in soiled clothes, guilty if all the germs behind the bathroom sink are not eradicated, guilty if they fail to notice the first signs of an oncoming cold, embarrassed if accused of having body odor, guilty if their sons go to school without good breakfasts, guilty if their daughters are unpopular because of old-fashioned, or unironed, or – heaven forbid – dirty dresses.[33]

Appeal to guilt was appeal to the morality of the 'inner-directed' person, the character type that David Riesman attributes to the nineteenth-century psychological alignment with the speed of change of industrialisation. That is, the character type that followed an inner-morality gyroscope that stressed honour, moral discipline, and a superordinate super-ego.[34]

But, as ascetic Protestantism's commitment to the moral discipline of labour emerged out of (but transformed) that of prior Catholicism, appeal to inner-direction produced its antithesis, 'other-direction'. That is, the need for consumer objects to satisfy inner-directed anxiety became transmuted into the cultural salience of the objects themselves, as mirrors of the person's morality, status and social bearing. Morality was judged by what other people judged. The emerging alignment of suburban living with consumerism increased isolation and privatisation of the individual's world. It increased the need for objects that stood for the person in providing messages to others of the person's worth within the anonymised world that stood outside the suburban front door.

Meanwhile, the basic roots of cultural stability were being torn out from underneath the society by the very *rate* of change that the people confronted in the early twentieth century. Human-scale reference points in everyday life were demolished as technological *systems* gained in power. The *scale* of objects, and of the production systems that housed daily labour and experience, was massive and ever-expanding. *Motion* was measured in automobile velocity which had crashed way past 'doing a ton', so it was no longer assessed against the speed of human perambulation. *Time* was not related to distance of human contact anymore, with the advent of the telegraph and thence radio communications. Being *bound* to earthly experience evaporated into the ether of air-conquest, and Einsteinian theories of relativity showed that Newton's apple would have behaved very differently if it were massively different in size and elsewhere in the cosmos. Even the existence or non-existence of God and the cosmos were not in reach of subjective consciousness, but arbitrated by experts who possessed a specialised knowledge way beyond the grasp of the layperson. And experience of nature, its rhythms and changes, was mediated by the substitute reality of machine-systems, and experienced as taps which gave water, electricity wires which gave energy, trucks which arrived before dawn and delivered food to be picked up in supermarkets, and alarm-clocks which signalled when the day began.

The result was a world of insecure cultural reference points, a reality that was in continuous flux, but an *order* that was commanded by technical systems and the artefacts that they produced. The 'system' delivered this order into everyday life through the consumer objects that could be individually possessed, and which stood *for* the person and their place in an anonymised and rapidly changing order.

So 'guilt' was transmuted into 'status anxiety',[35] the fundamental premise for a consumerist ideology to take off. As demonstrated in the previous chapters of this book, the culture forged alignment with the technological systems, called forth new technologies that enhanced the trajectory of alignment, and was in turn embedded within a continuous process of realignment as the technologies called forth came to bear down on the people's lives.

Alignments that Prepared the Way between the Technological Text and Everyday Life

The technology text advanced towards enframing culture right from the start of the Industrial Revolution through reaching into subjective life. Through direct coercion and co-optation at first, the rhythm and discipline of daily labour was brought into alignment with what was required to serve the factory-based machine system. But, as Chapters 6 and 7 point out, the surrounding reference points of cultural meaning were at the same time being transformed. Visibility of the new order, represented in dominating smoke-stacks and industrial towns, erected inescapable superordinate symbols to the order that was emerging. The patterns of interaction between people were transformed by the attachment of social relations of the home to the proximity of industrial employment. And legitimating ideologies emerged to make sense of the regimented 'calculated life' of a culture moving into alignment with mechanical control over its social relations of production. Thus, by the 1840s, the culture as a whole had forged an alignment with the factory system that now mediated the society's relationship to its ecological niche.

The dynamic properties of systems imply a much deeper penetration of subjective life however. At the core of system efficiency is order, and increased ordering of all the 'environments' from which the immediate technical system feeds – both in the smooth integration and standardisation of inputs (labour and materials), and in the smooth connection and standardisation of outputs, or markets. By the mid-nineteenth century, expansion of this ordering of environments confronted a critical reverse salient, and that was smoothly integrated transportation and communication to hold remote but interconnected factory and marketing systems together. Indeed, along with constraints on the expansion of both markets and employment – and thus on rates of profit – the British economy faltered into Depression in the late 1840s – until the 'bunching' of a series of core innovations concerned with railways (and steel) opened up a new horizon of interconnection between the separate factory and market systems.[36]

The Manchester and Liverpool Railway introduced the railways system to Britain in 1831, with 140 miles of track. By 1838, just seven years later, the size of the system had increased by a factor of four, and continued to expand throughout the length and breadth of the UK.[37]

With the widespread diffusion of the railways system, not only did employment and market potential expand, but also the social horizon for the society's culture radically transformed. The railways system implied 'calculated' and integrated time schedules – and thus, both abiding by precise time constraints and immediate communication between remote but connected parts of the system. Expansion of railways therefore directly aligned with the diffusion of precise time measurement into everyday leisure and travel. Expansion of the railways also aligned with immediate and remote communication connections through the telegraph, opening up the horizon of systematised (and anonymised) communication within everyday life. The railways joined town to country, and as superordinate symbol of the new wave of industrialisation, expanded the horizon of industrialism out of the factory towns and across the entire social and geographic landscape. The railways allowed business to expand across far distant but immediately connected locations, and implied anonymised communication within organisations to retain their smooth integration. Not only was communication separated from direct inter-subjective experience, but also the very speed of train travel disconnected concepts of distance and movement from everyday human reference points as well. The cultural alignment that was therefore actualised with the expansion of the railways system penetrated not only the culture of labour, but more deeply penetrated the culture of everyday life – ordering this as well into smooth harmony with the system's expanding technological frame.

Expansion of the railways system also aligned directly with the burgeoning urbanisation of society that directly paralleled the rise of industrialisation. As Henri Lefebvre observes, industrialisation could *only* find its fulfilment in urbanisation.[38] The shape and concentration of urbanisation was set initially by the labour demands of the factory system. But each new alignment of expanding technological systems with both labour and markets continued to shape the structure and concentration of city living. This was particularly the case with the railways, electricity and automobile systems. The seeds were therefore sown in the nineteenth century for the suburbanisation that followed in the early twentieth century, and for the contemporary 'spilling-over' of cities into merged metropolises. With a doubling rate of urban growth every 20 years,[39] the phenomenon that Jean Gottman observes, that is, the rise of the 'megalopolises' or giant merged cities is commonplace. Gottman has already named the East-Coast US amalgamation of Boston-New York-Washington as 'Boswash'.[40]

The emergent urbanisation of the nineteenth century therefore both aligned with the industrial systems that were developing, and prepared the way for the individualised culture that consumerism later depended upon. The power of the urban cultural 'code' over subjective life lies in cutting the person off from the inter-subjective dialogue that establishes and asserts personal identity, and setting the person adrift in a world that is dominated by anonymity. Paradoxically, what urbanisation does is to create simultaneity without discourse. That is, urbanisation draws more and more people into the same location – where they can see each other, be aware of the appearance they present, the lifestyle they lead, the objects they possess. But because of the sheer numbers of others, the individual is confronted continuously by others with whom it is impossible to have a continued meaningful discourse. The person in the modern 'systematised' city is surrounded in a sea of anonymous, but constantly experienced, humanity who can never be known inter-subjectively.

The physical structures of everyday existence in the modern city are beyond immediate legibility – by virtue of scale, and by virtue of the interconnection between urban structures according to the aesthetic of an external system rather than immediate human and community needs. As Kevin Lynch observes, 'in order to feel at home and to function easily we must be able to read the environment as a system of signs.' But the modern city environment renders it very difficult to 'relate these parts (of the environment) in time and space, and to understand their function, the activities they contain and the social position of their users'.[41]

Thus, with each new technological system encroachment on urbanised living, the reference points for inter-subjectivity, and for autonomous constitution of personal identity and culture, were further broken. And the reference points from which meaning is constituted consequently depend on the external systems and their spatial, social and lifestyle demands. Thus, throughout the nineteenth century, the technological frame increasingly extended its external order into inter-subjective life, and prepared the way for the subsequent consumerist alignment of commodities with signals of personal identity and values.

Furthermore, prior to the alignments of culture that followed the twin forces of electricification and automobiles, the machine itself had entered into the domestic sphere. This occurred via the sewing machine.

Up to 1854, sales of sewing machines were almost entirely to manufacturers, but then Wheeler and Wilson first conceived of introducing the machines into households, to release women from 'the thraldom of the needle'.[42] At first, sales were for cash, but a scarcity of ready money in certain districts caused the inauguration of a credit system that operated by means of promissory notes. As the wealthier market became saturated, the financial support system adjusted accordingly, and leasing systems and instalment plans were introduced, 'intended to reach the poorest class of people, who had no property of any shape, and no credit'.[43] The machine therefore diffused from the wealthy (for whom the machine was a source of easier leisure), to the poor (for whom the machine was a source of 'out-work' employment). By 1881, sewing machines were attached to low-voltage electric motors, and by 1887, 110 volt models were being produced that could take advantage of lighting circuits. Alongside the electric fan, the sewing machine therefore heralded the employment of electricity for domestic appliances.[44]

The sewing machine introduced the machine into the home, as a 'normal' and desired status object. The technical demand for a sturdy, smoothly-running, quiet and reliable machine that could continue to operate whilst remote from immediate technical repair, also set a pattern for industrialisation itself. The domestic machine required precision manufacture of a mass-produced commodity, and it demanded systems that could be repaired by interchangeable parts. These technical requirements were central to the further progress of the production system into the precision order that was necessary before mechanised, large-scale consumer production could take place.

Thus, the machine was introduced to the home. It brought the industrial system (with all its associated values) into the lounge-room, and set it alongside the mechanical clock that timed the rhythm of connection between home-life and the industrial system outside. The sewing machine heralded the possession of industrial machines as personal status signals. And it set in motion the alignment of commodity possession with credit, with commitment of the future against possession in the present. Furthermore, the sewing machine fed back new demands on the productive system itself. All of these technical and cultural alignments laid the ground for the subsequent development of a consumer-oriented society. As Maxine Berg observes, the sewing machine was, perhaps, the most powerful innovation in the production of consumer goods since the power loom.'[45]

Ideological Mechanisms Behind the Command of Commodities over Everyday Life

Technical and social alignments were set in place by the prior expansion of the technological frame throughout industrialising society before consumerism could take off. Yet, as was demonstrated in previous chapters, it was not alignment *per se* that created the *new* culture–technology alignment. The emerging consumer alignment was also housed in an ideological fabric, a fabric that signalled a new order that was emerging, a fabric that addressed the existential insecurity that the technological frame had visited upon the meaning of daily life. Marketing to housewives was based on appeal to the subjective character type that the nineteenth century had produced, that is, the 'inner-directed' person who could be made to feel guilty. But the conversion of this appeal into an alignment with the 'other-directed' character type it was instrumental in producing was set in a wider ideological grammar. This wider grammar was derived from the acceptance of the 'commodity' itself into its central location within the capitalist industrial system.

Following Marx, the 'commodity' is an object produced, not for its *use* value, or to be consumed by those who produce it. Commodities are objects that can be *exchanged* through the mediating circulation of money.[46] For Marx, the power of the commodity was a positive force within capitalism, for the commodity injected 'a civilising moment' into history. The search for new commodities shattered the constraints of tradition and 'encrusted satisfactions', thereby unleashing the progressive change on which subsequent communism could be based.[47] Thus the capitalist,

> searches for means to spur them (the people) on to consumption, to give his new wares new charms, to inspire them with new needs by constant chatter, etc. It is precisely this side of the relation of capital and labour which is an essentially civilising moment, and on which the historic justification, but also the contemporary power of capital rests.[48]

What makes an object of value in exchange is not only the cost of producing it, but more fundamentally its relative scarcity. As Marx implies, perception of scarcity is a product of fashion and persuasion. Perception of scarcity, and thus the value to marketers of the commodity is therefore fundamentally a psychological property. To take one recent example, 'Cabbage-Patch Dolls' are normally sold for around $50 each. But the craze to 'adopt' one developed into such an epidemic during 1983, that demand far outstripped supply, and 'original' dolls were selling in the United States for over $1,000 each.

The mobilisation of consumers in the early twentieth century fundamentally depended on recognising how to exploit the *perception* of scarcity, rather than to manipulate the factual reality of scarcity itself. The 'psychological' dimension of scarcity was central to the continuance of an expanding environment of more and more commodities, when every conceivable need could be satisfied by what already existed. The 'secret code' of commodities therefore consisted of erecting psychological scarcity on a framework of abundance. There are two dimensions to this code. The first is that people need to feel that each new commodity they purchase satisfies a *new* need, thus injecting a new source of scarcity into an existing consumer system. The second dimension of the code is that, whilst appearing to satisfy this need, the commodity is *inherently unsatisfying*, thus creating the platform for the next round of scarcity to stand on. 'Obsolescence' offered this code. 'Consumer credit' made it possible for an increasingly large proportion of the population to participate. And 'marginal differentiation' provided the symbolic meaning of participation, where the individual could signal his or her individuality within a systematised, mass produced consumer order.

Thus, the success of 'obsolescence' depended on attaching fashion and style to the basic dimensions of the scarcity code. As Jean Baudrillard points out, by purchasing a commodity model, one is acquiring not only the object itself, but asserting the series of which the model is one moment.[49] In the case of the 'leading-object', the automobile, the next model in the series is already designed and on its way to the production line before the current model can be driven out of the showroom. The commodity itself thus signals participation in the *process of accumulation*, a psychological mirror to the values underlying capitalism itself. The very act of 'consuming' a commodity lays the psychological foundation for continued accumulation. As soon as the current model is sold, the way is cleared for the next commodity in the series to appear. Possessing an earlier model in the series disenfranchises the owner from the full symbolic worth of being 'in-style'. We can never reach a point where we have 'enough', for the symbolic salience of our present possessions is outmoded with each passing day.

The 'series' forges the alignment between capital accumulation within the productive system, and commodity *accumulation* within subjective life. The 'set' injects alignment between the interconnected technological system, and the interconnected system of consumption objects. Within a vast array of commodities that are available, the purchase of one implies the need for others to match it, to complement it – to fill out the complete picture of the self that the commodity symbolises. The purchase of new clothing implies the purchase of fashion accessories that match. The purchase of make-up to maintain a healthy and cosmetically-nurtured skin implies the full set of cosmetic aids – cold-cream, moisturiser, skin-supplement, skin-repair, blusher, mascara, eye-shadow, kohl pencil, ultra-whip – so that a $3 purchase can quickly lead to a $300 shopping spree. With continuous change in all of these associated commodities, the obsolescence of one may outmode the entire set, in the way that the introduction of digitally-recorded, laser-read recordings makes the previously cherished record and tape collection both primitive and difficult to supplement.

Both the 'series' and the 'set' translate values of the system of the technological frame into values to be abided by in subjective life. Both devices provide a guidance system for negotiating consumer purchases within the vast array of products that appear before us. William Leiss observes, for example, that in North America alone, 1,500 new products appear on supermarket shelves each year, 80 per cent of which are withdrawn that same year, to be replaced by another assortment.[50]

The alliance between system-values and subjective life depends however on capitalising on the very mediation of reality that the 'text' of the technological system has injected into everyday experience. Scarcity, as a psychological phenomenon, depends on the erection of an artificial reality – both of need and its reference point. This is like an advertising billboard that portrays the scenery that the billboard itself obscures, but which can be repasted as soon as new commodities appear that can paint a new picture of the background reality. Whereas the real world is finite, there is an infinite number of ways to 'represent' it, and substitute for it – no end of possibilities for co-opting the consumer. As the commodity's 'scarcity' is not factually real, but an artefact, so too is its object-*reality* more a social symbol than a useful artefact by which to engage as a person-in-nature. Thus, as the accumulated heap of commodities available off the shelf grows larger and larger, the commodities increasingly block out the real world that stands behind them. The commodity stands *for* reality (both external and internal) and stands *in front* of it. An extreme (though perhaps apocryphal) radio story that William Leiss reports demonstrates this vividly. The story is of a multi-storey parking lot for camper vans in Texas City, 'where each vehicle stall is carpeted with plastic grass, and motion-picture images of wilderness scenery and wildlife are projected onto the surrounding concrete walls'.[51] As William Leiss comments, even if this is not true, it will be. The commodity world is therefore a world of objects that *signify* reality.[52] But what they signify refers only to the code of other commodities, to a 'substitute-reality' rather than the reality that lies beyond them. The reality is alienated from the active 'signifier' as their engagement with commodities is only within their 'exchange' and in their possession. The commodity-as-substitute-reality therefore assumes a passive market, active in making choices between the options offered within the code, but passive outside this frame of cultural expression. As passive recipients, the culture participants are therefore not engaged in actively constituting their culture, but only *receive* the culture within the cultural symbols they acquire, and which are constituted and fully articulated elsewhere. Like a pre-lingual child, the culture is offered therefore as a 'package' that cannot be opened to conscious scrutiny, and to the substitute-reality of which their actions need to align.

Thus, the reality code that locates personal identity for the individual is both artificial and in the future. The signals that are beamed out of the possession of commodities appear solid in *here-and-now* action, but the solidity of the meaning disappears as soon as we draw them into reach, as soon as we *possess* them. We live in the future, and the past disappears down the tunnel of the *past* models of the series that doesn't represent us any more. We *live* in imagination, and prop up its reality with 'personalised' objects that are transformed from providing satisfaction as soon as we grasp them. This situation is like Midas's decree that everything he touched should turn to gold. Everything we grasp turns into the 'code' – even the deepest, personal experiences of feeling and communicating with another, and with ourselves. It looks like gold, but is the source of the deepest insatiability of our humanness – because the real 'I' just is not there – only its image. There is no reality in a substitute future.

The consumer code is a code that commands. The integrated object-world of the modern commodity culture determines what we *can* experience. Our 'felt' external environment embodies the past actions and meanings of the society which predates us, and which have been sedimented into the immediate objects we experience. But what is sedimented is the product of the ever-expanding 'system' of commodities, which by their very essence represent alienation of the person from their subjectivity. We therefore confront an apparently solid and all-pervasive *set* of meanings, integrated as smoothly as is the technological frame itself. But we confront in the face of these objects both the history and the present of our own alienation from constituting culture. Our inability to intervene in an object-world that is so predominately fabricated elsewhere, and of such magnitude, is what Jean-Paul Sartre calls the 'practico-inert', a world we can only obey.[53]

The commodity code therefore commands us in the way a motorway commands where we drive, where we don't play with the children, how we behave, what we pay attention to – what we *need*. The past actions of people who participated in erecting the code (or the motorway) react back on us. They demand that we abide by the accumulated logic embodied in their fabrication of the written text of the system, and adhere to the inherent logic of 'progress' along lines that the technological frame determines. And what confronts us are not 'symbols', but 'signals'.[54] The meanings that lie behind the immediate commodities within the commodity code are not open to interpretation or manipulation, and are therefore not open to inter-subjectivity, as are symbols. Rather, we are confronted by meanings that are assigned by convention, by mutual agreement, and have nothing to do with our own subjective interpretation. Outside agreed convention, the red versus green versus amber lights of a traffic signal are meaningless. So too, with all signals. And, as with traffic lights, the messages portrayed by the signal are meaningful *only* in relation to an overall code (the traffic code), a code that is useful *only* if it commands us all. Consequently, living within the commodity-system world does not allow for negotiations of meanings in the same way that it is an entirely fruitless exercise to try and convince the traffic-policeman at the accident scene that a red light *should*, more appropriately, signal 'go'. The culture code simply stands there, alienated from our subjective engagement with it, and tells us, 'it is so!'

10

A Hall of Mirrors

'A Legend Of Our Time': The Danger of Atrophy of Subjective Life

In Greek and Roman mythology there is a legend that sums up the 'soullessness' and 'existential wobble' that the culture produced by the technological frame visits on contemporary society. This legend is the story of Echo and Narcissus.

Echo was a 'sportful' nymph who diverted the attention of Juno (Hera to the Greeks), the queen of heaven, whilst Juno's husband, Jupiter (Zeus) made love to other nymphs. When Juno discovered that Echo had been deceiving her, she transformed the nymph into an 'echo', depriving her of the power of speaking except when spoken to. Echo subsequently fell in love with Narcissus, a beautiful youth who was son of the river-god, Cephisus. But Narcissus did not return her passion. Venus, the goddess of love (who, incidentally was also a daughter of Jupiter by another marriage) sought retribution in the way that Greek and Roman gods were so fond of. To avenge Narcissus's offence against love, Venus caused him to fall in love with his own reflection in the waters of a fountain. Whilst Narcissus gazed only at his own image, Echo pined away until only her answering voice remained to perpetuate her name. The tragedy was completed, for Narcissus, unable to possess himself of his own reflection, eventually killed himself. Echo finally atrophied and died.

Jupiter, through his childhood conquests, was king of the heavens and of the earth. In present-day metaphor, Jupiter is the Technological Frame, with its god-like controller of nature, the cosmos and social life – instrumental rationality. Echo, the spontaneous, fun-loving servant, became co-opted into the Technological Frame's designs to play around with 'his' macho, patriarchal folly. Juno, the 'feminine' principle, the shadow side of human patriarchal values, was deceived into believing that Jupiter (or the Technological Frame) was still concerned about her. But, he wasn't. Juno could not seek revenge directly because 'he' was too powerful. But she could visit retribution on the servant of the 'system'. Echo, and all her fun-loving, passionate subjectivity, was thus locked into a prison from which she could only respond - to whatever messages that came her way.

Echo is one side of the modern-day consumer who is turned into *passivity* through their *activity* being co-opted into the designs of the Technological Frame. The other side of the consumer is Narcissus. He could not find true happiness in relating to what was no more than an echo of reality – an echo of the culture 'code' that sends out the signals of a reality that the Frame stands in front of and mediates. Narcissus could not love, so the goddess of love, of deep communicative understanding – of happiness – imprisoned him too. Venus put Narcissus in a space where he could only *seek* love and happiness in an *image* of himself, an image he could never possess as himself. Narcissus thus became the other side of the consumer, constantly looking for happiness in the image of himself in the objects he (or she) is surrounded by. But Narcissus, like the contemporary consumer, is never able to achieve this happiness in possession of the objects, because they provide no more than an ethereal, substitute reality, that calls forth the need for ever greater consumption to salve a hunger that intrinsically cannot be satisfied by mirrors.

According to the metaphor of the legend of Echo and Narcissus, both sides of the consumer died – at least in their autonomy to decide on meanings for themselves. The aspect of the consumer that only exists through response to a culture 'code' that is determined elsewhere, atrophied. The aspect of the consumer that searches for satisfaction and meaning in his or her own image as reflected in the objects of a substitute reality, self-destructed. Both aspects died by their own volition following their progressive demise due to the impossibility of ever being satisfied. Both had been set on a path to self-destruction through the command of the Technological Frame and its denial of love, caring and concern for others, whilst the 'system' marches patriarchally forward, playing around with its own power. The 'calculated life' observed from Charles Dickens of mid-nineteenth-century life in Chapter 6, has come to its final resting place in dependence, and soullessness of a culture that is defined by the Technological Frame rather than autonomously.

The Shape of the Mirror – 'Ordering' of Subjective Life

The command of the mass consumption culture did not arise simply because capitalism invented the devices of credit, obsolescence and marginal differentiation. Instead, the legitimation and acceptance of mass consumption aligned with the order of society that people were experiencing. This was an order that had evolved out of prior re-alignments of the culture against the increasing ubiquity of the technological frame within everyday experience – not only in work, but also in leisure, home-life and meanings.

On the one side, reference points for the human constitution of cultural meanings were being demolished – in, for example, the speed and power of the machine system compared with people, and in the illegibility of urban living environments that framed the people's social and cognitive landscape. Whilst deconstructing human reference points, the technological frame at the same time erected its own order to stand for these same reference points.

On the other side, the technological frame, by virtue of its penetration into daily life, offered immediately experienceable artefacts that could stand *for* the order that was becoming increasingly unintelligible in terms of *human* constructions of meaning. Thus, the sewing machine mirrored the machine system of production within the lounge-room; the electric fan, and subsequent electric appliances, offered the *power* of the productive system within the home.

The one hand of the technological frame destroyed. The other offered succour. But nurturance depended upon 'consuming' according to what was technically possible within the technological frame that lay outside the front door. And outside the front door, the technical systems were increasingly starting to align with each other across the social and geographic landscape, automobiles and electricity distribution in particular, creating the shape of the urban experience – automobiles and electrical appliances offering ubiquitous superordinate symbols of the technological order *within* daily life. It was within these cultural alignments with the technological frame that the 'inner-directed' character type that had built both empire and the technological frame was transformed. Originally through appeal to 'guilt', the character type of nineteenth-century society transmuted into the 'other-directedness' that sought self-worth through possession of commodities, and participation in the emerging cultural *code* of consumption.

Both marketers and consumers have been enmeshed within this same code. Max Horkheimer suggests, 'the early trapper saw in the prairies and mountains only the prospect of good hunting; the modern businessman sees in the landscape an opportunity for the display of cigarette posters.'[1]

Equally, when the culture signals of commodities are turned inwards, as vehicles to indicate to ourselves who we are and our relationship to the wider social order, they *mediate* our consciousness of self, in an identical manner to the way in which technologies mediate our relationship to, and engagement in, nature. The subjectivity of the

212 The Tragedy of Technology

individual is a *standing reserve* with the same properties that Heidegger attributes to nature as a technologically-mediated 'standing reserve'.[2] That is, human activity, and consciousness, are taken into the process of rationally *ordering* the inner psychic world – according to the mediating lenses that commodity objects allow. It follows then that the roadmap by which we have to gain access to our own subjectivity is therefore one of externally-derived image. Its grammar is the grammar of the code of substitute-reality itself. And the basic rules of this grammar are those of the background technological frame – that is, to do with 'rational' ordering of subjectivity, intellect and emotions, and use of a 'scientific' approach to mine anything below that which image permits us to see.

Through the medium of the commodity, the person therefore has come to *mirror* the technological frame, and the values that stand behind the production code of the commodities that have formed the bridge between system and subjectivity. The fundamental property of the technological system, order, is mirrored in ordered objectified signals to oneself and others of subjectivity. The system grammar of rational and instrumental efficiency is mirrored in the 'one-dimensional' ordering of emotion beneath a facade of 'cool' rational, calculative image.[3] The technological system's property of expansion and capital accumulation is mirrored in psychological commitment to the code of continuous accumulation of commodities, and the horizon of subjectivity that resides in the future rather than in 'here-and-now' action. The technological system property of complexity and interrelationship between specialised parts is mirrored in dependence on 'experts' rather than oneself for knowledge, even about the inner workings of one's own psyche – as with a self-conscious cog in a machine that could only make sense of its own motions in terms of *dependence* on all the other specialised parts of the machine as a whole. And the technological system property of reducing disorder through evicting labour out of its machine tissue, is mirrored in the labour-saving power of commodities – not only physical labour, but more particularly, labour on oneself. What is left of the person is image, a precarious shell that mirrors the technological frame and its assumptions, but is subjectively weak and insecure within.

That this transformation of subjectivity has occurred is reflected in the different kinds of patients that psychoanalysts are dealing with today compared to those that Freud analysed at the turn of the twentieth century. Freud confronted the powerful, repressive super-ego of inner-direction. The clinical manifestations of the repressive super-ego were presented in debilitating fixations, phobias and neuroses which arose out of psychic and sexual repression. Now, patients seeking psychoanalytic treatment present themselves far more commonly as psychically lost, with pervasive feelings of emptiness, depression and a violently oscillating sense of self-esteem. The contemporary psychic illness is pathological narcissism. Narcissism is a response to a world that has taken love away and replaced it with images of the very values that are opposite to love – possession and greed, power-hunger, fear and dependency. Narcissism is a response to a culture of double-binds where the path towards 'making-it' is through aggression, but aggression is masked behind images of responsibility and pseudo-authenticity. As in clinical studies of narcissism, the narcissist defends him- or herself against aggressive feelings by erecting a 'grandiose self' within a psychic world that is otherwise thinly populated by 'devalued, shadowy images of self and others, and potential persecutors'.

However, the grandiose self is a passively received 'legitimated' screen on which the culture code projects its messages. These are messages that say, 'By identifying with *this* object, with *this* commodity, with *this* "flavour-of-the-month" pop-star, political personality, self-development programme, or whatever ... you are OK! You can be fulfilled! You can *be* loved!' As but a screen of the self, when the culture code's projectionist goes home, and the person is alone with the barrage of emotional stimulation disconnected, the screen is empty. The person is left with a sense of inner vacuum, with perpetual restlessness, with fear of a dark wet hole that can only be temporarily filled with vicarious pleasures and borrowed warmth from others. Life is met with continuously trembling, grasping hands, and death – where all the material props of existence are torn away – is the ultimate, all-pervasive fear.

As Christopher Lasch points out, the cases of character disorder that confront the psychoanalyst reflect what is 'in a more subdued form' the character type that has become normal within everyday society.[4]

The *order* that commodities provide to subjectivity is *inherently* unsatisfying. With a need to find happiness in the object world and images that possession of objects signals, the psychological power of commodities is that they provide 'scarce' happiness. Nothing is produced that intentionally makes the person who possesses it unhappy. Thus the culture code ostensibly erases unhappiness by selling us only the white squares in a black-white game. This principle extends to the fine detail of subjective life. It is actualised in the commodities of 'personal development' packages, 'how to be a success and influence people' packages, 'sexual fulfilment' packages, and in the whole cartons that offer 'fitness', 'good diet', and a vision of perpetual youth. The operation performed on the human psyche is however like a frontal lobotomy. By cutting the left brain hemisphere off from the right, by separating the two parts of the self, the pain of depression goes, as do the heights of ecstatic happiness. The person from then onwards can only ever traverse the emotional middle territory – never again unhappy, but also, never again happy – just bland, perhaps complacent, but more likely, resigned. Thus the 'obsolescence' code offers the mirage of happiness in the reality of intrinsic unhappiness.

Ordering of subjective life inherently creates blandness. With the penetration of subjective life by the values of the technological frame, the society replaces each bit of the 'standing reserve' environment with objects that master it. Order replaces chaos and uncertainty. But in equal measure, order replaces spontaneity, novelty, freshness – the experience of the world that enlivens the senses.[5] The novelty of new commodities therefore mirrors spontaneity lost, and 'pricks' the need for the 'curious', the 'new' experience – as with those persons who must prick themselves to ensure that they are awake. Blandness persists as a background to all that is outside the 'freshness' that is offered by the new.

To *order* the world of experience means erecting object props that stand for and mediate this experience. As a substitute-reality for (both external and internal) nature, absolutes for human knowledge dissolve in a continuing series of masks. This 'places man in the country he creates with his own mind. In this country he is surrounded by brilliant, fantastic, wildly distorted images of himself'.[6] By replacing each part of the environment with a mirror, subjective life resides within a house of mirrors, and as Philip Slater observes, 'a house of mirrors is satisfying only to very sick people'.[7] But the cultural malaise of narcissism is cured by *depending* on the medicine that reglazing the commodity mirror provides.

Consequently, within the cultural world of ordered commodity mirrors, the society participates, and finds transitory fulfilment *within*, the commodity code. But active participation outside the code, in particular in the labour of autonomous self-consciousness independently of the commodity mirrors, has little cultural salience. As Herbert Marcuse notes of the Narcissus myth, Narcissus was punished for *not participating*.[8]

As a final example of the depth of penetration into subjectivity by the values of the the technological frame, one has only to consider the commodification of the deepest of subjective experience, the experience of love.

The Commodification of Love

Love, like all other subjective properties within a culture of narcissism, is owned, rather than given. Marx's observation about private property applies equally as well to love as it does to other commodities to be exchanged:

> Private property has made us so stupid and one-sided that an object is only *ours* when we have it – when it exists for us as capital, or when it is directly possessed, eaten, drunk, worn, inhabited, etc. – in short when it is *used* by us ... in the place of all physical and mental senses has therefore come the sheer estrangement of all these senses, the sense of having.[9]

'Having' is passive. 'Having' is opposite to 'giving'. Love in modern times is therefore often confused, as Erich Fromm points out, with the (passive) object-status the person *has*, and beams out as signals for the rest of the world to notice – a mixture of popularity and sex-appeal. To find love is, in most people's eyes, the quest to be loved, to be the object that others will find attractive.[10] On the social market-place this means presenting oneself in the best package *image* that one's social and economic resources will allow. For a man, this commonly means showing off the greatest success, power, and wealth as the social margin of his position in the culture makes possible. For a woman, the images that stand for 'being loved' often involve making herself as attractive an object – particularly in physical terms – as possible.

This is nowhere more clearly demonstrated than in the idolatry of love that is perpetrated by the Hollywood image-factories. As Jackie Collins reveals in her novel, *Hollywood Wives*, the wives of the successful, rich, popular film stars only survive socially by spending the majority of their waking moments paying for the massaging of their hips, breasts, and faces into youthful seductiveness. The wives disappear off the social 'hostessing' landscape as soon as their successful, rich, popular husbands turn their attention towards another love object. As Jackie Collins observes, the person most able to predict when this is likely to happen is the most prestigious local jeweller, where about-to-be-rejected love-objects shore up their future economic security before being evicted from the conjugal bed.[11]

Again, following the wider dynamics of the commodity-exchange system, finding a love-object and being loved follow the same pattern as do the commodity and labour markets. Two persons fall in love when they feel that they have found the best object available on the market, considering the limitation of their own exchange value.[12] As Peter

Berger observes,

> As soon as one investigates ... which people actually marry each other, one finds that the lightning shaft of Cupid seems to be guided rather strongly within very definite channels of class, income, education, racial and religious background. If one investigates a little further into the behaviour that is engaged in prior to marriage under the rather misleading euphemism of 'courtship', one finds channels of interaction that are often rigid to the point of ritual ... [and] ... a complex web of motives related in many ways to the entire institutional structure within which an individual lives his life – class, career, economic ambition, aspirations of power and prestige ... when certain conditions have been met or have been constructed, one allows oneself 'to fall in love'.[13]

'Falling in love' represents a crashing-through of the shell of aloneness that contemporary society inflicts on us in the name of individuality. To *be* loved is balm on the wound of isolation that is the basic human condition under a culture whose values are commanded by the technological frame. 'Falling in love' is the state of love that is most pervasively packaged on the commodity market – in everything from deodorant and toothpaste to the brand of cigarettes one smokes.

But 'falling in love' is a mirage that cannot last no matter what the commodity-advertisers tell us. It cannot last because 'falling in love' represents a sudden collapse of the barriers that existed until that moment between two strangers. 'Falling in love' is a collapse into sudden intimacy. The explosive force dies as the loved person becomes as well known as oneself – or, as little known. To rekindle this explosion requires continued labour, continued exploration of the subjectivity of the other that lies behind their front-stage image. This is what Erich Fromm calls 'standing in love'.[14]

However, in line with the imaging of subjectivity within the commodity world of labour-saving devices, images, and people as passively-acquired-objects, it is much easier to continue feeling that we are *being* loved by packaging *ourselves* into a set of socially-approved personae that do the work *for* us. The personae are masks that hide our deeper subjectivity from the labour that would have to be done to know ourselves, and so truly love, rather than merely seek to possess love.

For the 'Hollywood star' persona, the problem of 'falling in love' ceasing, is easily overcome. As a highly marketable commodity, once the explosion dies down, the persona puts itself back on the market, because the persona as an *image* on a screen of consciousness leaves nothing to explore behind the screen.

For the 'husband-wife' persona, 'falling in love' is transmuted into possession, and the ritual of bland normality. Fitting in to others' expectations means erecting appropriate social fronts, sharing drives for social prestige and conformity, sharing symbols of a person to be loved in the commodities that are jointly possessed – and *possessing* the expectation of 'appearing' to be loved by the persona's spouse. The persona *has* a marriage, no matter what the private hell that it may inflict on the persona, the spouse, or the children. The persona does not have to give, just exchange the pleasantries.

The 'Casanova-Delilah' persona may find that sexual desire and fulfilment may hold intimacy within reach. Sex can represent a crashing-through of the shell of aloneness, albeit briefly. Indeed without a good sexual relationship in marriage, the frost of continuing isolation can easily obscure the window through which the couple see each other. Sexual desire can be aroused however by any strong emotion – vanity, the need to conquer, to hurt or be hurt, fear of aloneness – or, love. Sexual fulfilment may require giving nothing of oneself, just the fantasising transference of desire onto the other as object, onto the image their body or behaviour arouses in one's own learned needs. The 'Casanova-Delilah' persona therefore images the wider culture values that align with the technological frame in power, whether it be exercise from a male (patriarchal) or female (seductive) perspective.

Finally, the 'team' persona seeks genuinely to share, to care, to grow, and to understand, by complementing the other's persona. This is a sharing of 'us-against-the-world'. The risk is that the 'husband-wife' persona images are invited in unexamined. That is, the male sees himself as contributing to the 'team' through imaging the practical, instrumental, powerful provider, and the female stops at the persona which prostrates itself to power whilst providing emotional, mothering, nurturing, home-supporting care – both aspects of a highly approved persona. The male interest is likely to dominate for it is more generally acknowledged as of 'value' within the 'oral text' that is played out within the 'written text' of the technological frame. But both sides of the 'team' persona are barriers to the self-discovery and giving that love represents. Both sides of the persona are still caught in an *exchange* family economy. Love remains a commodity that images the self.

Thus, the deepest of human emotions and subjectivity are penetrated by the values that derive from a culture that has forged alignment with the continuing advance of the technological frame. The 'standing reserve' of subjectivity is hidden behind commodity mirrors, and self-consciousness is mediated by the artificial reality that these mirrors image. Subjectivity is deeply embedded in the cultural alignment that has been woven into the advancing technological frame. Thus, as with Narcissus, happiness is only glimpsed in the next commodity image, which by its very existence *commands* unhappiness outside this image. As with Echo, happiness is only glimpsed in passive response, as participation is impossible. At a subjective level, the culture has adjusted very deeply to the continued 'remorseless working of things' that constitutes the Tragedy of Technology.

The Mirror World of Productive Action

As consumers, the society is passive. As participants within the labour of production, the society is active. But activity itself is enframed by the 'written text' of the technological frame, and therefore perpetuates its 'ordering' trajectory.

Participation in labour within the technological frame connects the person to the wider 'system' of the society. As Marie Jahoda demonstrates, beyond the 'manifest' function of employment in providing an income, lies a series of 'latent' functions. Employment provides *activity*, and *fills in time*, and therefore delivers *order* and structure to otherwise unordered life-experience. Employment provides *social connectedness* outside the nuclear family, where an in-group of people are brought together in social relations of production that are ordered by the demands of the productive system's technological requirements. Employment provides a sense of *personal worth and status* according to the specific prestige that is associated with the occupational position the individual assumes in service of the technological system. Employment provides direct and active engagement in the overall system of productive labour beyond the immediate factory or office, and thus connects the person into the fabric of social relations that are aligned with the technological frame as a whole. All of the 'latent' functions connect the 'oral' text of participation into the 'written' interconnected systematisation of society as a whole. Marie Jahoda demonstrates the importance of these 'active' mirrorings of the technological frame to personal identity and meaning, through showing the progressive personal identity crisis, anomie, and passiveness of the person who is suddenly ejected from the productive system into the dole queues.[15] What is also lost by the unemployed is the 'manifest' function of employment, to provide income, that allows them to participate in the wider commodity economy from which cultural meaning and location is derived. For the person who remains employed, these 'side-bets' on the consumer culture ensure *commitment* to the organisation within which the person is labouring.[16]

People tend to become increasingly committed to the purposes of whatever organisation they serve, the longer they remain there, and the higher up the internal status tree they are able to climb. Herbert Popper and Roy Hughson demonstrated this. They surveyed over 1,000 chemical engineers, giving them a series of case studies, and asking them how *they* would react. The case studies dealt with increasing levels of hypothetical conflict between the company's production interests, and the interests of the local community in having a non-polluted environment. The higher the status, or length of time of the respondent in the company, the greater was their commitment to corporate productivity, no matter what effect it had on the community.[17] Similarly, a 1972 review of 800 members of the National Society of Professional Engineers revealed that almost half felt 'restrained from criticizing their employer's activities or products'; over 10 per cent felt they were 'required to do things which violated their sense of right and wrong'. As Hannay and McGinn observe, the results demonstrate that people were more prepared to 'swallow the whistle' than be 'whistle-blowers'.[18]

However, the morality that results is not just one of passive resignation, but one of active proselytisation for the interests with which one's own interests are identified. Members of atomic energy establishments proselytise for more nuclear reactors, and deny the risks of reactor meltdown and radioactive emission that have been demonstrated so clearly at Three Mile Island and Chernobyl. Members of cigarette companies will deny the relevance of statistical data on smoking-related illness. Members of armaments companies will support the fantasy that to stockpile 20 times the nuclear arsenal that could annihilate the world, is a guarantee of peace.

The morality of the oral text is therefore one that is circumscribed by both the system demands, and the purposes of those who control productive labour. To break with these demands confronts the individual with the cost of not only losing his or her job, but also all the sources of connection and meaning within the interconnected society as a whole. To break the pattern precipitates the person into the existential insecurity that follows from not being able to participate in the commodity code. The dominant morality is therefore one that images the person as a dependent component in an otherwise technically-mediated, efficient system of organisation. Thus, *a*morality is normal, for morality is determined elsewhere, and by the demands for alignment between subjective action and cultural properties of the technological frame as a whole. The steroypical big businessman or politician can be amoral whilst operating within the system's frame – delivering polluted, unsafe factories to developing countries, aggressively destroying or undermining competitors or sectors of the community that stand in the way of 'progress'. Yet outside employment within the system, they may enjoy the image of being a loving provider for the family, a pillar of the church, and a concerned ecologist. The ideology that aligns with the properties of the technological frame, and participation within it, holds the whole order together, and decrees that such embedded amorality is normal.

The morality of the participant within the technological frame is remarkably similar to that of the psychopath. Robert Smith suggests that the generality of at least mild – or incomplete – psychopathy is not surprising, because many of the values that are associated with cultural alignment with the technological frame are a perfect nest for the psychopathic personality to rest within. As Smith comments, 'We have evolved a social order for which the psychopath is admirably fitted.'[19]

Classically, by Freudian analysis, the psychopath is a person with an inadequately formed super-ego.[20] Social morals have not been internalised to give the psyche an internal police-person to control the continuous set of negotiations that go on between the other two parts of the psyche – the id, or self-gratifying impulse, and the ego, or socially-reflected shell of self-perception. When the police are not watching, the person's behaviour is morally anarchic. But the anarchy is hidden behind a mask of self-presentation. The psychopath is radically out of touch with others' feelings, lives by surface appearances, and cannot empathise with, or feel, or love others. As Buss states, 'some individuals lack warmth and feeling for their fellow beings, but the psychopath is alone in his tendency to treat others as objects rather than as fellow beings.'[21] Psychopaths make perfect confidence tricksters because, with no internal moral court in which to appear, they must continuously weave ensnaring webs through superficial charm and good intelligence.[22]

Robert Smith points out that the approved cultural values of contemporary society accept (at least mild) psychopathic behaviour as appropriate. These values emphasise achievement, where the morality of the means disappears in the demonstration effect of the successful achievement of the end – calculated particularly in terms of objects, business take-overs, or social image that mirror subjective power and worth. Respect for people is measured more according to their 'market value' – as lovers, high status entertainment purveyors, or power-brokers – rather than according to their inner substance, wisdom, or integrity. Understanding of other people is mediated more according to their image rather than according to inter-subjective engagement. What is valued is the outside shell of the true human being. And the interpersonal skills that succeed are those of the post-World War II 'manager' – strong *manipulative* skills to capture others into the person's own orbit of power and support.[23]

What is particularly interesting though, is the parallel that can be drawn between the socialisation experience of the clinical psychopath, and the socialisation experience of a person entering an institution that is woven into the larger technological frame and its implied values.

In the case of the clinical psychopath, inadequate super-ego formation is, according to Freudian analysis, the result of the child receiving inadequate nurturing within the mother-father-child triangle at a critical early stage in their development. There are several scenarios that this triangle can represent, depending on their level of hate, violence, or insecurity, which accordingly end up as impulse-drives in the adult psychopath's make-up. The most common triangle for the less violent 'middle-class' psychopath however is one where the father is successful, distant, and authoritarian, whilst the mother is frivolous, indulgent, seductive – both, it should be noted, stereotypes of 'maleness' and 'femaleness' as valued in contemporary culture. The parents are self-centred rather than concerned enough with the child's needs to put their own images and needs to one side. Rather than being affectionate, they *indulge* the child to the extent that he or she mistakes appearances for feelings, and becomes charming and manipulative. And they punish the child the most strongly, when the child breaks the image of the family to outsiders. The psychopath therefore typically originates in a family culture of mirrors, and manipulation for self-gratification. As the parents never dealt in true feelings, or took the role of the child, or allowed the child to understand others – except through their appearances – the child grows up never capable of empathising with others, unable to take the role of others, and feel what they feel. The world becomes an unfeeling terrain of the appearance of objects to be manipulated for personal impulse gratification.[24]

The parallel to the modern organisational system is immediate. The organisational system is anonymous. The corporate entity cannot be aligned with particular people who can be dealt with at an interpersonal level, for all fit within the overall technological frame from which corporate purposes and actions derive. To learn the social norms that operate behind the organisational door the neophyte has entered, means that he or she must adopt them for themselves, trying the norms out as a moral topcoat, and later as a moral body. The organisational system provides a (metaphorical) surrogate father and mother to the child in the neophyte who is learning its way. The (abstract) father and mother bear a striking resemblance to the parents of the psychopath. The 'father' principle in the system is in the rational, the technically measured, the overarching authority of instrumental, unfeeling logic, by which the organisational child must live to be successful. The 'mother' principle in the system is the ineffectiveness of real emotion, and the seductiveness of 'cool', socially persuasive, artificial warmth that can be turned on and off as the 'father' principle in the system requires. Together, the two 'parent' principles *indulge* the organisational child for the appearance of handling the social and human skills necessary to 'perform' in their prescribed, subservient slot in the hierarchy. The organisational child is punished if he or she breaks the image that the combined system-family-unit presents to the outside world.

In time, the person becomes the 'system', and abides by the morality that aligns with dependence on the culture-defining properties of the technological frame. In turn, they are likely to play the morality back as a tape-recorded message to the others – meanwhile, finding psychic strength in an in-group appearance of a morality shared, and sustenance in a lifestyle supported. And the overall organisational system is legitimated because it fits into the total pattern of systems that are the (normal) whole organisational life of the society. The person is thus not alone in a society that is disturbed by fear of aloneness, and has power in a society where 'making it' puts the ego up at the right hand of God.

The Lesson of the Pharaohs: The Shaping of Social Protest by the Technology Text

Lewis Mumford observed of the pyramids built by the Pharaohs of ancient Egypt:

> In that feat of engineering, the most prodigious exercise of mathematical and engineering ability – combining exact measurement with the large-scale regimentation of labour – was placed at the disposal of an infantile fragment of the human personality seeking to achieve immortality by mummifying a corpse and heaping up a mountain of masonry.[25]

The process of industrialisation has built a set of interlocking, ubiquitous, efficient, pyramids across the entire social landscape of contemporary society, and called them 'systems'. Through a continuing series of alignments and realignments of culture with the values sedimented into the original factory 'pyramid', the systems have encroached on, and penetrated deeply into, subjective life within our contemporary industrialised culture. Ideological realignments both led the way for social adjustment, and at the same time, made sense of the order for everyday life and meanings that followed. But, as with the *passive* 'culture of narcissism', and the *active* 'psychopathy' of productive life, the result of subjective alignment with the technological frame evokes but 'an infantile fragment of the human personality' that seeks 'immortality' in 'progress' that 'mummifies' the subjective corpse under an ever-increasing 'mountain' of the technological frame.

The culture and subjectivity that align with the contemporary technological frame are ones that align with the continuing progress of this frame over any yet-to-be exploited elements of society that remain as 'standing reserve' for progress. For built into both cultural meanings and subjectivity is acceptance and psychic alignment. What is absent is autonomous departure from the cultural rules that follow from the technical properties of systems, and which have crossed the bridge into subjectivity that has been provided by the platform of commodities.

Excesses of the technological frame are dragged into the light, and perhaps put on a leash, by social protest. But the command of the technological frame is powerful, and co-opting of those interests who directly serve its progress. Social protest therefore only catches the system at the edge of its most visible excesses. It does not seem capable of altering the trajectory as a whole, for even the protesters are deeply aligned with the cultural order and meaning system of the technological frame itself. Social protest cannot irrevocably 'bury the truck' as the Cook Islanders could. It can just change the spiked tyres for rubber.

Social protest stands outside the culture-technology alignment of systematised industrial society. Social protest therefore stands metaphorically as an external 'governor' to a steam engine, rather than as an internal cybernetic control device to a complex system. There is a very big difference between the two controlling devices.

To follow the metaphor through, a machine-system is a closed system. All of its component parts interconnect, and influence each other. But they operate together in a wider environment that is fixed, or given, as far as the machine is concerned. The machine continues to operate, all its parts smoothly working with each other, as long as the environment does not move outside the limits of what the machine can tolerate as 'given'. At the same time however, the machine-system must have a *balancing* device, to keep its parts running smoothly, and to prevent one part of the system overrunning the next.

In the case of Watt's steam engine, *control* was achieved through a 'governor' – two metal balls on a central spindle that whirled faster as the engine ran faster, until the centrifugal force of their speed of rotation dragged them up the spindle past a point where a lever was tripped to let off excess steam. The point of a governor-controlled system is that it cannot achieve an easy balance between all parts of the system. An output of the system must reach a danger-limit before the governor triggers a change through the rest of the system, a change that drags the machine back from the edge of potential self-destruction. This sort of control system worked well for a steam engine.

In the case of a modern automated machine, balance is achieved through *continuous* measurement and control of each unit, and their relationship to the overall system. Thus, in a cybernetically-automated factory system, inputs are categorised and information fed forward to machines so that they can adjust as each input goes past. The system at the same time feeds back the flow of production to regulate the consequent flow of inputs necessary to keep the overall system operating at optimal speed. Automatic-control is thus the maintenance of a continuous equilibrium, whilst governor-control is control through recognition of limits.

Within the ubiquitous, interconnected technological frame of contemporary society, each of its units is regulated by social 'governors', not by automatic control. Pollution, genetic manipulation, nuclear energy systems, and nuclear proliferation – the most dangerous products of a rational technical system – are limited as they reach towards excess. They are limited by political protest and legislation, as a result of which an enforced 'should' acts as some kind of barrier to further excess. So chimneys and car exhausts 'should' have filters; scientists 'should' not work on cloning human embryo; nuclear energy systems 'should' have 'failsafe', error-prevention systems; and nuclear-warhead proliferation 'should' be negotiated.

But the system as a whole is not undergoing continuous 'automatic adjustment'. The systems adjust when their excesses reach public and political attention. They adjust only at the margin of visible excess, at the point where further growth is too (politically or economically) costly. This is so because the systems are ruled by that part of the human psyche that has forged alignment with greater power, more technical, instrumental logic, greater fear of the system not being in total control, and greed for continuing accumulation. The other parts of the human psyche are not aligned with the technological frame. They are not *in* the system. They can only act as a 'governor' from outside. Thus, the parts of the human psyche that are expunged by the technological frame can step in within street demonstrations, and letters to politicians, and litigation, and cry *stop!* But these actions can do no more than put a temporary curb on growth of the system as a whole, for the frame that is attacked is quickly outflanked by a larger, more pervasive frame that co-opts and incorporates the results of protest as well. Systems do not have the power to turn into non-systems. Solutions are 'system' solutions – new systems to control pollution, genetic manipulation, radioactive waste and nuclear arms proliferation. But these systems are also engraved with cultural values that have aligned with progress of the technological frame. And these values ultimately present image, appearance, and sanitising euphemisms, whilst the deeper system values of order, complexity, accumulation, and rational efficiency march forward relatively unhindered.

Within this frame, the culture of industrialism places a seemingly paradoxical salience on individual autonomy. Individuation however is a direct property of a system-atised order. On the one side, individuation aligns with privatisation, and thus produces status anxiety of the person seeking subjective meaning within a *system*-atically anonymised world, an anxiety that is fed by consumption of system-produced commodities. On the other side, individuation represents an ideology of 'equality', where all 'should' have equal power to participate. But the shadow side of equality is *sameness*, or interchangeability as components in an overall system.

Thus, the Black Rights, Feminist, and Liberationist movements that have grown in power over the last 20 years have kindled the fire of increased equality. Yet this is equality *within* the system, an equality that produces sameness of opportunity to participate and to consume. Furthermore, the assertion of active *human* power that is represented in these movements is itself at least partially co-opted into a passive synthesis as the wider system adjusts. Black Rights (particularly in the US) have been partially absorbed into middle-class 'black' television images. Feminism has been partially absorbed into the commodity market, opportunities to participate in constructing the system and, at the same time, serves to generalise the consumer market across both sexes. Feminism has been partially absorbed into equality of opportunities to participate in constructing the system, and being employed within it. Liberationist movements, whilst asserting power against direct repression, run the very real danger, at the same time, of being absorbed into an ideology of equality (and therefore sameness) rather than freedom (particularly from the command of the technology frame), into 'peace *and* a washing machine'.

Whilst active assertion of human power persists, individual freedom from system-atised definition of the person is maintained. But, the oral text of individualism is closely aligned with the written cultural text of systems technology. So protest and assertion of rights can be easily co-opted into a passive acceptance of the system itself, and into active assertion of the system's continuing power.

These co-optive powers of technological systems over cultural values reveal the end-play of *The Tragedy of Technology*. The 'Lesson of the Pharoahs' is yet to be learnt.

Part IV
Rewriting the Tragedy of Technology

11
Culture, Technology and Liberation

Liberation or Domination

It was recently reported to me that one of the most complex and sophisticated technological systems – a gas-turbine ship – would not function until the ship's engineer kicked it.

The ship was the first gas-turbine vessel to be commissioned out of Sydney, Australia, during the 1970s. The ship, once commissioned, embarked on its maiden voyage across the Tasman Sea to New Zealand. However, it had progressed only half-way when suddenly all systems cut out, and the ship was left wallowing in a seething ocean, with no engine power, no lights, no sirens, nothing.

As with all gas-turbine vessels, the degree of system complexity is such that to start and run the ship requires a highly sophisticated computerised control system. The chief engineer had been trained in the 'old' nautical engineering school of greasy engines and brass control devices. Though he had been through a subsequent 'crash' course in computerisation, he was in no way prepared to confront a computerisation problem amongst the myriad of interconnected computer systems that surrounded him on the ship's bridge. He tried the replacement of a few integrated circuits, and toyed with the information discs, all to no avail. The engineer then gave up, walking up to the mess to have a lukewarm cup of tea whilst he thought over the problem.

On his way out of the bridge however, in a gesture of frustration, the engineer kicked the central control panel. When he had finished his cup of tea, he returned to the bridge to try starting the engines one more time. They instantly sprang to life, and the ship proceeded unproblematically to harbour in New Zealand. The massive, highly sophisticated vessel had been started by a kick.

Subsequently it was found out what had gone wrong. The technician who was working on the final detail of the central control panel had inadvertently dropped a tiny length of pared wire into the panel. When the ship entered higher seas, its increased rocking movement caused the wire to fall across the critical wiring that commanded all other systems, thus creating a short-circuit in the ship's entire electronic system. By

229

kicking the control panel, the engineer had dislodged the wire and removed the short-circuit.[1]

As with the tiny discarded length of wire in the gas-turbine ship, the smallest of human errors can cause fundamental breakdown in highly sophisticated technological systems, particularly when associated with unexpected technical malfunctions. This was demonstrated with devastating consequences for Europe in the core meltdown of the Chernobyl nuclear reactor. Cases associated with the American nuclear deterrent system are legion. In one of the more frightening examples, America came to within six minutes of waging nuclear war on Russia because one of the personnel forgot to remove a war-game tape from the system's second back-up computer. The frontline computer had broken down due to technical failure. Operators switched to the first back-up system, and this also failed. When they then turned to the second back-up computer, the screens were filled with an invasion of missiles heading towards the US across the Arctic Circle from the Soviet Union. The countdown to firing America's retaliatory missiles started, and was only stopped – six minutes prior to world annihilation – when someone bothered to check, and found the war-game tape quietly beaming out invasionary messages from the second back-up computer.[2]

As the final end-play in the technological ordering of this (human) reverse salient in system efficiency, the US is now replacing human decision in the waging of systematised nuclear war. With only a four minute lead time between the sensing and impact of a nuclear strike in Europe, human decision-making is simply too inefficient. Thus, as the US Defense Advanced Research Projects Agency (DARPA) claims, weapons will be 'brilliant' rather than 'smart', will 'exhibit human-like "intelligent" capabilities for planning and reasoning', and will be operated 'with little human intervention, or even with complete autonomy'. And, as President Reagan's science adviser admitted, by the year 1990, the decision to wage war may be made automatically.[3] The technological system itself will determine whether the human race survives or is annihilated 90 times over.

The fact that this is possible is both the final act, and the criterion example, of the *Tragedy of Technology* – the submission of human purpose to the external systematic ordering of human affairs by the industrialised technological frame. The *tragedy* is experienced as a 'remorseless working of things', for individual human action appears to be so completely enframed within the technical properties of systems that there seems to be no way that the individual can stand outside and kick the system into new life or wrestle it into a trajectory that departs from the apparently intrinsic system expansion that has characterised industrial history. People can adopt the posture of social 'governors' and can shape the system's worst excesses. But, because of the very processes of 'enframement' that this book has identified, the people appear not able to act as 'cybernetic' balancing influences to redirect the trajectory fundamentally. For the cultural properties of systems have penetrated subjective life, and the meaning systems by which the system trajectory is judged. System cultural properties also mediate perceptions and practical transformations of the future – turning what is yet to be actualised into a standing reserve of limited options that can only apparently be mediated along the present general trajectory of change.

The power of technology to *command* culture is not universal, but is a relatively recent phenomenon, specifically associated with industrial history. The power *emerged* out of continuing cultural negotiations during the eighteenth and early nineteenth centuries in which technological change was one actor amongst culture-forming equals. These negotiations inscribed a world view into the first industrial technological system that is basic to the momentum of industrialisation, that is a world view that accepts system order over human autonomy. These negotiations finally produced an alignment between industrialisation's culture and this core cultural property of technological systems. From there on, the power and trajectory of industrialisation fundamentally depended on the fact that the culture mirrored and asserted this basic cultural property of technological systems. Progress of industrial technologies therefore both produced cultural alignment, and depended upon it, whilst both the technologies and the wider culture mutually mirrored the same ordering world view.

Explanation of how culture–technology alignment was forged lies in a view of technology as a cultural text, a text that according to the cultural values built into its original form and 'grammar', developed the power to emerge as a cultural *frame* for the constitution of cultural meanings across all reaches of contemporary life.

The technology text has been powerfully enframing, for in actualising the ordering world view of industrialism, it interacted with and transformed wider culture at the very roots from which the tree of cultural meanings grows. The technological systems text implied social relations of production and interaction within wider society, and it is within the patterning of discourse that cultural meanings are constructed in the first place. The technological systems text implied aligned stocks of technical knowledge, and institutions that produced them. And it is the society's stocks of knowledge that allow its people to construct meaning about the reality the society must deal with. The technological systems text brought forth a continuously changing reality, but this was one that was mastered by dominant symbolic evidence of the cultural values that were written into the system's text itself. Thus, the superordinate symbols of social order and ordering were those of the technology text or its products – a progression from clocks and smoke-stacks, to systematised energy and urban artefacts of power stations, high rise buildings, and suburban estates, to the transportation artefacts of automobiles and highways, to communication and media artefacts of computers and television. All stand in front of direct engagement with the natural world's reality. All progressively demonstrate the power of the cultural world view that places system order over direct human autonomy. As superordinate symbols of the society's order, the continuous accretion of these artefacts symbolised the apparent inevitability of technological system progress. As with all superordinate symbols, technology's master symbols hold the entire pattern of cultural meanings together within the symbols' superordinate signification of what the society's order means as a whole.

Clear evidence of the power of the technology text in drawing wider culture into alignment with the text's cultural values is presented to us both within history and within immediate experience. Where non-alignment of the technology text with wider culture has been confronted, the non-aligned culture has been smashed, or co-opted, into obeisance. This is equally the case, as this book has shown, in the fruits of Australia's 'outposted' history, as it is in traditional societies confronting modernised technological artefacts for the first time. Equally, the power of the technology text within industrialised society is revealed in the refashioning of social and class boundaries, knowledge alignments, ideology and power into ever closer alignment with system progress. Finally, the text's power is revealed in the rising and falling economic fate of industrial empires that progressively move into or out of alignment with the cultural and stock of knowledge demands that the industrial technology text requires. The technology text is powerful as its potency derives from its ability to reach deeply into culture and turn all that is yet-to-be-aligned into a passively constituted standing reserve for further system progress.

Thus the appearance of technological *autonomy* is very real. However, we cannot attribute this appearance of autonomy to the machine-systems themselves. Instead, the appearance of 'autonomy' must be attributed to *alignment* of the cultural properties of the technology text with, and actualisation of, a world view that wider society adopted as its own, and which must be sustained for the continued progress of technological systems into everyday life to be accepted. For as this book has demonstrated, it is this cultural 'alignment' that shapes the perception of machine-systems, their trajectory, and their possibilities *as if* machine-system progress were a remorseless undimensional tragedy.

The product is a culture of domination rather than liberation. However, domination is not by technological systems, but by the cultural values that these systems embody, and which industrial society has come to accept.

A technological determinist position offers little alternative to continuation of the present trajectory. For a position that attributes power to the machines rather than to cultural values reduces cultural constitution of meaning and action to automatic adjustment to technological command.

Such a total enframement of alternatives is *not* implied by the culture-technology alignment argument of the present book. When the power of the technology text is revealed as cultural power, then the power to question and transform the dominance of the technology text over everyday life is also revealed – in changing the cultural values that are taken for granted. For the power to reverse the flow of influence of the technology text lies where culture is ultimately constituted – in everyday life, action, and constructions of meaning.

Furthermore, in spite of the whole thrust of the argument of this book, there is considerable resilience in the recognition and acting out of cultural alternatives even within a society that is powerfully penetrated by the cultural values of the technology text. A theory that identifies *main* trends of technology domination, like all social theory, projects an image, or an 'ideal type' of the *tendency* of forces that lie behind social action, not the whole. The populace of an industrialising society is not totally and unconsciously embedded in the cultural trajectory that the theory implies. Otherwise, this book, and the many other critiques of the trajectory of industrial society that have been produced over the last 200 years in both literature and popular protest, could not be possible. Thus, the ability to perceive alternatives and to act them out exists within contemporary society, but only once the assumptions that have contributed to a collective unconsciousness are recognised. The primary social project of theory such as in the *Tragedy of Technology* is to help shape the consciousness from which the assertion of an alternative trajectory is possible.

It would be quite improper, and indeed highly pretentious, to move beyond this analysis to outline a programme of action about what to do, for such a programme would imply the ability to predict the intended and unintended consequences of a vast range of social forces that bear on the directions in which industrial society is heading, many of which are most certainly *not* dealt with in this book. At the same time however, it is legitimate to suggest the guiding principles for action that follow directly from the analysis that I have presented. The intention of the book is to project open-ended possibility rather than closed social determinacy.

The projection of open-ended possibility must immediately be qualified. The consideration of any 'guiding principles' can be made against no other field than the 'reality' of the society that exists in the late twentieth century. As a society that is deeply penetrated by technological systems, one cannot take the Luddite stand that denies that contemporary society is deeply dependent upon these systems for its survival, and pretends to be able to change the world by demolishing the machines. However, it is entirely practical to reshape the architecture of these systems, the development of new systems, or the knowledge that informs their design, in terms of an alternative set of values to those that have constrained the trajectory of industrial technological change to the present.

Equally, as this book has constantly asserted, the values context within which potency of the technology text of industrialisation is played out is fundamentally set within the trajectory and hegemonies of capitalism. The erection of any field of change possibilities cannot avoid recognition of the reality of this social force. Yet, it follows from the present book that even if the power of capitalism could be reshaped, unless the cultural power of the technology text itself is addressed, what is likely to be reinstituted is an order that is still bedevilled with the same technology text values that prevail now. Thus, whilst the communication of an open-endedness of future possibility requires suggestion of the specific (and limited) guidelines of action that follow directly from a 'cultural' analysis, reshaping the values of capitalism is also implied at many points along the way.

To return then to the analysis of culture-technology alignment, with these limitations in full view, entry points for change have already been demonstrated. These entry points lie most basically where the culture-forming power of the technology text penetrates wider culture. That is, in the patterning of communicative practices, in valuing and rewarding technical stocks of knowledge that align with the cultural values of the technology text, and in erecting superordinate symbols to the meaning and inevitability of the technology system-based social order. Choice can be asserted at each of these gates between technology and culture constitution. Given the alignment between ruling class power interests and the technological frame however, the action of choice is inherently political. And choice is only likely to be practical within the constraints that are imposed by the technological frame that already exists, and upon which contemporary society depends.

Thus, to confront the reshaping of communicative discourse for example, one is dealing with (amongst other factors) the influence and implied values of present computerised information systems. These systems directly intrude upon both the social relations of production and the social exchanges between people generally.

'Efficient' access to information is the source of power in commerce, and of State hegemonies over ideological submission. The use of information to retain hegemonic power depends however on the system 'control' value that is built into the information systems themselves, a value that aligns with vested interest (and the use of information to 'control') to the extent that access to the information system is limited. Thus, to reshape the power of 'domination' that is built into the use of these systems implies changing the purposes for which they are used. In turn, such a change implies open public access to centralised information systems that deal with social status vis-a-vis the State system (for example, information concerning social security, taxation, police records, health records and so on). Equally, the reshaping of system values implies open access to commercial credit-rating information, and open access to sources of political and commercial hegemony through, for example, access to literature and information about the performance of both State and commercial enterprise. Perhaps most importantly, the reshaping of values that lie behind the present use of information systems implies resisting the increasing centralisation of information, as it is through this expansion of systems that human autonomy is lost under the onslaught of the power of vested interests that align with expansionary system values. In other words, the *present* information systems can be used to enhance human engagement rather than deny it. And, it is within the enhancement of wider human engagement in the discourse that information systems foster, that cultural meanings and values can be constituted independently of the power interests that align with use of the technological systems for centralised advantage.

Furthermore, the 'right to know' follows easily from the 'ability to know'. Whilst information system architecture embodies the priority of centralised control over decentralised access, the *ability* to know will be retained in the hands of the powerful. And the morality of dependence, rather than assertion of human rights, is likely to be sustained. Different values *can* be designed into system architecture.

A similar principle can be applied to the design of organisations that *use* information *system*-atically, both to structure organisational discourse towards organisational purpose, and to control the organisational workforce.

The commanding principles of organisation design today mirror the core values of the technology text. That is, the design principles of human *organisation* are those of efficiency, instrumentally powerful, controlling *information flows* – and standardisation to make this 'system' work. The principles apply particularly within commercial enterprise, but also increasingly in government activity and provision of services.

Whilst such 'information' flows are indeed efficient in the transfer and use of specifically limited information, they also intrude directly on 'communication' flows within the organisation, as human 'communication' is replaced by impersonal and efficient 'information' systems. As the argument of Chapter 5 of this book demonstrates, *un*-powerful, *in*-efficient human communication captures a strength that is otherwise lost, for it is in this process that people jointly *constitute* their own (organisational) society. In displacing human communication by control-based information systems, organisations thus run a very real danger of eroding the very base from which organisation culture is constituted, yielding organisations where human purposes of the participants are only weakly aligned with organisation purpose. A case study that I completed recently of an Australian insurance company demonstrated that this occurred when a pervasive computerised system of operations was introduced without regard for its impact on previous patterns of communicative discourse.[4]

The result is a potentially weak organisation culture, a culture that is not only susceptible to increased encroachment of technique-mediated control, but also is unable to take command over a turbulent 'non-standardised' environment. In commerce, such weakness is ultimately likely to be visited upon bottom-line profitability. In government, such weakness is likely to be visited upon the State's coping mechanisms to deal with the social turbulence that is associated with the unintended effects of the technology frame's systematised ordering of social life and opportunity. Human *communication* design parameters *can* be built into the introduction of technological information systems into organisations, but this has to be a conscious choice at the outset.

To take but one example, in a metal-working company in Australia, computerised information was used to replace the 'craft' component of knowledge of numerically-controlled machine tool operators on the factory floor. The company sought to replace what they saw as an inefficiency. Previously, the operators had needed to reprogramme the machine tools several time each day to manage new runs of production.

What the company did was to interview each of the operators to find out the reprogramming actions that each operator separately performed.

Management then combined the operators' knowledge into a centralised computer information system. But they placed the computer on a desk remote from the shop floor, where it could only be viewed by a supervisor. Two foremen were hired then to tell the operators what they had previously known for themselves. Initially, the operators welcomed the computer information system for it potentially made their own job easier. But when the communication system became one of control rather than access – as management interests aligned with the values that system properties offered – the operators took industrial action. The *same* information could have been programmed into the computer system. The *same* use of this information could have been made in operations. But, for the operators to feel involved in contributing to the purposes of the company, rather than being dominated by them, required integrating the appropriate human communication system with the new information system that was introduced. Design parameters that modelled those embodied within the values of the computer technology text were imposed instead, to the detriment of the organisation.[5]

The design and use of stocks of technical knowledge are directly involved in each of the redesigns of communication structures that I have discussed here. At the present moment of alignment between the technological frame and society's primary stocks of technical knowledge, knowledge is mainly in the hands of specialised experts. However, as I pointed out in Chapter 3, as a 'non-phonetic' 'written' stock of knowledge, the sheer bulk of disconnected specialised knowledge is so vast that no individual expert controls its use. Instead, the use of knowledge is primarily in the hands of those organisations which have enough capital power to employ *groups* of experts to 'interpret' collectively the stock of technical knowledge in the interests of organisational performance. Application of knowledge is thus primarily in the hands of those with the capital resources to control organisational and technological architectures that can *select* what is relevant or profitable out of what is otherwise an 'information overload'. Such commercial and State interests are most likely to thrive in the contemporary competitive information ecosystem that the technology text has inspired, by focusing on what the organisation interests must know *now*. Otherwise, the organisation interests confront the spectre of enervation and depletion that must follow from information overload when dealing with immediate practical, commercial, problems. 'Knowledge' is thus converted into 'rational', instrumental, immediate 'information' to be mined as quickly and efficiently as possible.

What is so easily lost in the information-inspired race that now aligns with progress of the technological frame, is consciousness of what is *not* present in solutions to immediate problems. What is lost is a consciousness of the continuity of human purpose, and a consistent morality and wisdom that locates the immediate problems amongst all others. This wider understanding is largely excluded from the information systems of technical experts who must deal with that which is practical within constrained technical parameters, and therefore which is scientifically verifiable, rather than with that which is 'inefficiently' human. Furthermore, consideration of wider human issues is likely to be a severe disadvantage to those who must keep ahead of commercial competition in using new information to identify new products and services. Even the solution of social 'problems' that the technological trajectory itself produces must then be handed over to 'experts', for it is only they who have the technological efficiency to filter information, and command what constitutes 'knowledge' that can be applied. People in the wider community are excluded from this closed cycle. Instead, wider society stands at the end of a power-chain of technique that starts somewhere in the centre of technical efficiency, moves through links of increasing dependency for the population at large, and somewhere along the way, leaves human wisdom in the refuse bin. This series of dynamics directly aligns with further progress of the values of technological systems, and loss of human autonomy.

Entry into the way in which expert systems knowledge is created is therefore one of the gateways of change of the impact of the technological system as a whole on society. One key to entry lies in education.

Tertiary education systems are increasingly forging alignments with the competitive knowledge demands presently being imposed by keeping up with the trajectory consequences of the technological frame. In alignment with late twentieth-century high-technology economic competition, universities (and government support for them) are increasingly focusing on the teaching of knowledge that is instrumentally useful *now*, namely commercial, computer, engineering, and applied scientific knowledge. Few of these courses involve genuine integration of coursework with an understanding of the society we live in, its trajectory, or social alternatives. Indeed in the late 1980s, as academics, we increasingly have to apologise for 'liberal arts' as a luxury that may perhaps be justified in terms of some obscure commercial benefit of teaching philosophic ethics to doctors, sociologically manipulative mechanisms to businessmen, or English writing techniques to public relations personnel and journalists.

Thus the institutions that create the knowledge carriers of contemporary society are presently in very real danger of being unable to communicate a critical perspective, or a wider cultural understanding on the basis of which the knowledge carriers can contemplate their involvement in fostering the untrammelled progress of the technological frame.

Reshaping of the culture's stock of valued technical knowledge therefore implies fundamental reorientation of tertiary education practices towards integrating the wider cultural, critical, and historic perspectives into the education of the 'experts' of the future. This is a far-sighted principle that flies in the face of the immediate pragmatising trends. However, government policies and educational institutions *can* choose to deal with a longer-term horizon than that which appears in front of immediate 'pragmatic' vision.

Similar implications apply to the education of the young. Whilst education emphasises using established information systems and programmed learning of technical subjects, it will fail in fostering the ability to see technical subjects in their wider human context. And it will fail in promoting the ability of members of society at large to engage in creating their own world, rather than accepting passively whatever the advance of the technological frame implies. 'Inefficient' as it may be, it follows from a perspective that puts autonomy of choice above its command by technological expediency, that educators pay particular attention to allowing students to be involved in creating knowledge rather than passively receiving it. Equally, it follows that students need to be able to explore the human dimensions of technical subjects and problems rather than be rewarded simply for technically correct solutions. A reshaping guideline directs educators to foster students' exploration of their own human potential to engage in and create their world, and to question technological orthodoxy, rather than to accept passively what otherwise appears to be an inevitable path of dependency, system-aligned employment, or unemployment, that the present map of society may well lay out in front of them.

What I have described above are only limited examples of where choice at the gates of the culture-technology nexus is possible, and, according to a principle of reshaping technological domination, desirable. The point has only been to demonstrate that choice is *possible*, once a different set of values are applied to desirable action.

However, whilst the assertion of the possibility of alternatives has been limited to a small number of examples in the space of this conclusion, the central principle is clear. This is a principle that is derived directly from the historic and cultural analysis of this book. That is, that once accepted into industrial society, the cultural values of the technology text have had power to command the human constitution of cultural meanings into alignment with the central values of the text itself. The task of reshaping the culture-technology nexus is to break this alignment at the gateways where the values of the technology text have entered wider culture, and to reassert a culture of 'autonomy' within daily life.

Hopefully, the present book has at least contributed a perspective that might help to identify a path away from the domination of human culture by the culture-forming values of the industrial technology text. Equally, a culture-technology alignment perspective may be able to contribute to questions to be raised and explored in both sociological theory and theories concerning the social shaping of technological change – both scholarly pursuits that are central in providing a greater understanding of how the people within contemporary society can take a firmer hold on their future.

Culture, Technology and Sociology

Both Marx and Weber treat mature capitalism as a world where technological rationality reigns supreme within social organisation. The present book addresses this theme. However, whilst treating capitalism as background and core dynamic, the book has primarily been concerned with *industrialisation*. More particularly, the book has explored the *cultural* fabric and dynamic that underlies industrial progress.

In establishing a culture-technology perspective at the centre stage of analysis, the present work therefore adds a dimension that has not been applied before in either critiquing the Marxian or Weberian positions, or in rationalising the similarities and conflicts between the base theoretical positions that have informed sociology ever since.

As concluding notes to the present work there is not scope to develop fully the wider sociological implications of a culture-technology alignment perspective. Nor is there scope to locate the contributions within the rich stream of literature that has sprung from the well-springs of insight that Marx and Weber offered. These are substantial projects for later work. However, what I can do is to point the way, to identify some of the key implications for theories of industrialisation that have not been developed so far in the book but which are offered by a perspective that seeks to bridge so-called 'structural' and 'subjective' processes by erecting a platform of culture.

The prism through which the light of industrialising society is viewed in the present book treats industrialised technology as a cultural phenomenon that interacts with the wider culture of society in forming and reforming the society's overall *order*. Thus, the cultural 'text' of technology is directly implicated in the formation of the society's world views, horizons of collective interest (in class), ideologies and accepted legitimations of the authority of power. All of these ordering principles are nested within the society's collective patterns of meaning and action.

Interaction between the cultural 'text' of technology and the society's wider culture and order is played out in everyday life – within the social processes that produce a mirroring between culture, consciousness and action.

Thus, whilst there was prior machine-breaking and protest against direct capitalist repression, proletarian class consciousness only emerged once the wider culture was deeply penetrated by the order that the technology text implied, and not before. Class consciousness and action were formed within the technological frame to culture, not against it. For culture is constituted in daily life, and so too is the meaning of class within the overall social order. Thus, it was not until industrially-inspired 'discipline' had penetrated wider culture, that the discipline of union-based organisation was possible (as distinct from 'mob' protest), and proletarian class action *started* to have power to reshape worker repression *within* the wider order of industrial capitalism.

To follow this link between cultural alignment and class further, the emergence of *new* classes under industrialisation was aligned with a *cultural* transformation of the *whole* social order as it continuously rebalanced to align with the culture-forming consequences of technological advance. I should note at this point however what class means within the present analysis. In keeping with the cultural perspective of this book, class is viewed primarily in terms of what class horizons *mean* for the action and consciousness of those who reside within. As 'meanings' are set within the overall meaning system of the society, so too is class set within the overall *order* of the society.

Thus, cultural negotiations that produced the shape of an original industrial social *order* were those that produced the shaping of class boundaries. Not only were these negotiations between power interests, but they also involved those who were seeking to locate themselves within the emergent order, rather than specifically in terms of greater access to ownership of the means of production. What could collectively be called the bourgeoisie was therefore a fundamentally differentiated set of classes from the outset, for there was a variety of interest connections to the overall *order*.

It was not the emerging capitalists who were instrumental in providing legitimation for the emergent order. Instead, the burgeoning power of the capitalists was supported by interstitial groups who most feared *dis*order – as both the cultural reality and its meaning were undergoing transformation. It was the interstitial classes of the eighteenth and early nineteenth centuries that fostered the institutional means of *balancing* the interests of exploiters and exploited, through education, Mechanics Institute movements and so on. Their collective concern for order was drawn into collective action and consciousness from a variety of separate groups: from reformist elements of the aristocracy, from some capitalists, from progressive elements in the church, and from an emerging middle class. Collective interest was less in gaining access to control over the means of production, and was more in maintenance of the social order that their lifestyle and meanings fed upon. The disparate groups eventually clustered around 'middle-class' interest and definitions of reality, as the size of this class expanded in relation to their collective role in *balancing* the social relations of capitalist production, as their collective interest became increasingly central to the *order* of industrial society.

The emergence of a moving field of class interests depended on new technical stocks of knowledge that were called forth to support the march of industrial technology. It was here that the cultural values of the technology text encroached *directly* on class formation. The need for the employment of new stocks of machine knowledge at the turn of the nineteenth century, for example, produced professional classes whose interests were intimately connected with the technological text of the time (and therefore with *general* capitalist interest), but whose collective knowledge power provided independence from *particular* capitalist interest and control. The need for machine-skilled artisans called forth a class in the early nineteenth century that stood with separate identification and interest away from both unskilled proletarian 'survival' interest and from middle-class interest in order.

Equally, when the power of technology's cultural values to define wider culture is revealed, the merging of class interests today is explained. As this book has shown, the technology text increasingly became a frame for both the constitution and expression of cultural values, entering increasingly into subjective life and consciousness – entering through the cultural bridge of the commodity equally, therefore, into both middle-class and proletarian cultures. These cultures have merged into a shared culture of dependence – on a commodified subjective life that mirrors values of the technological frame. Thus working-class identification and action is quite specifically set within the domain of better salary and conditions for enhanced *participation* within commodified subjective life. Middle-class identification and action is merging with working-class forms of workplace confrontation – for the same reasons. And outside the domain of employed labour, the cultural demands, expectations and politics are only marginally distinguishable.

In all cases of class formation and change, the social relations of production are directly implicated. For the social relations of production represent the mode of sociality that bears on the society's reality and transforms it – and, as a cultural analysis suggests, social meanings and *experience* of reality are fundamentally connected. This view of the primacy of social relations in producing social order and its legitimation aligns with an orthodox Marxian position, but the focus is different, because, with culture formation at the centre of analysis, what is of primary concern is the way that social relations of production shape discourse, rather than the way that these relations are themselves shaped within the capitalist institution of private property. Thus in keeping with a culture-technology alignment position, the social relations are formed in the context of the technology text (which mediates the ownership values of capitalism). And, as the immediate culture-shaping property, the specific shape of class relations depends more directly on the technology text than on the shape of capitalist values *per se*. Furthermore, the specific shape of ideological legitimation within industrial society is also dependent more on the technological frame to culture (and order) than on capitalist values *per se*.

In line with Althusser, ideology is attached to legitimated order. Whilst social relations are one constitutive element in cultural order, there are others. Ideology therefore has some independence from the social relations of production, and indeed may be – as at the turn of the nineteenth century – instrumental in *shaping* the social relations of production, a position that is more in line with a Weberian than an orthodox Marxian view. However, as the argument of this book demonstrates, ideological legitimation *must* align with the overall order that the society experiences. If not, the ideology loses its legitimacy in everyday life experience, and will be transformed to align, or will fail as a meaningful justification of the way things are.

Under the technological 'enframing' of culture, *experience* of reality is mediated according to the values, assumptions, and focused capabilities that are sedimented into technological systems. Furthermore, the experience of *order* is enframed by the cultural import of technological system properties.

On the one hand these properties continuously expand through 'disordered' environments to capture these environments into technologically-inscribed order. On the other hand, cultural properties of the technological text penetrate culture at its constitutive roots – and therefore cause the *alignment* of cultural meanings with the newly expanded order that is set in place by the contemporary moment in the technological 'frame' itself. Thus ideologies – as *order* legitimations – must fundamentally align with the culture-constitutive properties of the technological frame, not with the social relations of production *per se*. Where there is non-alignment – as is most vibrantly demonstrated in the sudden encroachment of the fully articulated technological frame on Third World cultures – prior legitimations fail as do ruling classes whose interests in the social order are dependent upon them. The *power* lies in the cultural assumptions of the artefacts, and in the assumed system-cultural properties that stand as their shadow background.

Finally, to return to the starting point of this presentation of wider sociological implications of the present book, I should again emphasise that a culture-technology alignment perspective is an analysis of industrialism rather than of capitalism. I have not adopted this position because I am unable to see the fundamental social shaping force of capitalism. It is clear that capitalism stands as a contiguous background to everything about culture-technology alignment that the book has argued for. Rather, I have adopted the present perspective on the shape of industrialisation because when one focuses on the cultural order and meanings that people *experience* in daily life, it becomes clear that capitalism is not a *necessary* condition for progression of the industrial culture-technology alignment that shapes this experience.

If, following Weber, we are to perform a mind experiment on necessary conditions for the culture-technology alignment, capitalism is not the only social form for carriage of this alignment. The base property of the industrial order lies in its acceptance of the superordinacy of technological mediation and ordering of environments over human autonomy. The dynamic property of the social order is one that motivates action to *expand* technological mediation. Capitalism was perhaps the only form of command over the technological frame that *could* have emerged out of the trajectory of cultural negotiations that preceded it. This position is however arguable. It could well be posited that without the directly repressive drive of early capitalism, society would not have been shaken out of encrusted past ways and into such a fundamentally different relationship between human purpose and culture, and between culture and technological mediation. But the main function that capitalism performed was to actualise the base cultural properties of technological order to create the dynamic of the technological text. Once the process had been catalysed, carriage of the culture-technology alignment could equally occur under any other form of social/economic order that subscribed to the base properties of technological superordinacy and expansion.

Thus, under the influence of a drive to compete (both economically and ideologically), the shape of the culture-technology alignment in the Soviet Union (and increasingly, China) is emerging along remarkably similar trajectories to that of the capitalist West. The shape of progress may be retarded, or coloured in different tones, but the basic trajectory is the same – for the social orders of both the Soviet Union and China subscribe to the twin principles of technological superordinacy and expansion. Similarly, revolutionary movements that have succeeded in overthrowing repressive capitalist regimes – as in the Philippines and Nicaragua, where ruling class ideological legitimations were patently out of line with lived experience – have themselves been seeking a new order that is already enframed within the twin social order cultural properties of technological superordinacy and expansion. What is being fought for is more equal participation in the frame – 'peace and a washing-machine'. But whatever political colour the new revolutionary government may have, the base properties of the technological frame are likely to be assumed. And the progression of the culture-technology alignment is likely to follow the same basic trajectory as under capitalism – though with varying levels of participation and equality of opportunity.

Consequently, where the intention of sociological analysis is to critique the sources of unfreedom that prevail within contemporary society, analysis needs to focus not only on the structure and dynamics of capitalism, but also on the cultural ordering principles that lie beneath capitalism's umbrella of interests. It is to be hoped that the present analysis of culture-technology alignment may be able to contribute to this project.

The Social Shaping of Technology

Technology stands at the centre of the trajectory of industrialism. When a culture-technology alignment perspective is adopted, direct implications flow for the study of the social shaping of technological change within this trajectory. For, as the book has sought to demonstrate, it is the self-reinforcing cycles of cultural *alignment* with the technical properties of systems that shape the general trajectory of innovations that are introduced into society, as well as the impact of technology on the wider culture.

Thus, whilst specific innovations cannot easily be predicted, their general shape perhaps can be.[6] What 'fits' society is likely to be those innovations that abide by the 'new' cultural grammar of the technology text, and which move the next stage along the trajectory of system order.

The key to unlocking the general social shaping of technological innovation is the cultural grammar that lies beneath all negotiations that produce the innovation. This is the case even though at first-order analysis, relative power in negotiations appears to provide adequate explanation.

Each of the actors or institution interests that play a part in the negotiations that produce technological innovation can be seen to form into a social (and cultural) 'system' of production.[7] As interacting and self-referent subsystems of action, all other subsystems are environments to subsystem order. Other subsystems represent disorder to be ordered according to focal subsystem conditions of interest in order. Therefore, for example, politicians are likely to reach out to scientists to order scientists' action according to political system order; commercial managers are likely to reach out of their subsystem to order political action in terms of commercial order, and so on. The shape of innovation that results is likely to be a product of relative power within these subsystem negotiations to order the surrounding environments according to particular subsystem interests. Thus, for example in Paul Barrett's observation of the political shaping of Chicago's transportation system, the nexus between political and automobile lobby definitions of order dominated overall definitions of order to be achieved, and the shape of transport innovations that eventuated.[8]

However, as with the subsystems of a body, the negotiating social subsystems *can* only interact if they share a protocol at their interface. As with the body, this protocol is written not just at the edges of interaction, but more deeply in the compatibility of cellular and organic organisation.

For the body's systems, a genetic code that is shared across all subsystems determines overall balance. In the case of social subsystem negotiations towards innovation, a system culture-code provides an equivalent function to that of the genetic code within the system of an organic body. In other words, behind *all* subsystem negotiations a shared, fundamental culture-code or grammar is operating. Its manifestation will be seen as shaded by the particular interest groups' locations in benefiting from expression of the code – in, for example, political order, commercial order or scientific order. But given the culture-constitutive properties of technological systems, *no* group involved in innovation negotiations *can* depart from the culture code without being rejected from system negotiations – as an alien transplanted organ is expelled from the body by antibody reactions. This would be the case for example, with the rejection of 'alternative technology' interests from negotiations concerning the overall shaping of national energy systems to the extent that 'alternative technology' interests cannot be incorporated within the dominant system mode.

At any moment in industrial history the dominating cultural subsystem in the shaping of the overall innovation is likely to be the subsystem that has relative power to define the superordinacy of its own interest over other subsystems within the overall integrative protocol. Whilst immediate and independent sources of power may have a transitory shaping influence over the whole, the ultimate system that is likely to win out is that which best fits and actualises the cultural 'grammar' that underlies the whole system. Thus, for example, in the negotiations that produced the market dominance of an electrical refrigerator over gas-operated appliances,[9] relative power of the electric appliance lobby was a product of both co-opting consumers generally into the wider electricity generation *system*, plus the greater pervasiveness of this system itself in providing a shadow background to the choices that were the most viable.

Following the culture-technology alignment argument, one would expect that as the technological frame *started* to move across the face of industrial culture, considerable 'looseness' would be evident in subsystem negotiations – as the basic cultural grammar of the technological frame was still emergent *within* general social action and definitions of meaning. One could therefore expect that a greater range of innovation possibilities could be produced.

As the cultural grammar became more deeply implanted in the premises from which all culture is constituted however, one would expect the cultural grammar to place a much tighter clamp over the shaping of alternatives.

Thus, whilst alternative distribution systems for electricity were possible at the time of their inception in Germany and the US at the turn of the twentieth century, the alternatives, though shaped by local geographic, social and political interests, were still a limited range within an overall international template.[10] One would further expect that the overall international clamp of cultural grammar over innovation negotiations today would be much tighter still. It is the internationalised interconnected sophistication of technological systems that produces identical airport systems (though of different scale) in the Sultanate of Brunei as in the city of New York – thus producing, as Kenneth Boulding observes,[11] a coherent and uniform 'superculture' of internationalism, a superculture that in turn reinforces the singular shaping of subsystem negotiations into a severely restricted set of possible alternatives.

Buried deeply beneath the whole process of social negotiations that produce innovation one could therefore expect to observe the operation of the culture-technology grammar, a grammar that is *progressive*, that by its very essence produces an ever-more tightly constrained set of innovation alternatives from negotiations in the present.

As a result, whilst specific advances in computerisation may be difficult to predict, what can perhaps be predicted is the *shape* of these innovations. For, according to the culture-technology alignment argument, the shape is likely to expand technical power to order and control organisational and social environments. The shape is likely to redress whatever reverse salients that hinder expansion of order – in particular, any remaining vestiges of subjective human 'inefficiency' in productive labour or decision-making. The shape is likely to redress any reverse salients of complexity that the systems themselves produce or rely upon – through greater control that must intrinsically push direct human involvement into lower salience.

The shape of application of computerised systems, for example, to libraries and education, can equally be predicted. To follow the trajectory that is inscribed in the cultural grammar of the technology text, library systems are likely to become increasingly dependent on machine-ordered information. *Quantity* of information is likely to be handled effectively, but *quality* is likely to be reduced to that which can be ordered *system*atically. Use of libraries is likely to depend on privatised work stations where interrogative relationship between user and system is possible, but where serendipitous, *un*-systematised 'lateral' connections between sources is unlikely, and where reliance on the wisdom of people who 'know' what matters in the application of knowledge is increasingly excluded.[12]

These dimensions of innovation are likely because they all subscribe to the cultural grammar of the technological text that has been identified in the present book. Without a change in the values applied to the design of technological systems, the impact of the innovations will most likely be to further concretise and reinforce the culture–technology alignment, and therefore to create new demands for innovations that on the one hand cure the unintentional disorder that system-innovation creates, and on the other hand foster an even tighter alignment between technological order and cultural meanings.

All this is *likely* because the shape of the technology text's cultural trajectory has been predicated on the same basic culture-defining principles since its inception. Each step along the path has reinforced the grammar, rarely confronted it. Indeed, both innovations and social movements that have sought to confront the basic cultural grammar of the text have either been swept aside (as with systems of *communal* service in the early twentieth century),[13] or co-opted (as with 'alternative' technologies and movements that arose from the 1960s).

There are several consequences for research on the social shaping of technology that follow from these observations:

The first is that the shaping of social negotiations needs to be located historically – according to the moment of progress of the culture-technology alignment.

The second consequence is that in exploring the social negotiations that produce the particular shaping of innovation, the most essential project of research is to delve beneath the surface of the text that is being read and written in discourse to the grammar that lies beneath. According to proximity of allegiance of particular interest groups to this moment in grammar constitution, one would expect relative dominance of power to define by particular subsystems – and thus relative dominance as a force in the overall shape of the technological innovation produced.

The third consequence for research on the social shaping of technology and its impact follows from the observation that the cultural values of the technology frame penetrate the constitution of culture in different ways – in structures of communicative discourse; in creation, distribution and use of stocks of knowledge; and in the erection of superordinate symbols.

Different types of innovation are likely to affect these constitutive properties in different ways. High technology energy system innovations, for example, are likely to penetrate daily life only marginally, but at the same time are likely to rigidify and constrain further the background system frame of everyday life and opportunity for active constitution of meanings. Consumer media and communication system innovations are likely to penetrate immediate inter-subjective communication practices more directly. De-skilling technological innovations in industry and offices are likely to transform the content and distribution of technical stocks of knowledge and thus modify structures of social power. Technological innovation in any of the culture-constitutive properties is likely to call forth reverse salients in other elements that balance the overall culture-technology alignment. Therefore, research on the shaping of technologies needs to explore these wider culture alignments as frame for innovation, impact, and subsequent connected innovation. Furthermore, the particular shaping of impact and subsequent innovation can be seen more clearly if innovation is identified in its alignment with the *particular* form of culture constitution it penetrates.

Finally, a fourth consequence for research on the social shaping of technology follows from observation of the universality of the sociological process of culture-technology alignment under industrialisation. Studies of leading-edge technological innovations within technologically innovative cultures *can* only research one element in a general theoretical process. Such analyses need to be balanced against research on technological innovation and impact where the culture, and the content and distribution of stocks of technical knowledge, are radically different. This is the case, for example, in most developing countries. It is only from such a wider field of evidence that the most comprehensive and penetrating theories of technological innovation can be derived. Greater general theory power is as useful for studies of contemporary high technology innovation in the US or Japan as it is for research-based innovation in traditional agriculture in Indonesia or Brazil.

Final Note: The Last Act of the 'Tragedy of Technology'

'If the system's the answer, it must have been a bloody stupid question!', as an anonymous scribe wrote on a wall in Liverpool recently. But this is the question that this book, *The Tragedy of Technology*, has sought to understand.

In spite of the field of evidence that testifies to the apparent autonomy of technological systems, understanding does not lie in technology *per se*, but in cultural alignment. This is very important if we are even to glimpse alternatives to the present trajectory of industrialised society. What the 'alignment' position implies is that even though the technological frame has come to assume a position of enormous power in defining culture, *if* the culture could achieve a degree of independence, then the trajectory itself can be changed.

Thus the *ab*normality of the five late-1987 events reported in the Introduction to this book is exposed. The 'liberating' lessons from sociological theory and studies of the interactions between technology and society are indicated. And the 'myth of the machine' that Lewis Mumford identified in the 1930s is identified for what it is, a relatively 'plastic' cultural product.

What lies in front is the rewriting of the plot of *The Tragedy of Technology*. T.S Eliot's 'Choruses from "The Rock"'[14] provides a (frequently quoted) question to address, and an (infrequently quoted) introductory assertion to work from:

> The endless cycle of idea and action,
> Endless invention, endless experiment,
> Brings knowledge of motion, but not of stillness;
> Knowledge of speech, but not of silence;
> Knowledge of words, and ignorance of the Word.
> All our knowledge brings us nearer to death,
> But nearness to death no nearer to God.
>
> Where is the Life we have lost in living?
> Where is the wisdom we have lost in knowledge?
> Where is the knowledge we have lost in information?

Notes and References

Chapter 1

1. Alfred North Whitehead, *Science and the Modern World* (New York: Mentor, 1948) p. 17.
2. Lewis Mumford, *Technics and Civilization* (New York: Harcourt, Brace and Company, 1934); Jacques Ellul, *The Technological Society* (New York: Vintage Books, 1964); Langdon Winner, *Autonomous Technology: Technics-out-of-Control as a Theme in Political Thought* (Cambridge, Mass: MIT Press, 1977).
3. Jacques Ellul, 'The Power of Technique and The Ethics of Non-Power', in Kathleen Woodward (ed), *The Myths of Information: Technology and Postindustrial Culture* (London: Routledge & Kegan Paul, 1980), pp. 242–7.
4. For recent presentations of this position, see Donald MacKenzie and Judy Wajcman (eds), *The Social Shaping of Technology – How the Refrigerator got its Hum* (Milton Keynes: Open University Press, 1985); and W. E. Bijker, T. P. Hughes and T. J. Pinch (eds), *The Social Construction of Technological Systems – New Directions in the Sociology and History of Technology* (Cambridge, Mass: MIT Press, 1987).
5. Thomas P. Hughes, 'The Seamless Web: Technology, Science, Etcetera, Etcetera', *Social Studies of Science*, 16 (1986), p. 282.
6. Tine Bruland, 'Industrial Conflict as a Source of Technical Innovation: the Development of the Automatic Spinning Mule', in MacKenzie and Wajcman, *Social Shaping of Technology*, pp. 84–92.
7. Thomas P. Hughes, *Networks of Power – Electrification in Western Society 1880–1930* (Baltimore: The Johns Hopkins University Press, 1983), p. 405.
8. Charles W. Cheape, 'Moving the Masses: Urban Public Transit in New York, Boston, and Philadelphia, 1880–1912', *Harvard Studies in Business History*, 31 (Cambridge, Mass, 1980).
9. Paul Barrett, *The Automobile and Urban Transit: The Formation of Public Policy in Chicago, 1900–1930*, Technology and Urban Growth Series (Philadelphia: Temple University Press, 1983).
10. K. E. Bailes, 'Technology and Legitimation: Soviet Aviation and Stalinism in the 1930s', *Technology and Culture* 17 (1) (January 1976), pp. 55-81.
11. Mary Kaldor, *The Baroque Arsenal* (London: André Deutsch, 1982).
12. Hughes, *Networks of Power*, p. 79.
13. Melvin Kranzberg, 'Technology and History: "Kranzberg's Laws"' (Presidential Address, 19 October 1985, to SHOT), *Technology and*

Culture, 27 (3) (July 1986), p. 559.

14. Donald Schon, *Beyond the Stable State* (Harmondsworth: Pelican, 1975), pp. 61–79.
15. Jean Baudrillard, *Système des Objects* (Paris: Gallimard, 1968).
16. Ruth Schwartz Cowan, 'The "Industrial Revolution" in the Home: Household Technology and Social Change in the 20th Century', *Technology and Culture,* 17 (1) (January 1976), p. 14.
17. Mark H. Rose, 'Urban Environments and Technological Innovation: Energy Choices in Denver and Kansas City, 1900–1940', *Technology and Culture,* 25 (3) (July 1984), pp. 526–9.
18. Hughes, *Networks of Power,* p. 405.
19. F. M. L. Thompson, *English Landed Society in the Nineteenth Century* (London: Routledge & Kegan Paul, 1963), pp. 144–5.
20. J. B. Schneewind, 'Technology, Ways of Living, and Values in 19th Century England', in Kurt Baier and Nicholas Rescher (eds), *Values and the Future* (New York: The Free Press, 1969), pp. 110–32.
21. Ibid., p. 111.
22. A. Trollope, *The Duke's Children,* Ch. LXII. Quoted in J. B. Schneewind, ibid., `p. 110.
23. John Foster, *Class Struggle and the Industrial Revolution: Early Industrial Capitalism in Three English Towns* (London: Weidenfeld & Nicholson, 1974).
24. Maxine Berg (ed), *Technology and Toil in Nineteenth Century Britain,* (London: CSE Books, 1979), pp. 71, 127–48.
25. Fred E. H. Schroeder, 'More "Small Things Forgotten": Domestic Electrical Plugs and Receptacles, 1881–1931', *Technology and Culture,* 27 (3) (July 1986), p. 526.
26. Thomas Parke Hughes, 'Thomas Alva Edison and the Rise of Electricity', in Carroll W. Pursell (ed), *Technology in America* (Cambridge, Mass: MIT Press, 1981), pp. 123–5.
27. Malcolm MacLaren, *The Rise of the Electrical Appliance Industry During the Nineteenth Century,* (Princeton, N J: 1943), pp. 91–3.
28. J. B. Barrett, *Electricity at the Columbian Exposition,* Chicago, 1894, p. 154. Quoted in Schroeder, 'More "Small Things"', p. 527.
29. Schroeder, ibid.
30. Ibid.
31. This argument is developed in Chapter 9.
32. George E. Walsh, 'Electricity in the Household', *Independent,* 7 March 1901, pp. 556–9. Quoted in Schroeder, 'More "Small Things"', p. 528.
33. Cowan, 'The Industrial Revolution', p. 10.
34. Ibid., p. 14.
35. Christine E. Bose, Philip L. Bereano and Mary Malloy, 'Household Technology and the Social Construction of Housework', *Technology and Culture,* 25 (1) (January 1984), pp. 53–82.
36. Lynn White (Jr), *Medieval Technology and Social Change,* (New York: Oxford University Press, 1978) (first published, 1962), p. 28.

37. Dolores Hayden, *The Grand Domestic Revolution: A History of Feminist Designs for American Homes, Neighbourhoods and Cities* (Cambridge, Mass: MIT Press, 1981).

Chapter 2

1. Kranzberg, 'Technology and History', p. 558.
2. O. B. Hardison (Jr), 'A Tree, A Streamlined Fish, and a Self-Squared Dragon: Science as a Form of Culture', *Georgia Review*, XL (2) (Summer 1986), p. 372.
3. Martin Heidegger, 'The Question Concerning Technology', in David Knell (ed), *Basic Writings* (Harper & Row, 1977), p. 294.
4. Mikel Dufrenne, 'Art and Technology: Alienation or Survival', in Kathleen Woodward (ed), *The Myths of Information Technology and Post-Industrial Society* (London: Routledge & Kegan Paul, 1980), p. 165.
5. R. M. Bell and S. C. Hill, 'Research on Technology Transfer and Innovation', in F. Bradbury, P. Jervis, R. Johnston and A. Pearson (eds), *Transfer Processes in Technical Change* (Netherlands: Sijthoff and Noardhoff, 1978), p. 225.
6. Heidegger, 'The Question Concerning Technology', p. 294.
7. Philip Slater, *The Pursuit of Loneliness: American Culture at the Breaking Point* (Beacon Press, 1970), pp. 44–5.
8. Herbert Marcuse, *One Dimensional Man* (London: Sphere Books, 1970), p. 46.
9. Martin Heidegger, 'The Question Concerning Technology', pp. 296-8.
10. The association within *praxis*, or sensual activity, between consciousness and transformation of the world is presented in Marx's analysis of labour, in Karl Marx, *Capital*, I, (Moscow: Progress Publishers, 1974) (first published in German, 1867), p. 173.
11. See for example, Jurgen Habermas, *Theory and Practice*, trans. John Viertel (London: Heinemann, 1974).
12. Don Ihde, *Technics and Praxis* (Dordrecht, Holland: D. Riedel – Pallas Paperbacks, 1979), p. 59.
13. Ibid, p. 56.
14. As Durkheim observes, 'The god of the clan, the totemic principle, can therefore be nothing else than the clan itself, personified and represented to the imagination under the visible form of the animal or vegetable which serves as totem.' Emile Durkheim, *The Elementary Forms of Religious Life*, trans. Joseph Ward Swain (London: George Allen & Unwin, 1915, reprinted 1970), p. 206.
15. This alignment between 'machine text' and action is a view of the constitution of 'discourse' that Foucault's post-structuralism asserts. For Foucault, entities such as circumstances, events, objects and machines all embody texts that manifest as discourse. See M. Cousins and A. Hussain, *Michel Foucault* (London: Macmillan, 1984), p. 78.
16. Stephen Hill, 'Eighteen Cases of Technology Transfer to Asia/Pacific Region Countries', *Science and Public Policy*, 13 (3) (June 1986), p. 165.

17. For descriptions of Melanesian cargo cults see Peter Lawrence, *Road Belong Cargo: A Study of the Cargo Movement in the Southern Madang District, New Guinea* (Melbourne: Melbourne University Press, 1964); Peter Worsley, *The Trumpet Shall Sound: A Study of Cargo Cults in Melanesia*, 2nd edition (New York: Schocken Books, 1968); Glynn Cochrane, *Big Men and Cargo Cults* (Oxford: Clarendon Press, 1970); and Frederich Steinbauer, *Melanesian Cargo Cults: New Salvation Movements in the South Pacific*, trans. Max Wohlwill (St Lucia: University of Queensland Press, 1979).

18. This was an observation made by Peter Lawrence in *Road Belong Cargo*, ibid.

19. Tenney Frank, *An Economic History of Rome* (Baltimore: Johns Hopkins University Press, 1927), Chapter 14.

20. Lynn White (Jr), 'Technology in the Middle Ages', in Melvin Kranzberg and Carroll Pursell (Jr), (eds), *Technology in Western Civilization, Earliest Times to 1900* (New York: Oxford University Press, 1967), p. 72.

21. Lewis Mumford, *Technics and Civilization* (New York: Harcourt, Brace and Company, 1934), pp. 12–18.

22. Gerard Walter, *Caesar: A Biography* (New York, 1952), p. 544, quoted in Derek J. De Solla Price, 'Automata and the Origins of Mechanism and Mechanistic Philosophy', *Technology and Culture*, 5 (1964), p. 11.

23. De Vaucanson's mechanical duck is reported in Alfred Chapnis and Edward Droze, *Les Automates* (Paris: Neuchatel, 1953), pp. 239–46. Both the diagrams and description of de Vaucanson's automata are reproduced in Silvio A. Bedini, 'The Role of Automata in the History of Technology', *Technology and Culture*, 5 (1964), pp. 29, 36–8.

24. Wolfgang Krohn, 'Social Change and Epistemic Thought: Reflections on the Origins of the Experimental Method' (University of Bielefeld, Universitätsschwerpunkt Wissenschaftsforschung, mimeo, 1987), p. 9.

25. Francis Bacon, *Novum Organum, First Book*, Aphorism no. 49, in Francis Bacon, *Advancement of Learning, Novum Organum, New Atlantis*, ed Robert Maynard Hutchins (Chicago: Encylopaedia Britannica, Inc.), *Great Books of the Western World Series*, no. 30, p. 111.

26. Hardison, 'A Tree, A Streamlined Fish', pp. 372–4.

27. Observation of this shift in religious world view follows the familiar 'Protestant Ethic' position of Weber. I will show in Chapter 7 how transformations in religious views must be looked at within wider cultural-technological alignments if we are to understand the cultural dynamic of technology.

28. The direct association between science and technology at the time when English industrialisation took off was very weak. At that time, the science and technology stocks of knowledge were contained within quite separate cultural frames. It wasn't until alignment was achieved through industrial organisation practices at the start of the twentieth century that industry started to capitalise directly on scientific advance. I will develop and show the significance of this argument in Chapter 7.

29. T. K. Derry and Trevor I. Williams, *A Short History of Technology* (Oxford: Clarendon Press, 1960), p. 562.

30. Thomas Hughes draws the concept of 'reverse salient' from the definition of a 'salient' as a 'protrusion in a geometric figure, a line of battle or an expanding weather front'. In technological systems, Hughes shows, 'reverse salients' develop where 'there are components in the system that have fallen behind, or out of phase with, the others'. See Thomas P. Hughes, 'The Evolution of Large Technological Systems', in W. E. Bijker, T. P. Hughes and T. J. Pinch (eds), *The Social Construction of Technological Systems – New Directions in the Sociology and History of Technology* (Cambridge, Mass: MIT Press, 1987) p. 33 of preprint.

31. As I will go on to show later, early use of industrial technology was not intrinsically more efficient economically than alternative modes of production. One of the key reasons why the emerging capitalist class favoured factory systems was that the new technological system offered an effective means of social discipline and control over the workforce. See Stephen A. Marglin, 'What do Bosses Do? – The Origins and Functions of Hierarchy in Capitalist Production', in André Gorz (ed), *The Division of Labour: The Labour Process and Class-Struggle in Modern Capitalism* (Hassocks, Sussex: Harvester Press, 1976), pp. 13–53; and, Stephen A. Marglin, 'The Origins and Functions of Hierarchy in Capitalist Production', in T. Nichols (ed), *Capital and Labour* (Fontana, 1980).

32. Thomas Hughes identifies the idea of system 'momentum' as a product of prolonged growth and consolidation of the system's development. Hughes attributes system 'momentum' to social interests: 'Mature systems have a quality analogous, therefore, to inertia of motion. The large mass of a technological system arises especially from the organizations and people committed by various interests to the system.' See Hughes, 'The Evolution of Large Technological Systems', preprint, p. 39.

33. See Harry Braverman, *Labor and Monopoly Capital – The Degradation of Work in the Twentieth Century*, (New York: Monthly Review Press, 1974).

34. Hughes, 'The Evolution of Large Technological Systems', preprint, p. 39.

35. Some authors, in particular Langdon Winner, take a rather narrow view of 'forces of production', as comprising physical technology, but not labour or background cultural forces. Separating off cultural and human 'forces' leads however, as in Winner's case, to a rather 'technological determinist' view of progress in machine technology, a position that, as I demonstrate in this book, is quite wrong. Marx himself was not so limiting in his own concept of 'forces of production'. As William Shaw points out, central to Marx's concept is incorporation into the 'forces of production' of the past skills, knowledge, experience of labour power; as Donald MacKenzie emphasises, Marx fundamentally incorporated human consciousness within 'forces of production'. And, as the present book goes on to demonstrate, 'forces of production' must include the wider cultural frame in which labour, 'objectified labour' (embodied in present machines), and consciousness, are set. See, Karl Marx, *Poverty of Philosophy* (New York:

International Publishers, 1963), p. 109; Winner, *Autonomous Technology*, p. 78; William H. Shaw, '"The Handmill Gives You the Feudal Lord": Marx's Technological Determinism', *History and Theory*, 18 (1979), p. 158; Donald MacKenzie, 'Marx and the Machine', *Technology and Culture*, 25 (3) (July 1984), p. 477.

36. This quote is taken from Karl Marx, *Grundrisse*, in David McLellen, *Marx's Grundrisse* (St. Albans, Herts.: Paladin, 1973), p. 155. The term, 'objectification', as it was used by Marx, meant humans' natural means of projecting themselves through their productive activity on to nature – *in* the objects of their own creation. 'Objectivation' allowed the possibility of humans contemplating themselves in the world of their own making. But, under capitalism, what was objectified, what it was that stood *for* humans' relationship to nature, was the machine or 'fixed capital' that the worker confronted in the factory. What was objectified was under the private control of the capitalists. So, the world of humankind's collective making, the whole productive power of humankind's progress was alienated from the worker in each moment when he or she intervened in nature through labour. See Karl Marx, 'Economic and Philosophic Manuscripts', in Lucio Colletti, *Karl Marx – Early Writings* (Harmondsworth: Penguin, 1975), p. 329.

37. Karl Marx, *The Grundrisse* (1857–8), trans. Martin Nicolaus (Harmondsworth: Penguin, 1983), p. 693.

38. The ideas of 'complexity', 'scale', and 'ubiquity' were observed by Bruce Hannay and Robert McGinn. Their position is more a presentation of an 'anatomy' of technology, as the title of their article implies, than an analysis of interconnections and the sources of dynamics in basic systems properties. See N. Bruce Hannay and Robert E. McGinn, 'The Anatomy of Modern Technology: Prolegomenon to an Improved Public Policy for the Social Management of Technology', *Daedelus*, 109 (Winter 1980), pp. 28–34.

39. See Thomas P. Hughes, 'The Order of the Technological World', in A. Rupert Hall and Norman Smith (eds), *History of Technology – Fifth Annual Volume, 1980* (London: Mansell Publishing, 1980), pp. 2–3.

40. Marx, *Capital*, p. 362.

41. The case study of spinning and weaving is presented in Stephen Hill, 'Research Design Principles for Developing Countries', *Technology in Society*, 9 (1) (1987), p. 67. The case of the interaction between tractors and methane-gas production is presented in Hill, 'Eighteen Cases of Technology' p. 166.

42. Maxine Berg, *The Machinery Question and the Making of Political Economy 1815–1848* (Cambridge: Cambridge University Press, 1980).

43. Richard Oastler and others, 'Political Economy versus the Handloom Weavers', letter to George Poulett Scrope, Esq. MP, Bradford, 1835, in Berg (ed), *Technology and Toil*, p. 79.

44. For analyses of the dynamics of what Charles Reich identifies as a shift in consciousness, see Charles Reich, *The Greening of America*

(Harmondsworth: Penguin, 1971) (particularly, Chapters 9, 10, and 11); Herbert Gans, 'The Equality Revolution', in Wilbert E. Moore (ed), *Technology and Social Change* (Chicago: Quadrangle Books, 1972), pp. 208-21; and Beryl L. Crowe, 'The Tragedy of the Commons Revisited', *Science*, 166 (3909) (28 November 1969), pp. 1103–7.

45. This comment was made to a visiting Australian journalist by a woman supporter of the Philippine New Peoples Army in Ilo Ilo Province. See Louise Williams, 'Until Death (or a change in ideology) Do Us Part', *Sydney Morning Herald*, 14 February, 1987 p. 35.

46. Hughes, *Networks of Power*, p. 405.

47. Jonathan Swift, *Gulliver's Travels*, introduced by David G. Pitt (New York: Airmont Books, 1963, first published, 1726), p. 175.

Chapter 3

1. Reported by Jack Goody from unpublished field notes, in Jack Goody and Ian Watt, 'The Consequences of Literacy', in Jack Goody (ed), *Literacy in Traditional Societies* (Cambridge: Cambridge University Press, 1968), p. 32.

2. Eric Leed, '"Voice" and "Print": Master Symbols in the History of Communication', in Kathleen Woodward (ed), *The Myths of Information Technology and Post Industrial Culture* (London: Routledge & Kegan Paul, 1980), p. 43.

3. Walter J. Ong, *The Presence of the Word* (New York: Simon and Schuster, 1970), p. 33.

4. E. E. Evans-Pritchard, 'Time is not a Continuum', in Mary Douglas (ed), *Rules and Meanings – The Anthropology of Everyday Knowledge* (Harmondsworth: Penguin, 1973), pp. 75–81.

5. Benjamin Lee Whorf, 'Some Verbal Categories of Hopi', *Language*, 14 (1938), p. 277.

6. Goody and Watt, 'The Consequences of Literacy', p. 29.

7. Ibid., p. 71.

8. The Tongan gift-giving ritual was observed to me during a UNESCO Mission to the Kingdom of Tonga in 1985.

9. As McLuhan notes, 'When information is simultaneous from all directions at once, the culture is auditory and tribal, regardless of its past or its concepts': Marshall McLuhan, *Counterblast* (London: Rapp & Whiting Ltd, 1970), p. 142. Thus McLuhan observes that the human family now exists under conditions of a 'global village': Marshall McLuhan, *The Gutenberg Galaxy - The Making of Typographic Man* (London: Routledge & Kegan Paul, 1971 (1962)), p. 31. See also, Marshall McLuhan and Quentin Fiore, *The Medium is the Massage* (London: Allen Lane, Penguin Press, 1967).

10. Plato, *Phaedrus: and, the Seventh and Eighth Letters*, trans. Walter Hamilton (London: Penguin, 1973), p. 277c.

11. Friedrich Wilhelm Nietzsche, *Beyond Good and Evil: Prelude to a Philosophy of the Future*, trans. Helen Zimmern (London: George Allen

and Unwin, 1967, first published, 1909), pp. 9, 33.

12. V. Gordon Childe, *Man Makes Himself* (London: Watts, 1941), pp. 187–8.

13. Alfred Charles Moorhouse, *The Triumph of the Alphabet: A History of Writing* (New York: Schuman, 1953), pp. 90, 163.

Chapter 4

1. Lauriston Sharp, 'Steel Axes for Stone Age Aboriginals', in E. H. Spicer (ed), *Human Problems in Technological Change* (New York: Russell Sage Foundation, 1952).

2. This observation of the impact of employment at Bougainville on tribal society was made to me by a colleague working in the area at the time.

3. P. J. Pelto, *The Snowmobile Revolution: Technology and Social Change in the Arctic* (Menlo Park, California: Cummings, 1973).

4. This case of transformation of village life was reported to me by Esekia Solofa, a former resident of the village.

5. Paul Alexander, in Australian Broadcasting Commission, *Transcripts on the Political Economy of Development* (Sydney: ABC, 1977), pp. 140–5.

6. M. Perelman, 'Farming for Profit in a Hungry World', *Landmark Series* (1977), pp. 145–9.

7. Michael Howes, 'Knowledge and Power: The Transfer and Exploitation of Technology in a Rural Area in Thailand' (University of Sussex: PhD thesis, June 1977).

8. Perelman, 'Farming for Profit'.

9. Lynn Townsend White (Jr), *Medieval Technology and Social Change* (Oxford: Clarendon Press, 1962), p. 28.

10. Michael Howes, 'The Uses of Indigenous Technical Knowledge in Development', IDS Bulletin (Institute of Development Studies, University of Sussex), 19 (2) (January 1979), pp. 12–23.

11. This observation of the parallel between traditional and modern surgical practice was made to me by a surgeon in the Kingdom of Tonga.

12. C. Lévi Strauss, *The Savage Mind* (London: Weidenfeld & Nicolson, 1966), p. 17.

13. The significance of 'learning by doing' is developed in R. M. Bell and S. C. Hill, 'Research on Technology Transfer and Innovation', in F. Bradbury, P. Jervis, R. Johnston and A. Pearson (eds), *Transfer Processes in Technical Change* (Netherlands: Sijthoff and Noardhoff, 1978), p. 258.

14. Arthur Koestler, *The Call Girls* (London: Pan Books, 1976).

15. Marion Christie, 'The Human Impact of Cash Cropping of Coffee in the Highlands of Papua New Guinea: A Case Study', in Stephen Hill *et al.* (eds), *Development with a Human Face* (Canberra: Australian Government Publishing Service, 1981), pp. 51–69; and Marion Christie, *Changing Consumer Behaviour in Papua New Guinea: its Social and Ecological Implications* (Canberra: Centre for Resource and Environmental Studies, Australian National University, Report no. 3, 1980).

16. Paul Zimmet, 'The Fatal Impact: The Medical Effects of Social Progress in

the Pacific Populations', in Stephen Hill *et al.* (eds), *Development with a Human Face*, pp. 117–27, and also from private correspondence with the author.

17. This observation was made by Dr David Puloka, and is recorded in the *Meeting Report* of the 'UNESCO-SPEC High Level Regional Meeting on Policy and Management of Science and Technology for Development in the South Pacific Region', Apia, Western Samoa, 16–19 March 1987 (Canberra: Australian National Commission for UNESCO, May 1987), Appendix.

18. These observations were reported by Mr Tai Manuela, Director of Economic Development of the Cook Islands, at the 'UNESCO-SPEC High Level Regional Meeting on Policy and Management of Science and Technology for Development in the South Pacific Region', held in Apia, Western Samoa, 16–19 March 1987.

19. J. R. K. Standingford, 'How Appropriate is "Appropriate Technology"?', First International Conference on Technology for Development, Canberra, 1980, p. 77.

Chapter 5

1. Ralph Linton, *The Study of Man* (New York: Appleton, 1936).
2. A. L. Kroeber and Clyde Kluckhohn, *Culture – A Critical Review of Concepts and Definitions* (New York: Random House (Vintage Books), 1963).
3. Clyde Kluckhohn, 'The Concept of Culture', in D. Lerner and H. D. Lasswell (eds), *The Policy Sciences* (Stanford: Stanford University Press, 1951).
4. Clifford Geertz, 'Ethos, World View and the Analysis of Sacred Symbol', in Alan Dantes (ed), *Every Man His Way* (Englewood Cliffs, NJ: Prentice Hall, 1968), p. 314.
5. Ibid.
6. Alfred Schutz and Thomas Luckmann (trans. Richard M. Zaner and H. Tristram Engelhardt (Jr)), *The Structures of the Life-World* (London: Heinemann, 1974), pp. 35–7 particularly; and Thomas Luckmann, 'Personal Identity as an Evolutionary and Historical Problem' (Constanz, August 1977 (mimeo)), p. 10.
7. Schutz's 'general thesis' of 'the reciprocity of perspectives' assumes two idealisations, 'the interchangeability of standpoints', and 'the congruence of relevance systems'. Schutz and Luckmann, *The Structures of the Life-World*, pp. 59–61.
8. George Herbert Mead, *Mind, Self and Society* (Chicago: University of Chicago Press, 1934).
9. Both the evidence, plus this 'pneumatic hand' proposal, are contained in Lesley A. Albertson, 'Telecommunications as a Travel Substitute: Some Psychological, Organizational, and Social Aspects', *Journal of Communication*, 27 (Spring 1977), pp. 32–43.
10. See Jean Piaget and Barbel Inhelder, *The Psychology of the Child*, trans.

Helen Weaver (London: Routledge & Kegan Paul, 1969). Studies of 'aphasia' are particularly pertinent as evidence of the connection between cultural language and consciousness – hence the essential capability that Piaget refers to, of representing 'absent' things symbolically. As a result of brain damage to the frontal operculum, the aphasic patient is unable to represent to consciousness either complex ideas or objects that are not in immediate view. Thus whilst an aphasic patient may be able to throw a ball quite accurately into a basket in front of them, they are unable to do so when a screen is placed between themselves and the basket. Aphasia is directly associated with speech disorder. As Head explains, aphasia is a disorder of 'symbolic thinking and expression ... Behind every propositional expression lies recognition of the meaning of symbols.' H. Head, *Aphasia and Kindred Disorders of Speech* (Cambridge: Cambridge University Press, 1926).

11. For Schutz, 'the ego lives in its acts. Its attentiveness is concentrated upon the realization of its projects' ... in particular those acts ... 'that gear into the external world and alter it; ... the condition of wide-awakeness outlines every pragmatically relevant province of the world. This relevance for its part determines the form and content of our life of consciousness.' Schutz and Luckmann, *The Structures of the Life-World*, p. 26. On Marx's association between sensual activity in transforming the world, and consciousness, see Marx, *Capital*, Volume 1, p. 173.

12. As Mumford observes, Christopher Columbus had the self-confidence to circumnavigate the globe in 1492 because of the invention of the sea-astrolobe, magnetic compass, and sailing charts that were framed in terms of latitude and longitude. The voyage of Columbus brought together two modes of 'exploration', and represented a world view that was to characterise change in European society from the fifteenth to nineteenth centuries. The first mode of exploration was through abstract symbols, rational systems, universal laws and predictable events, and objective mathematical measurements of the structures behind the world of immediate appearances. This mode sought to understand, use and control the forces that derive ultimately from the cosmos and the social system. The second mode of exploration 'dwelt on the concrete and the organic, adventurous, the tangible', and involved the sailing of great oceans, the conquering of new lands, and the discovery of new foods and medicines. Lewis Mumford, *The Myth of the Machine: The Pentagon of Power* (New York: Harcourt, Brace, Jovanovich, 1970), Chapter 2. See also Stephen Hill, 'Technology and Society', in Stephen Hill and Ron Johnston (eds), *Future Tense? – Technology in Australia* (St Lucia, Queensland: University of Queensland Press, 1983), pp. 29–30.

13. Edmund Husserl, *Cartesian Meditations*, trans. Dorian Cairnes (The Hague: Nijhoff, 1960). For a more detailed discussion of the role of active and passive synthesis in socialisation, see Stephen Hill, 'In Search of Self – The Social Construction of Meaning in Scientific Knowledge through the Formation of Identity as Scientist', in M. R. Pusey and R. E. Young (eds),

Control and Knowledge: The Mediations of Power in Institutional and Educational Settings (Canberra: Australian National University Press, 1979), pp. 134–6.

14. As Alfred Schutz comments, 'the anonymity of a typification is inversely proportional to its fullness of content ... the fullness of content of the individualized social type conforms to the relative immediacy of the experiences from which it is constituted.' Schutz and Luckmann, *The Structures of the Life-World*, pp. 80–1. See also Luckmann, p. 10.

15. As Luckmann and Berger observe, in modern industrial society, where personal identity is largely anonymised, 'an important part of identity reaffirmation is directly played by material objects rather than human beings'. Luckmann and Berger term this process, 'the sacramentalism of consumption'. Thomas Luckmann and Peter Berger, 'Social Mobility and Personal Identity', *Humanitas*, 7 (1) (1971), p. 103.

16. E. B. Tylor, *Primitive Culture* (London: John Murray, Publishers, 1871), p. 1.

17. Durkheim describes the 'contagiousness of sacredness' as follows: 'The sacred world is inclined, as it were, to spread itself into this same profane world which it excludes elsewhere: at the same time that it repels it, it tends to flow into it as soon as it approaches.' Emile Durkheim, *The Elementary Forms of Religious Life*, trans. Joseph Ward Swain (London: George Allen & Unwin, 1915, reprinted 1970), pp. 321, 318.

18. Geertz, 'Ethos, World-View', p. 303.

19. Ibid., pp. 305–6.

20. See Peter L. Berger and Thomas Luckmann, 'Secularization and Pluralism', in *Sociology of Religion*, Vol. II (1966) (Opladen: Westdeutscher Verlag), pp. 73–84; Bryan Wilson, *Religion in Secular Society* (London: Watts, 1966); Thomas Luckmann, *The Invisible Religion: The Transformation of Symbols in Industrial Society* (New York: Macmillan, 1967).

21. Durkheim, 'The Elementary Forms', p. 206.

22. Henri Lefebvre, *Everyday Life in the Modern World*, trans. Sacha Rabinovitch (London: Allen Lane – The Penguin Press, 1971), p. 100.

23. Thomas P. Hughes, 'The Science-Technology Interaction: The Case of High-Voltage Power Transmission Systems', *Technology and Culture*, 17 (4) (October 1976), p. 647.

24. See for example, Rose, 'Urban Environments', pp. 503–39.

25. Schwartz Cowan, 'The "Industrial Revolution"', and Christine E. Bose, Philip L. Bereno and Mary Malloy, 'Household Technology and the Social Construction of Housework', *Technology and Culture*, 25 (1) (January 1984), pp. 53–82.

26. See Geoffrey Barraclough, *An Introduction to Contemporary History* (Harmondsworth: Pelican Books, 1967), pp. 50–1. Great Britain, in 1850, contributed 40 per cent of the world's economic output, but this fell to only 20 per cent by 1900, and continued to slide – to 14 per cent in 1914, thence 4 per cent by 1963. Barry Jones, *Sleepers, Wake! Technology & The Future of Work* (Melbourne: Oxford University Press (new edition), 1984), p. 12.

27. Universities in Britain for example remained largely theological in character and hostile to the 'new' philosophies of science throughout the nineteenth century. It was not until 1894 that *mechanical* science (engineering) was introduced at Cambridge. Stephen Hill, 'Work and Technological Change in Australia', in John Western and Jake Najman (eds), *A Sociology of Australian Society* (Melbourne: Macmillan, 1988), preprint, p. 249.

28. Lefebvre, *Everyday Life*.

29. Baudrillard, *Système des Objets*.

30. Weber originally outlined the dependence of authority – in any form of social order – on legitimation. H. H. Gerth and C. Wright Mills (eds), *From Max Weber: Essays in Sociology* (London: Routledge & Kegan Paul, 1974), pp. 294–301.

31. This definition of ideology is drawn from a Marxian perspective that identifies ideology with 'any form of thought which has been invaded by the vested interests of a ruling class or the aspiring intentions of subordinate classes'. Marx and Engels' position is derived in their critique of the Young-Hegelians' ideology, and is based on the premise that 'Life is not determined by consciousness, but consciousness by life', so that 'Men are the producers of their conceptions, ideas, etc. - real, active men, as they are conditioned by a definite development of their productive forces and of the intercourse corresponding to them, up to its furthest forms.' See, Karl Marx and Frederick Engels, *The German Ideology*, ed C. J. Arthur (New York: International Publishers (New World Paperbacks), 1974) (1970), pp. 65–6. Karl Mannheim's use of the concept is similar in its distortive effects, though Mannheim's concept focuses more on ideology's ordering principle than its materialist and class-based derivation. For Mannheim, ideology is 'all thought distorted by the desire to conserve the present social order or restore the past: ideology is the manifestation of the vested interest or the program of action.' Karl Mannheim, *Ideology and Utopia*, trans. L. Wirth and E. Shils (London: Routledge & Kegan Paul, 1972).

32. Gwynn Williams develops the idea of 'hegemony' from Gramsci, as 'an order in which a certain way of life and thought is dominant, in which one concept of reality is diffused throughout society in all its institutional and private manifestations, informing with its spirit all taste, morality, customs, religious and political principles, and all social relations, particularly in their intellectual and moral connotations.' G. A. Williams, 'Gramsci's Concept of Egemonia', *Journal of the History of Ideas*, 21 (4) (1960), p. 587.

33. Ralph Milliband, *The State in Capitalist Society – The Analysis of the Western System of Power* (London: Quartet Books, 1973), pp. 190, 194.

34. See for example, Louis Althusser, *Reading Capital*, trans. B. Brewster (London: New Left Books, 1975), p. 66; Louis Althusser, *For Marx*, trans. B. Brewster (London: New Left Books, 1977), p. 232.

35. K. E. Bailes, 'Technology and Legitimacy: Soviet Aviation and Stalinism in the 1930s', *Technology and Culture*, 17 (1) (January 1976), pp. 55–81.

36. *One Hundred Great Lives* (London: Oldhams Press, 1954), pp. 341–57.

37. J. Nehru, *The Unity of India: Collected Writings (1937–40)* (London: Lindsay Drummond, 1948); V. V. Bhatt, 'Development Problem, Strategy and Technology Choice: Sarvodaya and Socialist Approaches in India', *Economic Development and Cultural Change*, 31 (1) (October 1982), pp. 88–99. For a contrast with Gandhi's village-centred position, see M. K. Gandhi, *Socialism of My Conception* (Bombay: Bharatiya Vidya Bhawan, 1966); and, M. K. Gandhi, *An Autobiography or the Story of My Experiments With Truth*, trans. Mahadev Desai (Ahmedabad: Navajivan, 1927).

Chapter 6

1. Charles Dickens, *Hard Times* (1854) (Harmondsworth: Penguin, 1969), p. 65.

2. Ibid., p. 108.

3. Marx, *Capital*, Volume 1, pp. 360–1.

4. Ibid., p. 364.

5. This quote is presented by Marx on p. 341 of *Capital* as a quote from an author writing in the very earliest days of the Industrial Revolution, Adam Ferguson, *An Essay on the History of Civil Society* (Edinburgh, 1767), p. 280.

6. Karl Marx, *The Grundrisse* (1857–8) trans. Martin Nicolaus (Harmondsworth: Penguin, 1973), p. 693.

7. Thomas Carlyle, *Sartor Resartus*, Collected Works, Volume III, p. 114, quoted in Maxine Berg, *The Machinery Question and the Making of Political Economy, 1815–1848* (Cambridge: Cambridge University Press, 1980, 1982 paperback), p. 12.

8. S. Pollard, 'Factory Discipline in the Industrial Revolution', *Economic History Review* (2nd series), XVI (1963–4), pp. 245–9.

9. Eric John Hobsbawn, *Labouring Men: Studies in the History of Labour* (London: Weidenfeld & Nicolson, 1964), p. 347.

10. T. K. Derry and Trevor I. Williams, *A Short History of Technology* (Oxford: Clarendon Press, 1960), p. 562.

11. E. P. Thompson, 'Time, Work-Discipline and Industrial Capitalism', *Past and Future*, no. 38 (1967), p. 81.

12. Ibid., p. 83.

13. Ibid., p. 71.

14. Ibid., pp. 73–6.

15. Stephen A. Marglin, 'What do Bosses Do? – The Origins and Functions of Hierarchy in Capitalist Production', in André Gorz (ed), *The Division of Labour: The Labour Process and Class-Struggle in Modern Capitalism* (Hassocks, Sussex: Harvester Press, 1976), p. 39.

16. Ibid., p. 40.

17. Ibid., p. 14.

18. S. Pollard, *The Genesis to Modern Management* (Harmondsworth: Penguin, 1965); William Lazonick, 'The Self-Acting Mule and Social

Relations in the Workplace', in MacKenzie and Wajcman (eds), *The Social Shaping of Technology*, pp. 94-5.

19. P. Mantoux, *The Industrial Revolution in the Eighteenth Century* (New York: Harper and Row, 1962), p. 375.

20. E. Baines, *History of the Cotton Manufacture in Great Britain* (London: Cass, 1966).

21. Reinhard Bendix, *Work and Authority in Industry* (New York: Harper and Row, 1963), Chapter 2.

22. Andrew Ure, *The Philosophy of Manufactures* (London: Charles Knight, 1835), reprinted in Thomas P. Hughes (ed), *The Development of Western Technology Since 1500* (New York: Macmillan, 1964), p. 91.

23. William C. Preston, 'Parliament's Battles for the Children – in Factory, Chimney and Brickfield – First Paper', *The Sunday Magazine* (London: Isbister and Company, 1889), pp. 301-3.

24. William C. Preston, 'Parliament's Battles for the Children – in Factory, Chimney and Brickfield – Third Paper', *The Sunday Magazine* (London: Isbister and Company, 1889), pp. 619-20.

25. Ibid., p. 621.

26. William C. Preston, 'Parliament's Battles for the Children – in Factory, Chimney and Brickfield – Fourth Paper', *The Sunday Magazine* (London: Isbister and Company, 1889), p. 708.

27. Ibid.

28. Ibid., p. 709.

29. Ibid., p. 707.

30. Preston, 'Third Paper', p. 619.

31. Berg, *The Machinery Question*, p. 11.

32. This observation of the changing character of the toyshop was made in 1806 by John Edwards Stock, and was printed as his Appendix to *Memoirs of the Life of Thomas Beddoes M.D.*, published in 1811. The Appendix is reproduced in Mary-Lou Jennings and Charles Madge (eds), *Humphrey Jennings – Pandemonium, 1660-1886: The Coming of the Machine as seen by Contemporary Observers* (London: Picador, 1987), pp. 125-7.

33. Whilst 'mob' destruction of machines came into being some time earlier, one of the first descriptions of mob violence against capitalist machinery was made by Josiah Wedgwood in 1779 (in his letter to Thomas Bentley, published in Eliza Meteyard, *A Group of Englishmen*, 1871). Jennings and Madge reproduce this letter, and observe in connection with it, that, 'the mob was one of the principal actors in the great struggles of the next seventy years'. See Jennings and Madge, *Humphrey Jennings*, pp. 76-7.

34. Berg, *Technology and Toil*, p. 36.

35. John Jewkes, David Sawers and Richard Stillerman, *The Sources of Invention* (London: Macmillan, 1958), pp. 45-6.

36. Berg, *Technology and Toil*, p. 73.

37. George Burges, 'Plain Sense and Reason: Letters Addressed to the Present Generation on the Unrestrained Use of Modern Machinery – Letter IV', Norwich, 1831. Reprinted in Berg, ibid., p. 77.

38. Raphael Samuel, 'The Workshop of the World', *History Workshop*, no. 3, 1977, p. 51.
39. Richard Oastler and Others, 'Political Economy versus the Handloom Weavers', letter to George Poulett Scope, Esq., MP, Bradford, 1835. Reprinted in Berg, ibid., p. 79.
40. Preston, 'First Paper', pp. 300–1.
41. Berg, *Technology and Toil*, p. 71.
42. Eric John Hobsbawn and George Rudé, *Captain Swing* (London: Lawrence and Wishart, 1969), Appendix IV, 'The Problem of the Threshing Machine', pp. 359–63.
43. Phyllis Deane and W. A. Cole, *British Economic Growth, 1688-1959: Trends and Structure*, 2nd edition (Cambridge: Cambridge University Press, 1969), pp. 191–2.
44. Berg, *Technology and Toil*, pp. 127–32.
45. Alexander Hay, 'The Sewing Machine', in *Industrial Curiosities* (London, 1880). Reprinted in Berg, ibid., p. 229.
46. Nathan Rosenberg, 'The Direction of Technological Change: Inducement Mechanisms and Focusing Devices', in Nathan Rosenberg (ed), *Perspectives on Technology* (Cambridge: Cambridge University Press, 1976), p. 117.
47. Lazonick, 'The Self-Acting Mule', p. 95.
48. Thomas P. Hughes, 'The Evolution of Large Technological Systems', in W. E. Bijker, T. P. Hughes and T. J. Pinch (eds), *The Social Construction of Technological Systems – New Directions in the Sociology and History of Technology* (Cambridge, Mass.: MIT Press, 1987), p. 33 of preprint. Hughes' concept of 'reverse salient' is discussed in Chapter 2 of the present book.
49. Tine Bruland, 'Industrial Conflict as a Source of Technical Innovation: the Development of the Automatic Spinning Mule', in MacKenzie and Wajcman, *The Social Shaping of Technology*, pp. 84–92.
50. John Foster, *Class Struggle and the Industrial Revolution: Early Industrial Capitalism in Three English Towns* (London: Weidenfeld & Nicolson, 1974).
51. J. H. Clapham, *An Economic History of Modern Britain*, 2nd edition (Cambridge: Cambridge University Press, 1939), p. 74.
52. G. N. Von Tunzelman, *Steam Power and British Industrialization to 1860* (Oxford: Clarendon Press, 1978), pp. 27–36.
53. David S. Landes, *Unbound Prometheus: Technological Change and Industrial Development in Western Europe from 1750 to the Present* (Cambridge: Cambridge University Press, 1969), p. 122.
54. Hobsbawn, *Labouring Men*, p. 347.
55. Berg, *Technology and Toil*, pp. 14, 207.
56. As Jennings and Madge observe, 'the transformation of the mob into the ordered and disciplined demonstration of the nineteenth century is one of the clearest signs of increasing political consciousness.' See Jennings and Madge, *Humphrey Jennings*, p. 77.

57. The 'Union Club Oaths' were reprinted in the *Cambrian Newspaper*, 11 November 1831, and are reproduced in Jennings and Madge, *Humphrey Jennings*, pp. 179–80.

58. Louis James, *Fiction for the Working Man, 1830–1850* (Oxford: Oxford University Press, 1963), pp. 99, 102, 109.

59. Estimates of the pervasiveness of levels and distribution of literacy in the 1830s and 1840s are very difficult to ascertain. One indicator is what was happening in formal schooling. There were a large number of ostensibly free schools in the early nineteenth century. But there were very few genuinely free spaces available, so education was restricted to those who could pay. A survey of education in Westminster in 1837–8 demonstrated that the length of schooling for a child depended on the parents' economic circumstances: children were removed from school when employment was offered for them, or when their parents' incomes did not allow the payment of fees (usually one penny a week). Consequently, although the proportion of children attending school doubled between 1818 and 1851, at any one time only one-third of the children enrolled were in attendance. Meanwhile it took 12 months to teach basic reading skills, and three to four years to teach children to write well, together with some simple arithmetic skills. Given the economic circumstances of even the better-off members of the working class, the average amount of time a student spent at school (at the Borough Road School in London) was 13 months – enough time to acquire a basic ability to read, but not enough time to learn to read well or to write. See Robert K. Webb, *The British Working Class Reader, 1790–1848: Literacy and Social Tension* (London: Allen and Unwin, 1955) particularly p. 17; R. K. Webb, 'Working Class Readers in Early Victorian England', English Historical Review, LXV (1950), pp. 333–51; and Frank Smith, *A History of English Elementary Education, 1760–1902* (London: University of London Press, 1931), p. 220.

Meanwhile, the Sunday School Society founded by Robert Raikes, a newspaper proprietor of Gloucester in 1785, proved very popular, in spite of their low level of teaching competence. These schools (that taught for two to three hours per week) would probably be able to teach very basic reading skills but little more, but they were aimed quite specifically at the working classes. In the first ten years after 1785, 750,000 pupils had enrolled; by 1833, 1,550,000 pupils were attending 16,828 schools; and, according to the 1851 Religious Census, 2,400,000 pupils were on the registers, and 1,800,000 were in attendance. The impact of Sunday Schools (whose prime purpose was religious instruction) was complemented by strong initiatives amongst working-class adults to educate themselves outside formal instruction. The difficulties were great, for as James Watson (born 1799) reported at the time, 'there were no cheap books, no cheap newspapers or periodicals, no Mechanics Institutions to facilitate the acquisition of knowledge'. But the spirit of self-improvement was strong. Thus, although the *level* of literacy amongst the working classes was likely to be quite low, an elementary level of literacy was quite widely distributed. See Smith, *A History of English Elementary Education*, and John Burnett (ed), *Destiny Obscure – Autobiographies of Childhood, Education and Family from the 1820s to the 1920s* (Harmondsworth: Penguin, 1984), pp. 136–41.

60. Burnett, ibid., p. 136.
61. Charles Shaw, *When I Was a Child, by an Old Potter*, 1st edition, 1903 (facs. edition, 1977), p. 21. Reprinted in Burnett, ibid.
62. Webb, 'Working Class Readers'.
63. This interpretation of the analogy of *Frankenstein* is contained in *A Popular History of the Arts* (London: Cavendish House, 1984), p. 156.
64. Landes, *Unbound Prometheus*.
65. John H. Lienhard, 'The Rate of Technological Improvement before and after the 1830s', *Technology and Culture*, 20 (3) (July 1979), p. 527.
66. Charles Kingsley, *True Words for Brave Men*, 1848, reprinted in Jennings and Madge, *Humphrey Jennings*, p. 240.

Chapter 7
1. R. S. Schofield, 'The Measurement of Literacy in Pre-Industrial England', in Jack Goody (ed), *Literacy in Traditional Societies* (Cambridge: Cambridge University Press, 1968), p. 316.
2. E. P. Thompson, 'Time, Work-Discipline and Industrial Capitalism', *Past and Future*, no. 38 (1967), p. 88.
3. W. Turner, *Sunday Schools Recommended* (Newcastle, 1786), pp. 23, 42. Cited in Thompson, 'Time, Work-Discipline', p. 84.
4. Benjamin Franklin, 'Poor Richards Almanac' (January 1751), in L. W. Labaree and W. J. Bell, *The Papers of Benjamin Franklin* (New Haven, 1961), pp. iv, 86–7. Cited in Thompson, 'Time, Work-Discipline', p. 89.
5. Schofield, 'The Measurement of Literacy', p. 316.
6. See note 59 in Chapter 6.
7. Max Weber, *The Protestant Ethic and the Spirit of Capitalism*, trans. Talcott Parsons (London: Allen & Unwin, 1930, first published in German, 1904).
8. George Ovitt (Jr), 'The Cultural Context of Western Technology: Early Christian Attitudes toward Manual Labour', *Technology and Culture*, 27 (3) (July 1986), pp. 477–500.
9. Ibid., p. 498.
10. Ibid., p. 500.
11. Ibid.
12. See Mary-Lou Jennings and Charles Madge (eds), *Humphrey Jennings – Pandemonium, 1660–1886: The Coming of the Machine as seen by Contemporary Observers* (London: Picador, 1987), p. 158.
13. Reported by Sir John Lubbock, in 'Science in Schools', *Leisure Hour* (London, 1875), p. 48.
14. Martin F. Tupper, 'Of Industry and Idleness', *Leisure Hour* (London, 1875), pp. 342–3.
15. The 'God is Dead!' movement that Bishop Robinson highlighted accepted

the radical secularisation of modern society, stressed the irrelevance of traditional beliefs in God, and sought to build a new theology on these premises. J. J. Altizer and William Hamilton, *Radical Theology and the Death of God* (Indianapolis, Ind.: Bobbs-Merrill, 1966), pp. 23–50.

16. Thomas Luckmann, *The Invisible Religion: The Transformation of Symbols in Industrial Society* (New York: Macmillan, 1967); Peter L. Berger and Thomas Luckmann, 'Secularization and Pluralism', in 'Sociology of Religion: Theoretical Perspectives – I', *International Yearbook for Sociology of Religion*, Vol. II (1966) (Opladen: Westdeutscher Verlag), pp. 73–84; Bryan Wilson, *Religion in Secular Society* (London: Watts, 1966).

17. Jennifer Tan, 'The Textile Millwright in the Early Industrial Revolution', *Textile History*, V (October 1974), p. 81.

18. William Fairbairn, *A Treatise on Mills and Millwork* (2 vols) London, 1861 (2nd edition, 1865). Cited by Maxine Berg, *The Machinery Question and the Making of Political Economy, 1815–1848* (Cambridge: Cambridge University Press, 1980) (1982 paperback) p. 153.

19. This splitting off of 'conception' from 'execution' was capitalised on by F. W. Taylor's 'scientific management' movement in the early twentieth century. As with all other aspects of the culture-technology alignment, the movement was an extension of what went before, not an entirely new concept. The scientific management movement however focused a basic feature of the social-technological alignment into management thinking. With its clear expression of the system efficiency and labour ordering principles that followed however, the scientific management movement (or 'Taylorism') underlay the de-skilling process that followed in work design thereafter. Braverman attributes the alienation of conception from execution to the social dynamics of capitalism *per se*, but as the present book seeks to demonstrate, this split was a necessary product of the *alignment* between the capitalist social form and the technological frame rather than capitalism *per se*. See Frederick Winslow Taylor, *The Principles of Scientific Management* (New York: Harper and Brothers, 1911); Frank Bunker Gilbreth, *Primer for Scientific Management*, 2nd edition (introduced by Louis D. Brandeis) (Easton, Pa.: Hive Publishing Company, 1973); H. Braverman, *Labor and Monopoly Capital – The Degradation of Work in the Twentieth Century* (New York: Monthly Review Press, 1974).

20. Maxine Berg, *The Machinery Question*, pp. 153–4.

21. Ibid., pp. 146–7.

22. Ibid., p. 151.

23. John Burnett (ed), *Destiny Obscure – Autobiographies of Childhood, Education and Family from the 1820s to the 1920s* (Harmondsworth: Penguin, 1984), p. 138.

24. Katrina Honeyman, *Origins of Enterprise: Business Leadership in the Industrial Revolution* (Manchester: Manchester University Press, 1982).

25. Berg, *The Machinery Question*, p. 160.

26. W. P. Gaskell, 'An Address to the Operative Classes, being the Substance of

a Lecture Explanatory and in Defence of the Nature and Objects of the Cheltenham Mechanics Institute', Cheltenham, 8 May 1835, pp. 4-7. Cited in Berg, *The Machinery Question*, p. 160.

27. Thomas Chalmers, 'On Mechanics Schools and on Political Economy as a Branch of Popular Education', *Glasgow Mechanics Magazine*, V (3 June 1826), pp. 217–21. Cited in Berg, *The Machinery Question*, p. 163.

28. Berg, ibid., p. 154.

29. Ibid., p. 173.

30. Communication from Dr William Chambers to the editors, 'American Ideas versus British Ideas', *The Leisure Hour* (London, 1875), pp. 47–8.

31. Honeyman, *Origins of Enterprise*.

32. Eric Roll, 'An Early Experiment in Industrial Organization, being a History of the Firm of Boulton and Watt', London, 1930. Reprinted in Berg (ed), *Technology and Toil*, pp. 27–35.

33. Honeyman, *Origins of Enterprise*.

34. Jewkes, Sawers and Stillerman, *The Sources of Invention*, pp. 44–7.

35. Ibid., pp. 46–7.

36. *One Hundred Great Lives* (London: Oldhams Press Ltd, 1954), pp. 74, 78.

37. Berg, *The Machinery Question*, p. 174.

38. Ibid., p. 176.

39. Ibid., pp. 176–7.

40. T. K. Derry and Trevor I. Williams, *A Short History of Technology* (Oxford: Clarendon Press), pp. 623–5.

41. Jewkes, Sawers and Stillerman, *The Sources of Invention*, p. 49.

42. Derry and Williams, *A Short History of Technology*, p. 623.

43. John L. Beer, 'Coal Tar Manufacture and the Origins of the Modern Industrial Research Laboratory', *ISIS*, 49 (1958), pp. 123–31.

44. J. Clarke, C. Freeman and L. Soete, 'Long Waves and Technological Developments in the twentieth century', paper presented to the *Bochum Conference on 'Wintschaftliche Wechsellagen und Sozialer Wandel'* (University of Sussex, Science Policy Research Unit, September 1980), p. 15.

45. Hill, 'Technology and Society', pp. 40–2.

46. Ibid., pp. 42–3. The further a corporation, an economic sector or a nation is removed from the leading edge of technological progress, the more tenuous is the link between industry and science. The marginality of science to industry is therefore particularly seen in developing countries. See Stephen Hill, 'Basic Design Principles for National Research in Developing Countries', *Technology in Society*, 9 (1) (1987), pp. 63–73.

47. Althusser's concept of ideology was discussed in Chapter 5. See Louis Althusser, *Reading Capital*, trans. B. Brewster (London: New Left Books, 1975), p. 66; Louis Althusser, *For Marx*, trans. B. Brewster (London: New Left Books, 1977), p. 232.

48. J. S. Mill, *Principles of Political Economy with Some of their Applications to Social Philosophy* (1848), in *Collected Works of J. S. Mill*, Volumes II and III (Toronto, 1965), pp. 104, 109.

49. Boulding observes the 'superculture' as the internationalised 'culture of airports, throughways, skyscrapers, hybrid corn and artificial fertilizers, birth control, and universities'. Kenneth E. Boulding, 'The Interplay of Technology and Values – The Emerging Superculture', in Kurt Baier and Nicholas Rescher (eds), *Values and the Future* (New York: The Free Press, 1969), p. 348.

50. Alvin Toffler coins the word 'cognitariat' in his book *Previews and Promises*. Toffler argues that, as the 'Second Wave' of the Industrial Revolution produced the proletariat or working class, the 'Third Wave, or high-speed information revolution is producing the "cognitariat", a group 'based on knowing, on the use of mind, rather than on muscle'. Alvin Toffler, *Previews and Promises* (London: Pan Paperback Original, 1984).

Chapter 8

1. Evidence and sections of the text in this chapter have been revised from a recent chapter I published in *A Sociology of Australian Society*. The chapter in the earlier book contains some detailed statistics, tables and figures that are not presented here, in particular, concerning technology in contemporary Australian society. Evidence presented here also refers to both the overall continent of Australia and to the former colony, New South Wales (NSW). Prior to 1901 when the separate states of Australia were federated, statistics were collected within each separate colony or state, not for Australia as a whole. Indeed in some areas the statistics across the separate states during the nineteenth century were not comparable, their mode of collection being the subject of some debate between the state statisticians. Thus, the historic evidence that is presented in the present chapter refers to Australia where overall data is available and comparable. The colony of New South Wales (NSW) is referred to most frequently for the earliest data however, as it was the first colony to be established, and throughout the nineteenth century generally represents the leading edge of what was happening in other colonies. See Stephen Hill, 'Work and Technological Change in Australia', in John Western and Jake Najman (eds), *A Sociology of Australian Society* (Melbourne: Macmillan, 1988).

2. Arthur H. Corbett, *The Institution of Engineers, Australia – A History of the First Fifty Years, 1919–1969* (Sydney: The Institution of Engineers, Australia), with Angus and Robertson, 1973, p. 2.

3. Ibid., p. 6.

4. *NSW Statistical Register, 1901 and Previous Years* (Sydney: NSW Government Printer), p. 146.

5. Sources of data used on nineteenth century NSW industry are the following: *NSW Statistical Registers: 1860*, p. 167; *1861*, p. 190; *1863*, pp. 111–12; *1867*, Table No. 74; *1876*, pp. 188–9; *1895*, p. 618; *1901*, pp. 626–9.

6. R. A. Buchanan, 'Engineers in Australia, 1788–1890: A Preliminary Analysis', *Journal, Institution of Engineers, General Engineering Transactions*, 1982, p. 54.

7. *NSW Statistical Register, 1938–39 and Previous Years* (Sydney: Government Printer, 1941), p. 445.

8. Buchanan, 'Engineers in Australia'.

9. T. A. Coghlan, *Statistics, Six States of Australia and New South Wales, 1861 to 1900* (Sydney: William Applegate Gullick, Government Printer, 1901), Table no. 51, p. 18.

10. Walter Rostow comments on the nineteenth-century impact of railways in the US: 'as the leading growth sector in American growth from the 1840s to the 1880s, closely linked to the emergence of the steel industry after the Civil War, the railroads were surely connected in one way or another with immigration, with population increase, internal population movement, and almost everything else that mattered in the American economy.' See Walter W. Rostow, 'Kondrateiff, Schumpeter, and Kuznets: Trend Periods Revisited', *Journal of Economic History*, 35 (1975), p. 725.

11. *NSW Statistical Registers: 1867*, Table no. 74; *1876*, pp. 188–9.

12. Sources of data used on the development of energy technologies are the following: *NSW Statistical Registers: 1892*, p. 483; *1895*, pp. 606–7; pp. 618–19; and pp. 625–9; *1904*, pp. 234–5; and, *1938–9*, p. 445.

13. Geoffrey Barraclough, *An Introduction to Contemporary History* (Harmondsworth: Pelican Books, 1967), p. 51.

14. Coghlan, *Statistics*, Table no. 93, p. 32.

15. *NSW Statistical Register, 1901 and Previous Years*, p. 146.

16. Figure 1 is prepared from original sources. Barry Jones comes to the same conclusion as the figure demonstrates, that is, concerning the relationship between agricultural, services and manufacturing employment in Australia's history. But Jones identifies the time of cross-over to services somewhat earlier in the nineteenth century. I have been unable to replicate Jones' data from the original statistical sources. Figure 1 demonstrates the results when reasonably safe assumptions are applied to colonial, census and Australian Bureau of Statistics data on the labour force, and its classifications. For data sources, see Figure 1. For Jones' analysis, see Barry Jones, *Sleepers, Wake! Technology & the Future of Work* (Melbourne: Oxford University Press (new edition), 1984), p. 55.

17. This figure is calculated from data presented in the *Official Yearbook of the Commonwealth of Australia, 1924*, no. 17, p. 938; and *1911*, vol. III, pp. 1284–5.

18. Buchanan, 'Engineers in Australia', p. 56.

19. H. J. Brown, 'Trends in Higher Technological Education and Development in New South Wales', *Journal, Institution of Engineers*, Australia, 21 (9) (1949), p. 151.

20. Ibid., p. 152.

21. Gene I. Rochlin, 'The Technological Imperative – Introduction', in Scientific American, *Scientific Technology and Social Change* (San Francisco: W. H. Freeman and Company, 1974), pp. 150–1.

22. R. A. Buchanan, 'The Diaspora of British Engineering', *Technology and Culture*, 27 (3) (July 1986), p. 504.

23. Brown, 'Trends in Higher Technological Education', p. 143.
24. Ibid., p. 142.
25. Ibid., p. 149.
26. Ibid., p. 152.
27. J. R. Moore, 'Survey of the Engineering Profession - Tabulated Results and Statistics – I', *Journal, Institution of Engineers*, 11 (7) (July 1939), pp. 259–62; and J. R. Moore, 'Survey of the Engineering Profession – Tabulated Results and Statistics – II', *Journal, Institution of Engineers*, 11 (9) (September 1939), pp. 331–4.
28. Buchanan, 'Engineers in Australia, p. 55.
29. *NSW Statistical Register, 1895*, p. 744.
30. *Official Yearbook of the Commonwealth of Australia*, 1901–1907, No. 1 (1908), p. 508.
31. S. Brogden, *The History of Australian Aviation* (Melbourne: The Hawthorn Press, 1960), pp. 20–33.
32. Sources of data used here are the following: *NSW Statistical Registers: 1893 and Previous Years*, pp. 608–9; *1895 and Previous Years*, pp. 744–5; *1901*, p. 263; *1904*, p. 426.
33. Sources of early data are those for 1893, 1895, 1901 and 1904 *NSW Statistical Registers* cited above in note 32.
34. Australian Bureau of Statistics, *Research and Experimental Development, Business Enterprises, Australia, 1981–1982* (Canberra: ABS Catalogue no. 8104.0, Table 18), p. 23.
35. Buchanan, 'Engineers in Australia', p. 55.
36. Peter Stubbs, *The Australian Motor Industry, A Study in Protection and Growth*, University of Melbourne, Institute of Applied Economic and Social Research Monograph no. 5 (Melbourne: Cheshire, 1972), pp. 1–29; Gerald Bloomfield, *The World Automotive Industry* (Newton Abbot: David & Charles, 1978), p. 256.
37. E. J. Hobsbawn, *Industry and Empire* (Harmondsworth: Penguin, 1968).
38. R. MacLeod, 'Scientific Advice for British India: Imperial Perceptions and Administrative Goals: 1893–1923', *Modern Asian Studies*, 9 (3) (1975), pp. 382-3.
39. R. MacLeod, 'On Visiting the "Moving Metropolis": Reflections on the Architecture of Imperial Science', *Historical Records of Australian Science*, 5 (3) (1982).
40. Haldane Committee, *Report of the Machinery of Government Committee* (London: HMSO, 1918).
41. F. Sagasti and M. Guenero, quoted in R. MacLeod, 'On Visiting the "Moving Metropolis"'.
42. MacLeod, ibid.
43. Asa Briggs, 'Technology and Economic Development', in Scientific American, *Scientific Technology and Social Change* (San Francisco: W. H. Freeman and Company, 1974), pp. 95–7.
44. Rohan Rivett, *David Rivett: Fighter for Australian Science* (Australia: The Dominion Press, 1972).

45. In Australia, only 23.5 per cent of R&D is performed in the business sector; by way of contrast, in the US 71 per cent, in West Germany 69.2 per cent, and Japan 60.7 per cent respectively of R&D is performed in the business sector. The Australian figure (for 1981-3) is taken from the *Australian Bureau of Statistics, Research and Experimental Development, All-Sector Summary, Australia, 1981–83* (Canberra: ABS, Catalogue no. 8112.0, 1984), p. 5. The United States figure (for 1981) is taken from C. E. Barfield, *Science Policy from Ford to Reagan – Continuity and Change* (Washington: American Enterprise Institute for Public Policy Research, 1982), p. 130. The Japanese figure (for 1981) is taken from *The Statistical Handbook of Japan 1983* (Statistics Bureau, Prime Minister's Office, 1984). The figure for West Germany (for 1979) is taken from *OECD Economic Surveys* (Paris: OECD, July 1981).

46. For a detailed analysis of the way that the internal culture of research laboratories reflects the laboratory's institutional location within the wider technological frame and within the wider national culture, see V. V. Krishna, *Scientists in Laboratories: A Comparative Study on the Organisation of Science and Goal Orientations of Scientists in CSIRO (Australia) and CSIR (India) Institutions* (University of Wollongong, Australia: PhD Thesis, 1987); and S. C. Hill, 'Contrary Meanings of Science: Interaction Between Cultural and Personal Meanings of Research in a Developing Country Research Institution', in S. S. Blume (ed), *Perspectives in the Sociology of Science* (Great Britain: John Wiley & Sons, 1977), pp. 195–230.

47. Australian Bureau of Statistics, *Research and Experimental Development, All-Sector Summary, Australia, 1981–83* (Canberra: ABS, Catalogue no. 8112.0 1984) p. 5.

48. For comparative data on Australia relative to the other nations of the Asian region, see A. Rahman and S. Hill, *Science, Technology and Development in Asia and the Pacific: Progress Report, 1968–1980* (Paris: UNESCO Document SC 82/CASTASIA II/REF 1, 1982).

49. Ron Johnston, 'The Critical Barriers to the More Effective Appropriation of Research Results', paper delivered to the Australian National University Public Affairs Conference, *Science Research in Australia: Who Benefits*, 23-24 June 1983 (University of Wollongong: Department of History and Philosophy of Science, mimeo) p. 10.

50. The 'laissez-faire' political-economic interest of the postwar Liberal Government in Australia was finally brought into an 'uneasy alliance' (as Jarlath Ronayne terms the relationship) with the demands of scientists for research autonomy. As a result, the scientists won the day, and the disconnection of science from national political or economic interests persisted. See J. Ronayne, 'The Uneasy Alliance: Science and Politics in Australia', *Search*, 7 (3) (March 1977), pp. 85–9; V. V. Krishna, *Scientists in Laboratories*, pp. 258–64; J. Ronayne, 'Science Research, Science Policy, and Social Studies of Science and Technology in Australia', *Social Studies of Science*, 8 (1978), pp. 361–84.

51. OECD, *Economic Surveys*, Table 3, 'Distribution of GERD in the OECD Area', p. 20.
52. Ron Johnston, 'The Control of Technological Change', p. 104.
53. See Rahman and Hill, *Science*, Table 3.7 (p. 116), Table 3.8 (p. 117), and Table 4.1 (p. 150); Neville Hurst, 'Indicators for S & T Policy Formulation and Monitoring', paper presented to the ASEAN/COST High Level Meeting on *Science and Technology Policy and Program Management*, Canberra March 1985 (Canberra: Australian Department of Science, 1985), pp. 207–29.
54. OECD, Group of National Experts on Science and Technology Indicators, *Science and Technology Indicators*, Working Paper No. 2, *Indicators of the Technological Position and Performance in OECD Countries During the Seventies* (Paris: OECD, DSTI/SPRI/84, 1984), Table 8, p. 29.
55. Australian Bureau of Statistics, *Research and Experimental Development, Business Enterprises, Australia, 1981–82*, (Canberra: ABS, Catalogue no. 8140.0), Table 18, p. 23.
56. Three-quarters of these exports are of completely unprocessed materials. Australian Bureau of Statistics, *Foreign Trade, Australia, 1982–83*, (Canberra: ABS, Catalogue no. 5410.0, 1984), pp. 76–8.
57. Australian Bureau of Statistics, *Overseas Trade, 1974–75* (Canberra: ABS, Catalogue no. 5410.0, 1976); *Overseas Trade, 1978–79* (Canberra: ABS, Catalogue no. 5410.0, 1980); *Overseas Trade, 1981–82* (Canberra: ABS, Catalogue no. 5410.0, 1983). For a detailed presentation of the data and trends, see Hill, 'Technological Imperialism', Table 3.
58. This conclusion follows simply from projecting trends. Payment costs for all forms of technical know-how have steadily increased since the late 1970s – from A$69.5 million in 1976–7, to $108.6 million in 1978–9, to $126.6 million in 1981–2 across all industries. Over this time, the ratio of payments to receipts has remained around seven to one. See Australian Bureau of Statistics, *Research and Development, Business Enterprises, Australia* (Canberra: ABS, Catalogue no. 8104.0, 1984), p. 21.
59. In the mining sector, foreign ownership rose to 27.3 per cent in 1963, to 57.8 per cent in 1974–5. See Greg Crough, 'The Political Economy of the Mineral Industry', in G. Crough et al., *Australia and World Capitalism* (Melbourne: Penguin, 1980). Since that time, the level of foreign ownership appears to have plateaued. See Australian Bureau of Statistics, *Foreign Ownership and Control of the Mining Industry, Australia, 1982–83* (Canberra: ABS, Catalogue no. 5329.0, 1984). Foreign ownership of food processing, the other industry where foreign control comes close to the heart of Australia's main exports, is lower (at 31.5 per cent), and also has remained fairly stable since the early 1970s. Here, less sophisticated technologies are required. See Australian Bureau of Statistics, *Foreign Ownership and Control of the Manufacturing Industry, Australia 1972–73* (Canberra: ABS, Catalogue no. 5322.0 1974), and *Foreign Ownership and Control of the Manufacturing Industry, Australia, 1982-83* (Canberra: ABS, Catalogue no. 5322.0, 1985).

60. Australian Bureau of Statistics, *Foreign Ownership and Control of the Manufacturing Industry, Australia, 1982–83*, ibid., Table 5.

61. Hill, 'Work and Technological Change in Australia', Figures 5 and 6.

62. Australian Bureau of Statistics, *Research and Experimental Development, Business Enterprises, Australia, 1981-82* (Canberra: ABS, Catalogue no. 8104.0, 1984), p. 22.

63. For sources of data on Australian urbanisation during the nineteenth century, see T. A. Coghlan, *Statistics*, Table 2, p. 1; and Table 14, p. 5. For the figure on the present level of urbanisation in Australia, see Jones, *Sleepers*, p. 16.

64. The assessment that more than 75 per cent of leading contemporary Australian artists are drawn from an overseas culture is derived from analysis of the painters represented in one of the most authoritative recent accounts of Australian painters, *Modern Australian Painting, 1950–1975*. Of the 162 'Australian' painters represented in the collection, 46 were born and educated overseas (41 per cent of whom were British); 82 were born in Australia, but studied, travelled and lived extensively overseas; and only 34 were born in Australia, and primarily lived and studied in Australia. The observation is supported by the representation of artists in major recent exhibitions of Australian art. In the 'Australian Visions' Exhibition (selected by the Visual Arts Board of the Australia Council), only two of the eight artists were born, educated, and lived primarily in Australia. In the 'Subject of Painting, 1985' Exhibition (selected by the Art Gallery of NSW and the Contemporary Art Society of NSW), only one of the twelve artists selected was born, educated and lived primarily in Australia. See Kym Bonython, *Modern Australian Painting, 1950–1975* (Adelaide: Rigby Publishers, 1980); Diane Waldman, *Australian Visions: 1984 Exxon International Exhibition* (New York: The Solomon R. Guggenheim Foundation, 1984); and Art Gallery of New South Wales, *The Subject of Painting* (Sydney: Art Gallery of NSW and the Contemporary Art Society (NSW), 1985).

Chapter 9

1. Jean Baudrillard, *The Mirror of Production*, trans. Mark Poster (St Louis: Telos Press, 1975), p. 144.

2. E. Mercer, 'The Houses of the Gentry', *Past and Present*, No. 5 (1954), pp. 11–32.

3. R. Konig, *The Restless Image* (London: George Allen and Unwin, 1973).

4. Dorothy Davis, *History of Shopping* (London: Routledge & Kegan Paul, 1966).

5. Harold C. Whitford, 'Expos'd to Sale – The Marketing of Goods and Services in Seventeenth Century England as Revealed by Advertisements in Contemporary Newspapers and Periodicals', *New York Public Library Bulletin* 71 (1967), pp. 496–515.

6. The ability of US manufacturers to produce clocks for one dollar was observed by an English group of Commissioners who were sent to observe

the American 'system' in 1853. In their report back to the British Parliament the Commissioners attributed the success of America's increasing world competitiveness (the clocks were now being sold widely throughout Europe) to the American 'manufacturing principle', that is, 'the production in large numbers of standardised articles on a basis of repetition in factories characterised by ample workshop room and "admirable system".' The Commissioners' Report is quoted in D. L. Burn, 'The Genesis of American Engineering Competition, 1850–1870', *Economic History*, 2, (1930–3), pp. 292–311.

7. James J. Flink, *The Car Culture* (Cambridge, Mass: MIT Press, 1975), pp. 148-9.
8. Ibid.
9. Henri Lefebvre, *Everyday Life in the Modern World*, trans. Sacha Rabinovitch (London: Allen Lane – The Penguin Press, 1971), p. 100.
10. Flink, *The Car Culture*, p. 160.
11. Robert S. Lynd and Helen M. Lynd, *Middletown in Transition: A Study in Cultural Conflict* (New York: Harcourt Brace, 1937), p. 245.
12. Flink, *The Car Culture*, p. 174.
13. Tibor Scitovsky, *The Joyless Economy – An Inquiry Into Human Satisfaction and Consumer Dissatisfaction* (New York: Oxford University Press, 1976), pp. 255, 275.
14. Harlow Curtice's speech is quoted in Jules Henry, *Culture Against Man* (London: Social Science Paperbacks, 1966), pp. 22–3.
15. Jean Baudrillard, *La Société de Consommation – ses Mythes, ses Structures* (Paris: Gallimard, 1970) p. 123.
16. Robert S. Lynd and Helen M. Lynd, *Middletown: A Study in Modern American Culture* (New York: Harcourt Brace, 1929), p 257.
17. Ibid., pp. 64–5.
18. Donald Schon, *Beyond the Stable State* (London: Temple Smith, 1971), p. 37.
19. John W. Dyckman, 'Transportation in Cities', in Scientific American, *Cities – Their Origin, Growth and Human Impact* (San Francisco: W. H. Freeman and Company, 1973), p. 197.
20. This estimate of how much of Los Angeles is devoted to 'automobilia' was presented in Ian Breach and Stuart Reid, 'Do You Really Need A Car?', *Sunday Australian*, 23 April 1972, p 8.
21. John Steinbeck, *Cannery Row* (New York: Viking Press, 1945).
22. Siegfried Gierdion, *Mechanization Takes Command – A Contribution to Anonymous History* (New York: W. W. Norton, 1975), p. 42.
23. These observations were made by Siegfried Gierdion through identifying when each of the products first appeared in mail-order catalogues. See Siegfried Gierdion, ibid.
24. Rose, 'Urban Environments', Table 8, p. 536.
25. Susan Strasser, *Never Done: A History of American Housework* (New York: Pantheon Books, 1982).
26. Christine E. Bose, Philip L. Bereano and Mary Malloy, 'Household

Technology and the Social Construction of Housework', *Technology and Culture*, 25 (1) (January 1984), p. 76.

27. Geoffrey Barraclough, *An Introduction to Contemporary History* (Harmondsworth: Pelican Books, 1967), p. 51.
28. Bose, 'Urban Environments', pp. 525–7.
29. Schwartz Cowan, 'The "Industrial Revolution"', p. 10.
30. In 1900, household servants formed 98.9 out of 1,000 of the population; in 1920, 58.0 out of 1,000 of the population. D. L. Kaplan and M. Claire Casey, *Occupation Trends in the United States, 1900–1950*, US Bureau of the Census, Working Paper no. 5 (Washington, DC, 1958), Table 6. Cited in Schwartz Cowan, ibid.
31. Schwartz Cowan, ibid., pp. 1–23.
32. A. Michael McMahon, 'An American Courtship: Psychologists and Advertising Theory in the Progressive Era', *American Studies*, 13 (1972), pp. 5–18.
33. Schwartz Cowan, 'The Industrial Revolution', p. 16.
34. David Riesman, with Nathan Glazer and Reuel Denney, *The Lonely Crowd – A Study of the Changing American Character* (Garden City, New York: Doubleday–Anchor Books, 1953).
35. Thomas Luckmann and Peter Berger, 'Social Mobility and Personal Identity', *Humanitas – Journal of the Institute of Man*, 7 (1) (Spring 1971), pp. 93–109.
36. For discussion of the 'bunching' of innovations and its relationship to long (Kondratiev) cycles of economic expansion and recession, see Gerhard Mensch, 'Institutional Barriers to the Science and Technology Interaction', in H. F. Davidson, M. J. Cetron and J. D. Goldhar, *Technology Transfer* (Leiden: Noardhoff, 1974); Gerhard Mensch, *Stalemate in Technology: Innovations Overcome the Depression* (Cambridge: Ballinger, 1979); Ernest Mandel, 'Explaining Long Waves of Capitalist Development', *Futures*, 13 (August 1981); J. J. van Duijn, *The Long Wave in Economic Life* (London: George Allen & Unwin, 1983); Christopher Freeman et al., *Unemployment and Technical Innovation* (London: Francis Pinter, 1982); Nathan Rosenberg and Claudio R. Frischtak, 'Technological Innovation and Long Waves', in C. Freeman (ed), *Design, Innovation and Long Cycles In Economic Development* (New York: St Martin's Press, 1986), pp. 5–26. For an analysis of the social alignments that are associated with long waves of economic development, see Hill, 'Technology and Society', pp. 27-46.
37. B. R. Mitchell, *Abstract of British Historical Statistics* (Cambridge: Cambridge University Press, 1962), p. 225; Wolfgang Schivelbusch, *The Railway Journey: Trains and Travel in the 19th Century* (Oxford: Blackwell, 1980).
38. Lefebvre, *Everyday Life*, p. 135.
39. Kingsley Davis, 'Man's Adjustment to Cities', in Scientific American, *Cities – their Origin, Growth and Human Impact* (San Francisco: W. H. Freeman & Co., 1973), p. 3.

40. Jean Gottman, *Megalopolis* (New York: Twentieth Century, 1961).

41. Kevin Lynch, 'The City as Environment', in Scientific American, *Cities* (Harmondsworth: Penguin, 1967), p. 204.

42. Alexander Hay, 'The Sewing Machine', in *Industrial Curiosities* (London, 1980). Reprinted in Berg, *Technology and Toil*, p. 230.

43. Hay, ibid., p. 227.

44. Malcolm MacLaren, *The Rise of the Electrical Appliance Industry During the Nineteenth Century* (Princeton, New Jersey, 1943), pp. 91–3.

45. Berg, *Technology and Toil*, p. 225.

46. Marx, *Capital*, Volume 1, p. 145.

47. Karl Marx, *Grundrisse: Introduction to the Critique of Political Economy*, trans. M. Nicolaus (Harmondsworth: Penguin, 1973), p. 410.

48. Ibid., p. 286.

49. Baudrillard, *Système des Objets*.

50. William Leiss, *The Limits to Satisfaction: An Essay on the Problems of Needs and Commodities* (Toronto: University of Toronto Press, 1976), pp. 14–15.

51. Ibid., p. 23.

52. For central discussions of the alienation of the 'signifier' from the 'signified', and the constitution of a substitute reality, see particularly, Lefebvre, *Everyday Life*, p. 135; and Baudrillard, *Système des Objets*.

53. Jean-Paul Sartre, *Critique of Dialectical Reason*, trans. A. Sheridan-Smith (London: New Left Books, 1976); and Jean-Paul Sartre, *The Problem of Method*, trans. H. Barnes (London: Methuen, 1963).

54. Henri Lefebvre presents an example of the way that the 'code' signifies the link between the technological production system and subjective life through the example of television. As Lefebvre observes, television signals that, 'You are being looked after, cared for, told how to live better, how to dress fashionably, how to decorate your home, in short how to exist; you are totally and thoroughly programmed, except that you still have to choose between so many good things, since the act of consuming remains a permanent structure ... the whole of society is with you, and considerate into the bargain, for it thinks of you, personally, it prepares for you personally specially personalised items.' Lefebvre, *Everyday Life*, p. 107.

Chapter 10

1. Max Horkheimer, *The Eclipse of Reason* (New York: Oxford University Press, 1947), p. 104.

2. Martin Heidegger, 'The Question Concerning Technology', in David Knell (ed), *Basic Writings* (Harper and Row, 1977), p. 294.

3. Herbert Marcuse, *One Dimensional Man* (London: Sphere Books, 1970).

4. Christopher Lasch, *The Culture of Narcissism – American Life in an Age of Diminishing Expectations* (London: Sphere Books-Abacus, 1982), Chapter 2.

5. Philip Slater, *Earthwalk* (Garden City, New York: Anchor Press-Doubleday, 1974).

6. Edward Harrison, *Masks of the Universe*, 1984. Quoted in Hardison (Jr), 'A Tree, A Streamlined Fish', p. 390.

7. Philip Slater, *Earthwalk* , p. 10.

8. Herbert Marcuse, *Eros and Civilization* (London: Sphere Books, 1969), p. 168.

9. Karl Marx, *Economic and Philosophical Manuscripts*, *in Karl Marx, Early Writings*, introduced by Lucio Colletti, trans. Rodney Livingstone and Gregor Benton (Harmondsworth: Penguin Books, 1975), p. 351.

10. Erich Fromm, *The Art of Loving* (London: Unwin Books, 1962).

11. Jackie Collins, *Hollywood Wives* (London: Collins, 1983).

12. Fromm, *The Art of Loving* .

13. Peter Berger, *Invitation to Sociology – A Humanistic Perspective* (Harmondsworth: Penguin Books, 1971), p. 48.

14. Fromm, *The Art of Loving*, p. 48.

15. Marie Jahoda, *Employment and Unemployment: A Social-Psychological Analysis* (Cambridge: Cambridge University Press, 1983).

16. Howard S. Becker, 'Notes on the Concept of Commitment', *American Journal of Sociology*, 59 (1960), pp. 235–42; and Howard S. Becker, 'Personal Change in Adult Life', *Sociometry*, 27 (1964), pp. 40–53.

17. Herbert Popper and Roy Hughson, 'How Would *You* Apply Engineering Ethics to Environmental Problems?', *Chemical Engineering*, 2 November 1970, pp. 88–93; and Herbert Popper and Roy Hughson, 'Engineering Ethics and the Environment: The Vote is In!', *Chemical Engineering*, 22 February 1971, pp. 106–12.

18. N. Bruce Hannay and Robert E. McGinn, 'The Anatomy of Technology: Prolegomenon to an Improved Public Policy for the Social Management of Technology', *Daedelus*, 109 (Winter, 1980), p. 41.

19. Robert J. Smith, *The Psychopath in Society* (New York: Academic Press, 1978), p. 79.

20. Sigmund Freud, *Psychopathology of Everyday Life* (London: Ernest Bonn, 1914) (reprinted, 1960).

21. A. H. Buss, *Psychopathology* (New York: Wiley, 1966).

22. These symptomatic descriptions of the psychopath are drawn from H. Cleckley, *The Mask of Sanity* (4th edition) (St Louis: C.V. Mosby, 1964).

23. Robert Smith, *The Psychopath*.

24. See A. H. Buss, *Psychopathology*, H. Cleckley, *The Mask of Sanity*, and H. G. A. Gouch, 'A Sociological Theory of Psychopathy', *American Journal of Sociology*, 53 (1948) pp. 359–66.

25. Lewis Mumford, 'From Erewhon to Nowhere', *The New Yorker*, 8 October 1960, p. 182.

Chapter 11

1. This event was reported to me by Doug Taylor, the engineer who was reponsible for commissioning the ship in Sydney prior to its departure.

2. This, and other examples of the technological/human error risk in nuclear warfare 'defence' were reported in Ground Zero, *Nuclear War: What's In It For You* (New York: Pocket Books, 1982), p. 242; and Andrew Mack, 'The Risk of Nuclear War', in Jim Falk (ed), *Preventing Nuclear War – Australia's Role* (Australia: University of Wollongong, Monograph, 1982), p. 12.

3. Reported by Jonathon Jacky, 'Why Star Wars Won't Compete', in *Weekend Australian*, 29–30 June 1985, p. 17.

4. Stephen Hill, Robin Horne and Stewart Carter, 'White Collar Factory: Information Technology and Transformations of Corporate Culture – The Case-Study of an Insurance Corporation in Australia', in *Prometheus*, 1988 (forthcoming).

5. This case was reported by the union official who had dealt with the industrial conflict. The report was made to the Australian *1986 Conference of Manufacturing Industry*, entitled, 'Technology for the Future', NSW Department of Industrial Development and Decentralisation, Wollongong, August 1986.

6. In presenting this position, a very clear distinction needs to be made between 'invention' and 'innovation'. Invention implies an act of individual creativity, but innovation implies the acceptance and application of this inventive genius within technical and social systems. The shape of invention is very hard to predict. Individual inventors may well stand at the far distant margins of what is accepted as psychological sanity. As never-used patents testify, what is *invented* may well bear very little relationship to demand, or to received opinion of what has value within the culture-technology alignment. Innovations on the other hand embody what is taken from the field of possible invented alternatives, and *accepted* into the womb of cultural creation. Thus, whilst invention of the electrically-heated toilet seat or balloon-carried armchair have never come into application, invention of the mechanical calculator by Liebniz did form the basis for innovation some centuries later when 'calculated' life of the burgeoning technological system required it. The appearance of a reverse salient in system progress may well call specifically shaped inventions into being. But those inventions that emerge into application will be those that best redress the reverse salient of system progress. That is, the *innovations* will be *shaped* according to the properties that are already sedimented into the culture-technology alignment, and according to critical stumbling blocks for the progression of technological order.

As a consequence, whilst invention is likely to be shaped according to a very wide field of cultural and conceptual alternatives, innovation is likely to be shaped according to a severely constrained field of opportunity. Once we understand the underlying grammar that shapes the culture-technology alignment and its progress, it is thence possible to delineate the general territory within which innovation is likely to be shaped. By identifying the critical reverse salients at any moment in the evolution of alignment, and by identifying the pre-existing forms of mediation by technological systems of alternative perceptions, it should be possible to predict rather more specifically the shape of the particular innovations that will then be called into being. With innovation rather than invention as the focus, the key to prediction lies in understanding the underlying grammar of alignment.

7. This application of a 'culture-technology alignment theory' to theories of 'self-referent systems' is informed by fruitful discussions of self-referent systems theory with Professor Peter Weingart and his colleagues in the Centre for Science Studies at the University of Bielefeld. Through the seminar series that I presented there under the auspices of West Germany's Stifferverband in May–June 1987, I was provided with stimulating and critical review of the culture-technology alignment ideas that I have presented in this book.

8. Paul Barrett, *The Automobile and Urban Transit: The Formation of Public Policy in Chicago, 1900–1930* (Philadelphia: Temple University Press, *Technology and Urban Growth Series*, 1983).

9. MacKenzie and Wajcman, *The Social Shaping of Technology*.

10. Hughes, *Networks of Power*, p. 405.

11. Kenneth E. Boulding, 'The Interplay of Technology and Values – The Emerging Superculture', in Kurt Baier and Nicholas Rescher (eds), *Values and the Future* (New York: The Free Press, 1969), p. 348.

12. Stephen Hill, 'Information Technology and the Culture Club', Keynote Speech, International Conference of Librarians, Brisbane, August 1984.

13. Dolores Hayden, *The Grand Domestic Revolution: A History of Feminist Designs for American Homes, Neighbourhoods and Cities* (Cambridge, Mass.: MIT Press, 1981).

14. T. S. Eliot, *Collected Poems, 1909–1962* (London: Faber & Faber, 1963), p. 161.

Index

205; *see also* commodity, theory of
morality, and image, 164, 198; of
dependency, 219; of systems, 222;
industrial, *see* discipline, industrial
Morrow, James (Australian inventor),
174
Mount Hagan Dispute (Papua New
Guinea), 82
mule spinner strikes, 126; *see also*
resistance to industrialisation

National Register of Professional
Engineers (Australia), 173
narcissism, pathological, 213–4
Narcissus, legend of, *see* Echo and
Narcissus
Nauru, Island of, health problems, 16,
83–4
Nehru, Jahawarlal, 106
neo-colonialism, Australia's
susceptibility to, 163
Neolithic society, 45
'New Sociology of Technology', *see*
sociology of technology
New South Wales (colony of), *see*
Australia
Niagara Falls electricity generation
system, 102
Niue, Island of, outmigration, 85
Northampton (as early industrial
shoe-making town), 127
nuclear power, 26, 27, 59, 219, 230
nuclear weapons, 27, 98, 99, 219, 230
Nuer tribe (Nigeria), 60
nylon fishing nets, impact on
traditional village, 78

objectification, definition of, 257; of
self in commodities, 12, 96–7; of the
past in artefacts, 28, 56, 92; of wider
system values in artefacts, 40, 75, 86,
136; of stocks of knowledge in
artefacts, 48, 51–2; of labour skill, 54,
57, 70; of cultural symbols in written
texts, 65, 67; of spiritual labour, 140
objectivations, and consciousness, 93;
and culture, 99; *see also*
objectification
observation, disciplined, *see*
disciplined observation

obsolescence, ideology of, 17, 26; social
mechanisms for promoting, 190–3,
204; *see also* commodity, theory of the
Oldham (as early industrial cotton
manufacturing town), resistance to
industrialisation in, 32, 127–9, 134
oral cultures, *see* text (cultural), oral
orality, secondary, 62
order, social, *see* social order
Order in Council (for the
establishment of the colony of
NSW), 165
organisation, design, 236–8; culture,
236, 274
'other-directed' character type, *see*
character type
Owenist Movement, 122; *see also*
resistance to industrialisation

Papua New Guinea, and cargo cults,
44–5; impact of industrial artefacts
on, 74
Parliamentary Committee of 1817 (on
child labour), 119–20
patents, early industrial, 122, 144; early
Australian system of, 174–5;
Australian science and, 180;
Australian expenditures on, 275
Peel, Sir Robert, 121
'penny novel' themes, as indicator of
culture change, 131–2
personal identity, *see* self
Phaedrus, 63
'picture galleries', as havens from
early industrial town life, 135
political economy, ideology of, 15, 50,
86, 89, 146, 150, 159
political power, *see* social power
Poor Laws, 128
power, *see* social power
practico-inert, 207
pragmatic motive, 94, 261
pragmatism (economic), 104
praxis, 9, 39, 52, 54, 71, 94, 254
printing press, impact of the, 46
privatisation, effect of automobiles on,
194; and the technological frame,
225
production, craft, 116; forces of, 9, 48,
51, 70; material conditions of,

114; social process of, 53; social
relations of, 9, 10, 47, 51, 67, 77–8, 80,
86, 87, 101, 104, 132, 135, 200, 231, 243
profane symbols, 99, 103, 262; *see also*
symbols
professionalisation of engineers, 143,
242; US growth in, 172
progress, ideology of, 45, 65, 71, 120–3,
131–2, 142, 145, 146, 149, 151, 157, 192,
220, 225, 232, 239
proletariat, *see* working classes
Protestant Ethic, 139; *see also*
schooling, religious; and
protestantism
protestantism, 31, 49, 58, 137–40; *see
also* Protestant Ethic
protocol (in system interaction), 246–7
psychoanalysis, change in client
disorders for, 212–3
psychopath, pathology of, 220–1;
parallel in organisations of the,
221–2
public transport systems, decline in
US, 194
'putting–out' system (of early capitalist
production), 116
pyramids, symbolism of, *see* Egyptian
society
Pythagorus, 37

railways systems, effect in Australia,
167; early British, 200; industrial
symbolism of, 201; US impact of,
272; *see also* technological systems
Raikes Sunday Schools, 138–9, 267; *see
also* schooling, religious
rational logic, *see* rationality, ideology
of; and action, instrumental
rationality, ideology of, 49, 71
reactions against industrial
technology, *see* resistance to
industrialisation
Reagan, President Ronald, 230
reality, and culture, 61, 90–1, 94, 95, 98,
136, 158, 164, 231–2;
substitute, 206–7, 214, 218
reciprocity of perspectives, 92, 260
reformist movements, 119–120, 131,
143–5, 147, 223–5; *see also*
resistance, to industrialisation

religion, secularisation of, 100, 269
Religious Census, 1851 (Britain), 267
religious education, *see* schooling,
religious
Renaissance, 49
repression, early industrial, 112–3, 130,
133; *see also* labour, child
research, scientific, *see* scientific
research
research laboratories, early industrial,
155
resistance, to industrialisation, 55,
125–6, 128, 133, 265; to the
technological frame, 223–5, 233, 249
reverse salient, 50–1, 116, 126, 155, 161,
200, 230, 248, 250, 281;
definition of, 256
Ridley, John (Australian inventor), 174
Rivett, Sir David (Australian scientist),
178
Robinson, Bishop, and the 'God is
Dead' movement, 141, 269
Royal Commission of 1840 (on child
labour), 120
Royal Scientific Society, 57
ruling classes, sources of atrophy, 14,
28–34, 104, 244; cooptation of
subordinate classes, 113, 158;
legitimacy, 133–4, 158; and ideology
of order, 157; and politics of change,
234–5

sacramentalism of consumption, 262;
see also consumer culture
sacred symbols, 99–101, 103, 104, 262;
see also symbols
'Saint Monday', industrial work
practices and, 115
Salt Laws (imposed by British on
India), 106
Samoa, Western, impact of modern
technologies on, 76, 87, 88
scarcity, psychological use in
marketing of, 204, 206
Schneider–Dreusot Company
(France), 168
schooling (eighteenth–nineteenth
century), religious, 137–8, 157;
introduction of science into, 141;
literacy and, 267